The Craft of
SCIENCE FICTION

the text of this book is printed
on 100% recycled paper

A Symposium on Writing Science Fiction and Science Fantasy by

Reginald Bretnor
Poul Anderson
Hal Clement
Norman Spinrad
Alan E. Nourse
Theodore Sturgeon
Jerry Pournelle
Frank Herbert
Katherine MacLean
James Gunn
Larry Niven
Jack Williamson
John Brunner
Harlan Ellison
and
Frederik Pohl

The Craft of SCIENCE FICTION

Edited by

REGINALD BRETNOR

BARNES & NOBLE BOOKS
A DIVISION OF HARPER & ROW, PUBLISHERS
New York, Hagerstown, San Francisco, London

 For information address Harper & Row, Publishers, Inc., 10 East 53d Street, New York, N.Y. 10022. Published simultaneously in Canada by Fitzhenry & Whiteside Limited, Toronto.

Designed by Gloria Adelson

First BARNES & NOBLE BOOKS edition published 1977

ISBN: 0–06–463457–4

80 81 10 9 8 7 6 5 4 3 2

For Rosalie, again

Contents

TRADE SECRETS

Foreword

It is almost axiomatic that writing cannot be taught, not in any Training Manual sense, like simple plumbing, running a poodle launderette, or dentistry. There are elements of writing that the Training Manual approach can convey, and convey effectively, but these are basics: sentence structure, essentials of dramatic conflict, characterization, plotting. None of these, nor all of them together, can make anyone a writer, especially a writer of science fiction and science fantasy—for writing good sf demands much knowledge and many new perspectives not essential to what is generally called "mainstream" fiction. The knowledge is that which man has already gained through the exercise of the scientific method, and the perspectives are those which advancing science and technology are now forcing all men to develop, often for their own survival.

One of this book's primary purposes is to help writers, new or long-established, to understand the importance of these factors, to see the possibilities they offer for the practice of the craft, and to avoid the still too prevalent delusion that science really has little or nothing to do with science fiction and that literary emotionalism and wishful thinking can somehow whisk science and technology away.

Therefore we shall deal here less with "how to write sf" than with *how sf is written*

—in other words, with *how to become* a science fiction writer (which, in the long run, of course, comes to pretty much the same thing).

Individuality—the individual's native intelligence and sensitivity and talent, his cultural and literary background, his awareness of his own capabilities and limitations and of the world around him, his writing goals and the drive with which he hopes to reach them—all these play too important a role for the success of any stereotyped instruction to be guaranteed. Something more is needed.

To employ a military analogy, what we have here is the difference between peacetime Basic Training, sometimes from instructors who themselves have "learned it by the book," and a close association with soldiers of experience, combat veterans who have had to solve in the field the problems posed and played with in the theoretical atmosphere of camp and classroom. "This is how I did it and how it worked" or "This is how so-and-so tried to do it, and it didn't work" usually are more useful guidelines than "This is how it should be done because *I* say so." They leave the ultimate solution of every writing problem to the individual writer instead of trying to prescribe the solution in advance. They teach him not so much how to solve his problems but how to arrive at his own solutions.

This is not to denigrate good courses in writing and good Training Manual texts. They are fine as far as they go, but the purpose of this symposium is to go beyond them and to provide guidance and instruction that otherwise *cannot* be acquired except through experience. The writers who have contributed its chapters were selected because their special knowledge, their particular perceptions, and the nature and quality of their work seemed to me to qualify them especially well in each instance; and I have not tried to dictate or to influence their personal methods or opinions in any way. They have, I think, produced a stimulating book which will be extremely valuable to anyone who sets out to write sf, whether he is a learner or an experienced writer trying to move into the field, and of course to teachers of science fiction courses and writing courses on every educational level.

Any credit for the book, therefore, belongs more to its authors than to its editor. Their work required much thought and effort and was done largely out of their interest in and devotion to the sf field. I am indebted to Ms. Victoria Schochet, then of Harper & Row, who started the book on its way, and to M. S. Wyeth, Jr., their editor-in-chief, and his assistant, Ms. Lynne McNabb, who bore with me through the many hindrances that can plague a symposium prior to its birth. I am very grateful to Dr. Robert L. Forward, Senior Scientist in the Exploratory Studies Department at Hughes Research Laboratories, for permission to quote the challenging subject headings from his speech on "Far Out Physics," delivered to an S.F.W.A. Convention in 1974 and printed subsequently in *Analog*. And also I must thank Mrs. BetteLynn Johnson of Medford, Oregon, who did the final typing beautifully.

REGINALD BRETNOR

Medford, Oregon

The Science Fiction Spectrum and Its Sources

REGINALD BRETNOR

SF: The Challenge to the Writer

Ours is an age of vast and rapidly accelerating changes, technological, social, psychological, sometimes scarcely understood, sometimes not even recognized, only too often perilously close to being cataclysmic, affecting almost every aspect of our lives and of our world. Many of us, aware of one or another of these changes, have tried to use them, to manage them for our own power or profit. Others have attempted to "explain" them in terms of pre-scientific or pseudo-scientific maps of structure and process, of how and why: almost any economist's explanation of the causes of recession and inflation, or any sociologist's for the violent crime and other social evils besetting us can serve as an adequate example. In many areas, scientifically sound attempts to get down to the real bedrock of cause and effect, to understand great man-made changes as clearly as we understand the devices man has made, have scarcely started, and it is hard to see how, unless they receive far more support than they have hitherto, they can now win the race between understanding and control and disaster.

These are truisms and trite enough. But they do describe today's world accurately—and they also tell us why it offers sf writers unprecedented opportunities for the exercise of their imaginations, their intelligence, their skill.

That is a wonderful and terrible challenge. Any writer who would make the most of it must meet it well equipped, trained, prepared—not necessarily with exactly the same understandings and opinions as his fellows, or with identical skills, but with his own natural abilities and aptitudes developed to their optimum (something that is very largely up to him)—and this applies not only to the new and unpublished writer but to each of us who looks out on the world as it is and the universe as we are finding it to be and sets his or her mind to adventuring among the dangers and difficulties and strangenesses we know or suspect are there.

There is one essential difference between sf and what we generally accept as mainstream literature, and it arises from the fact that, in this century especially, most mainstream writers and critics have rigidly excluded science—that is, man's use of the scientific method as an agency of change—from their area of awareness, often damning it as cold and inhuman and denying it artistic respectability. By doing so they have confined themselves to the world as it appears "always" to have been and have limited their own opportunities and the opportunities open to their characters to the conditions of a cosmos which quite literally does not exist, for the living world is more than an *existence;* it is and always has been a *becoming.* Over many centuries its ordinary changes themselves appeared unchanging and eternal: ebbing and flowing tides, the seasons of the year, war and peace, famines, plagues, prosperities, success and failure, birth and death, the rise and fall of conquerors and their empires. Especially after God and the gods were made unfashionable, these changes could be proclaimed as the enduring verities of life and the greater process, of which they are a part, ignored. This was called *realism,* and as science made more and more basic changes in the world it became more and more unreal.

That is why science fiction and science fantasy, in our own century, emerged as a separate literary stream: to try to cope, in fiction—in the imaginations of its authors and its readers—not just with life as it had "always" been but with the world as it promises, or threatens, to become tomorrow, next week, next year, or as it may become if new and unanticipated doors into knowledge or into other worlds suddenly are opened by men using the scientific method and its technologies.

Other writers on the subject[1] *have pointed out that this separation

*Notes will be found at the end of chapters.

and emergence came about as a direct result of the mainstream's artificial self-restriction, but the point cannot be made too often or too strongly, for the restrictive voices are still with us. They are often prestigious and invariably insistent, and their nuisance value in inhibiting the development of sf as a literary art lies largely in their attempts to restrict its scope, very much as they did that of the mainstream. Sf writers, whether students or professionals, should ignore them assiduously; so should teachers of sf courses and of associated courses in what the academics are pleased to call "creative writing."

The reason is a simple one: sf cannot and should not be restricted in its scope. It has developed from the mainstream; it can use all those themes which are the mainstream's stock in trade, making them its own and treating them with its many deeper perceptions and wider visions. Its scope is universal, and the degree to which its promise will be realized can be limited only by the limitations of its writers, publishers, and readers.

Yet the arguments for restriction are repeated endlessly. They still echo in the remnants of the New Wave, that attempt to inflict on science fiction the hysterical illogic characterizing so much of this century's "intellectual" writing, and also in the spate of avid academic criticism following the discovery that sf, instead of being untouchable, was an untapped source of ready raw material for the Ph.D. mills.

They reappear constantly, sometimes seeping through on strange levels. *Science Fiction, Today and Tomorrow,* the discursive symposium which preceded this more specialized one, was reviewed, oddly enough, in one of the crotch magazines; and partly because the review's introductory paragraphs are so typical of what I have been discussing and partly for the very special flavor of their wit and prose, I shall quote them in full, omitting only the accompanying illustration of two space-suited figures attempting sexual intercourse:

> We can take science fiction too seriously. This is not Tolstoy. Science fiction is written by people who want to *entertain* and *make money.* It's pulp writers, balding guys with bad teeth and three children, lost among the pod creatures of the planet Xenon. Science fiction is forgettable, like toothpaste, like Johnny Nash. Quality seems to be random, nurtured almost solely by novelty. One good twist is all you need. Eternity is gravy.
>
> Still, longevity inspires high seriousness. Is there an *auteur* theory of nickelodeons? Did George M. Cohan have a soft spot for Keynesian economics? Do you care? They will assemble in the plaza below, waving copies of *1984* and

Brave New World. Wonderful, wonderful, but hardly . . . prescient. Can anybody read Olaf Stapleton without laughing? Doesn't Heinlein strike you (seriously now) as a writer for boys? Frank W. Dixon lives again. This ain't exactly the Renaissance, space freaks.

This ain't exactly Tolstoy either, but it's a sample of the sort of drivel that can inhibit sf's future Tolstoys before they ever get a start, urging them into now-sterile fields of writing—especially when presented on a slightly higher plane, with professorial authority or the clout of some nationally known literary huckster backing it.

There is nothing intrinsic to sf that limits it either in its scope or potential literary quality. There is no theme—Homeric, Sophoclean, Shakespearean, or Tolstoian—that sf cannot make its own and treat with originality and power.

But there is one difficulty every writer of sf must, and every critic should, bear in mind. Because sf so often deals not with life and the world as they have always been but with lives and worlds yet unborn, undreamed of hitherto, alien and therefore unfamiliar to the reader, it is much harder to write really well than mainstream fiction. It poses problems of characterization and verisimilitude unknown to the mainstream writer: the problem of creating far and future worlds, worlds which have themselves shaped beings and societies utterly different from our own; and then the the problem of making these beings and societies emotionally and intellectually believable, so that alien readers—we ourselves—can share their hopes and fears, their dreams and their excitements, their strivings and adventures.

It is always more difficult to blaze new trails than to drive down a familiar freeway—but that does not mean that it can not be done, given the talent, the training, the equipment, and the will to do it.

The Writer's Art: Basic Ingredients, Basic Skills

"It is perhaps unwise," wrote John Cowper Powys,[2] "to attempt any single dogmatic definition of culture; but . . . one rather felicitous definition runs as follows—'Culture is what is left over after you have forgotten all you have definitely set out to learn'—and in this sally you get at least a useful warning against associating culture too closely with the academic paraphernalia of education."

Much the same thing can be said about the writer's art, for all the skills he must acquire, the rules with which he must become familiar, the faces and mannerisms and intonations of all the people he has met, the emotions he has experienced and observed, the treasures of his vocabulary, and his entire fund of knowledge—all these must be integrated into his individual personality and into the actual act of writing. Once this integration is achieved, his dramatic subject matter can itself spontaneously determine his style and technique, with no necessity for a self-conscious copying of other writers as his model, or for uncritically obeying critical *dicta.*

The importance of this integration cannot be too strongly emphasized. In my own chapter for *Science Fiction, Today And Tomorrow,* I wrote (page 163):

> Any artist, unless we abandon all traditional definitions of what this means, must be like the accomplished fencer, the finished horseman. The fencer must practice and absorb all those exercises of cut, thrust, lunge, and parry which over several centuries have proven their effectiveness. The horseman similarly must understand his aids: reins, legs, weight, and voice. The sculptor and the painter must first master the chisel and the brush, must learn the texture of hard stone and the way colors combine on the palette. But once any of them have attained these masteries, then their preoccupation must be with what they have in hand: the bout with sabre or *épée,* the steeplechase or polo game, the statue or the portrait. Any underlying reasonings, any underlying drives, must be subordinated into the act of skill, the act of art, the act of love. In all this, the role of the doer's intellect must be an *editorial* one, monitoring the act the whole man is performing while itself remaining, not uninvolved, but—as far as possible —unswayed and undisturbed.
>
> Nothing is so destructive of the arts as self-consciousness in the artist—which cripples both intuition and spontaneity. . . .

The catch here is that the basic skills of writing *must* be acquired and, as far as the individual writer's native talent and intelligence and taste permit, perfected; and these skills are even more important to the writer of sf than to the mainstream writer, again because his task is harder. The writer without some sort of good general education, the writer who has himself read almost nothing (or almost nothing not badly written), the not quite literate writer with a deficient vocabulary, can't be expected to turn out very much worth reading, regardless of any native genius he may consider himself blessed with or the number of creative-writing courses he can stumble through.

The basic skills of writing cannot be separated from the basic ingredients of the writer's craft, for neither can exist without the other. Without the resources of the language, any knowledge of technique is meaningless; therefore the writer must build a vocabulary and keep adding to it, and he must master the fundamentals—though not necessarily memorizing the formal rules—of grammar and usage. Much of this may come to him through his exposure to intelligent, well-educated adults —both in and out of school—during his childhood and youth. As much or more can be acquired through reading, as Joseph Conrad once acquired it.

Anyone who wants to write *must* read; he must have read continuously and he must continue reading. What he reads should either be informative or of at least passable literary quality—for all writing (as indeed all art) is to a great extent derivative, and if you pour garbage in a blender you'll get blended garbage out. Personally I do not think that he should force himself to read *anything* simply because someone in authority proclaims it essential. If, in his youth, he prefers Dumas to Dostoevski, or Bartolomé de las Casas to Henry James, well and good. I myself couldn't get interested either in Jane Austen or the Brontës until after I'd turned forty, which was fortunate, because then I read them willingly, and they enriched me instead of boring me to death.

Just because the writer or would-be writer intends to dedicate himself primarily or solely to sf does not exempt him from this necessity for reading in the mainstream. To the contrary. That is where he can learn how great the English language is, how infinitely flexible, how noble when called upon to tell all that men hold most sacred or most terrible. That is where he can experience and absorb its vast variety of tastes and textures, from the majestic prose and poetry of the King James version to the quickening dialogue of George Bernard Shaw; from the subtle, beautifully shaped sentences of Thomas Fuller to the involvements of George Meredith or James Joyce; from the intricacies of Shakespeare's sonnets to the harsher nobility of Middle Scots in, for example, Dunbar's "Lament for the Makars."

It does not really matter whether, once read, he forgets all of them; they will be with him still, to make their presence felt whenever he sits down to write and especially when he writes something he feels strongly. They will, to my mind at least, stand him in better stead than any gimmicks he may memorize from writing courses or "training manual" texts. These do have their uses, largely because a good teacher or a really good text can frequently illuminate what a writer has been doing wrongly (or not at all).[3] By doing so, they can help him to find his blind spots and, sometimes, when even then he fails to see the way out of a dilemma, can point the way for him. They can also communicate something of that structural sense of story which some more fortunate writers seem to absorb automatically from life and from their reading. Of course, bull sessions with sincerely interested fellow writers can accomplish much the same sort of thing and, unless a writer happens to be introverted and solitary by nature, can play a tremendously important part in developing his skills.

Let me make one point clear: the *basic* ingredients and skills of the writer's craft are precisely the same, whether one is dealing with the "mainstream" or with sf, even though the two may still be officially separated today. Stories about people are stories about people, even when the people are thin reflections of people, distortions of people, or non-people or anti-people or sort-of-people seen (as they always must be) through people's eyes.

The equations are the same. Only the values and their consequent relationships are different. And that brings us to a most important question: *what does the sf writer need that today's mainstream writer almost never has?*

The World of the Sf Writer

I have already spoken of the difference between the sf world of change and the as-always world of mainstream fiction. Both, of course, differ from the world as currently accepted or acceptable scientific assumptions show it to be, the sf world because it allows more latitude, the world of mainstream fiction because it remains decades or even centuries behind today's realities. Bearing in mind that we are dealing with a spectrum rather than with discrete entities, we can say that there are three languages or sets of languages: those of hard science, those of sf, and those of mainstream literature. The sf writer should try to have a smattering of the first, but he must be fluent in the other two.[4]

It is possible to know nothing of scientific progress and still to write good, and indeed great, mainstream fiction as mainstream fiction is presently defined. The writer's cosmology need be no vaster than Shakespeare's; his knowledge of physical structure and process no more comprehensive than Milton's; his concept of man's role in the Universe and of his destiny no deeper than Goethe's or Thomas Mann's. But the writer today lives in a world greatly changed from theirs.

Let us take one example: our view of what, intrinsically, we are. I do not mean from any teleological point of view. We can confine ourselves to how we see ourselves biochemically, mechanically. Let us take Hamlet's "too too solid flesh," for that is just how our languages describe our own: they show us as very "real," solid objects moving in a world and universe of other solid objects, some of them—for instance, air and water—not quite as solid as are we, and we ourselves not quite as solid as stone or metal or even living wood. Yet what are we really? What do we now know ourselves to be? One writer, Charles Panati,[5] puts it this way:

> Proportionately, there is more empty space inside an atom than there is in our entire solar system. If all that empty space were squeezed out of a person, the amount of solid matter remaining would be no larger than a speck of dirt. This space of which we are almost entirely composed is filled with three types of fields —electromagnetic, nuclear, and gravitational. In the words of the biologist Dr. Lyall Watson, "We are hollow men and our insubstantial bodies are strung together with electromagnetic and nuclear forces that do no more than create the illusion of matter."

Both Mr. Panati's book and Dr. Watson's deal primarily with the new scientific frontiers of parapsychology (a field of great present importance to sf writers and about which I shall have more to say), but the physical fact they state here does dramatize the great gap between any modern concept of structure and process and those built into the languages we grow up with in and out of school.

This means, essentially, that in the majority of cases the sf writer must educate himself. Often his reeducation will consist primarily of unlearning, or at least trying to forget, those narrow alleged "relevancies" inflicted on him by the educationist middlemen who have made anything resembling a good general education practically a thing of the past, at least in our public school systems. Any education designed for "relevance" to a limited environment, average or lower-than-average IQs, any restricted subcultural situation, or assembly-line life patterns will be of very little use to the sf writer unless he can himself, in school or out of it, acquire the immensely broad view of the world and man which he almost certainly has been denied. What he has learned is never worthless, but its design has been fundamentally centrifugal, concentrating on the small self in its petty environment, and becoming more and more diluted and inaccurate as it attempts to comprehend greater entities: man, life on Earth, the Universe, the vastness of the Cosmos, the mystery of Time.

How can he go about this? Obviously, there can be almost as many varied ways as there are writers, but it seems to me that the first essential is to learn something about how we learn, how we communicate, and how the scientific method works. It is not necessary to *be* a scientist (though, when the preparation hasn't been too restrictive, it's certainly a help); nor is it necessary to be a mathematician. What is really necessary is to understand that mathematics are languages which can describe natural processes and relationships far more accurately than those often false-to-fact accretions that constitute everyday speech and that the scientific method, used in alliance with that other human characteristic, intuition, is a far more reliable way of learning and predicting than intuition used alone, or blind experimentation, or purely verbal logic.

Above all, the sf writer must start out by disabusing himself of the anti-scientific heresy that science is cold and inhuman, for (as far as we know, at least) only humans use it, and it is no more cold and inhuman than they themselves (though, considering recent history, that may not seem too much of a saving grace). If he cannot renounce this notion, if he persists in asserting the false dichotomy between "cold science" and "the warm human emotions," he can seldom advance beyond the writing of fear-of-science fiction, which (as the New Wave has shown) is a dead end intellectually, a fiction of despair, a confession of intellectual impotence.

Let us assume, then, that the writer or would-be writer examines his own attitude toward science and decides that it could with profit be revised. How should he go about it? To my mind, the best work he can turn to is Count Alfred Korzybski's *Science and Sanity, An Introduction to Non-Aristotelian Systems and General Semantics,* about which I had quite a bit to say in my chapter for *Science Fiction, Today and Tomorrow.* ". . . a profound, revolutionary, and seminal work which has had considerable influence, not only on scientists but on science fiction writers—Robert Heinlein and John W. Campbell, for example."

Science and Sanity is not an easy book to read; some of its scientific "facts" and theories have been disproved or modified by new discoveries (as Korzybski himself, who *dated* every statement of fact or theory, of course expected); but it is well worth the effort, for even a single, uncritical reading of it can change one's entire view of the world and man, opening uncounted new outlooks and perspectives. One does not read Korzybski to "learn about science"; one reads him to learn about the human mind and human meaning and the human importance of the scientific method.

After one has read him, one's mind can no longer be confined to a single city, a single campus, a single culture, a single set of acquired assumptions, or any single small sector of the mighty cosmos in which we live.

A picture of the living sciences and their advancement can be acquired later, and the non-scientist can scarcely make a better start than by reading Isaac Asimov and accepting his guidance for further reading.

The frontiers of science are, to a great extent, contiguous with the frontiers of the mind, and the mind—except perhaps where saints and the greater gurus and Zen masters are concerned—cannot attain its own frontiers without exploring them. Just where, today, do these frontiers lie? And how closely contiguous are they with those frontiers of thought science fiction has delineated and started to explore?

In the August 1975 issue of *Analog*, editor Ben Bova published the text of a speech made by physicist Dr. Robert L. Forward, Senior Scientist in the Exploratory Studies Department at Hughes Research Laboratories, to the Science Fiction Writers of America at their 1974 annual meeting in Los Angeles. Its title is "Far Out Physics," and I wish that I could reprint it here in its entirety, for I can think of no single article as important or as challenging to the sf writer.[6]

Though Dr. Forward carefully qualified the speculative ideas he discussed as "only speculations," he documented the theoretical and experimental bases from which they were adduced with more than twenty references; and the scope of these speculations can best be suggested by listing his subjects:

FUTURISTIC POSSIBILITIES IN GRAVITY/INERTIA
Speculations About a New Theory of Gravity
Gravitational Radiation
Black Holes
Hawking Black Holes (named after a scientist, S. Hawking)
Antigravity—Six Ways
Newtonian Antigravity
General Relativistic Antigravity

Antinewtonian Antigravity
Inertia Reversal Antigravity
Inertia Redistribution Antigravity
Dr. Forward went on to speak of
FUTURISTIC POSSIBILITIES IN SPACE/TIME
Space Travel
Gravity Catapults
Space Warps
Tachyon Tunneling
Inertia Control
Negative Mass Propulsion
Fifth Dimensional Hypervelocity
Time Travel
General Relativistic Time Contraction
Tipler Two-Way Time Machine
Negative Matter Time Machine
FUTURISTIC POSSIBILITIES IN MASS/ENERGY
New Forms of Matter
Unconventional Nuclear Reactors
Superperformance Organic Materials
(Non)conservation Laws
Interconversion of Mass-Energy-Momentum Tensor
The final topic was
FUTURISTIC POSSIBILITIES IN INFORMATION/COMMUNICATION
Communication Media
Communication Without Media

I have refrained deliberately from commenting on any of these topics—many of which are already sf commonplaces—partly because they are sufficiently suggestive in themselves and partly because I hope that every reader of this book will seek out the issue of *Analog* in which they appeared and read what Dr. Forward had to say to his audience of "balding guys with bad teeth and three children" who "want to *entertain* and *make money.*"

Those readers who take the trouble to do so will discover that science and science fiction have a common frontier expanding along an exponential curve and that this frontier should be taken very seriously indeed.

Here is where science and science fiction meet—or almost meet—and it is here that the great "what ifs" that go into the making of great science fiction first are found, those which gave us Stapledon's *Last and First Men*, Cordwainer Smith's Underpeople, Murray Leinster's "First Contact," Ted Sturgeon's "Killdozer," Arthur Clarke's *Childhood's End*, and all the rest. Science fiction and science fantasy simply take the next step or two beyond the known, the suspected, the perhaps barely possible. That step may not always seem precisely placed; sometimes, especially when new discoveries and hindsight enter in, it may appear to have been downright stupid. So did man's first attempts to fly.

The important thing, for the writer especially, is that the frontiers of science and of science fiction and science fantasy cannot be divorced. Had the velocity of light never been determined, had Einstein not presented that velocity as an absolute limit to the speed with which anything in the physical universe can move, the sf commonplace of "faster than light travel" (Fifth Dimensional Hypervelocity?) could not even have been imagined—not even in a doctoral dissertation on science fiction proving that science really doesn't have very much to do with it.

The sf writer can find this basic material in a thousand places—in *Sky and Telescope*, *Science*, *Scientific American*, *Nature*, or more rarely in *Harper's* or the *Reader's Digest* or his daily paper. Or of course—don't we all?—he can absorb much of it at secondhand from the reading and writing of his fellows. The most important thing, at least in my opinion, is that he should not forget where it comes from and not attribute to myth, magic, or Marxism that for which only the exercise of the scientific method is responsible.

Yet what of that shadowy area where science is now meeting what was once classified as myth and magic? (We can dismiss Marxism as a mid-Nineteenth Century pseudo-science and therefore a horse of quite a different color.) Dr. Forward's final topic, "Futuristic Possibilities in Information/Communication," which he discussed only briefly, had to do with the possibilities of ESP and so can serve to introduce this entire subject.

Many phenomena which, prior to the Age of Reason, were (often in fear and trembling) believed in almost universally—phenomena which the late Charles Fort catalogued so meticulously in his four curious, questioning books[7]—have finally been brought into the laboratory and, in varying degrees, subjected to scientific testing and verification. Where the impossibility of reproducing a phenomenon on demand has, in the past, apparently precluded the application of the experimental method (as in the case of poltergeists), new approaches have been developed serving the same purpose (as they have in the case of bursting stars); and of course new scientific and technological devices and techniques have made completely new experiments possible. Electroencephalography, for instance, has measured altered states of consciousness produced by Zen meditation, "Transcendental Meditation," and other similar disciplines and has established, under rigorous laboratory conditions, the existence of telepathy between identical twins. Similarly, the Kirlian method of photographing the "auras" of living organisms has corroborated the ancient belief in their existence. I myself believe that we now definitely can state that the following phenomena are proven—even though most of them are still seldom predictable or producible on demand: telepathy, psychokinesis, clairvoyance, dowsing, precognition, the "green thumb" in horticulture, and what, for lack of any more precise term, we can call faith healing.

Science fiction, naturally, has already explored and exploited many of these areas. (John W. Campbell, as editor of *Astounding Science Fiction,* which he later renamed *Analog,* was especially active in encouraging sf writers to do so.) But the explorations have hardly scratched the surface. If we accept the existence of telepathy and all the other "wild talents," limitless fictional opportunities open up before us, in interpersonal relations first and foremost, in our possible relations with other beings and cultures, in the relationship of God and man (or gods and men), in how we view the past and future (or futures), in how we see ourselves.

Books on "the occult" have proliferated mightily during the past few years, most of them "quickies" hacked out to capitalize on the sensational and on sudden public interest. Therefore the interested writer should be careful of where he seeks his introduction to today's parapsychology. I will suggest a few titles—first and foremost, former astronaut Edgar D. Mitchell's symposium *Psychic Exploration, A Challenge for Science* (G.P. Putnam's Sons, New York, 1974). Since his retirement from the Navy, Dr. Mitchell has headed the Institute for Noetic Sciences, which he himself founded and which is dedicated to this area of research; and the book, to which more than thirty authorities contributed, is the most comprehensive introduction available. Next there is Mr. Panati's work, already mentioned. The other two titles, both by Sheila Ostrander and Lynn Schroeder, are *Psychic Discoveries Behind the Iron Curtain* (Prentice Hall, New York, 1970; Bantam Books, 1970) and *Handbook of Psi Discoveries* (Berkley Publishing Company and Putnam, New York, 1974).

Reference, Research, and the Sf Writer

The sf writer does *not* have to know everything about everything. (The platitude about the Universal Man of the Renaissance—that in his day he could know everything there was to know and that universality no longer can be aimed at because there's so much more to know today—is sheer nonsense. The world of the Renaissance was not that simple; in some ways—where local dialects and weights and measures were concerned, for instance—it was vastly more complex.[8] The Renaissance Man simply had the good sense to *attempt* universality—to study the Cosmos and the world instead of just his own petty corner of it—but then he didn't have any Authorities with Doctorates of Education to tell him that such an effort was not relevant to becoming an effective used-car salesman or lawyer or plumbing contractor or urban guerrilla.) Like the Renaissance Man, the sf writer must, therefore, strive for universality—and for a universality that reflects his individual bent. His map of the world—of structure and process, of how and why—will be incomplete; it will be inaccurate; it may sometimes display his personal quiddities as facts. But it will be vastly better than no map at all, or one of those contemporary maps that show the world restricted to a single slum, a single cultural cranny, a status notch, or a thatch of pubic hair.

The sf writer must either know, or else learn, how to use those very important tools of his trade, *questions:* questions asked of books, questions asked of people who will, in turn, ask them of books (reference librarians), and questions asked of people who simply know more than he does (experts). *Books* come first. In them, he can usually find what he does not know; they will explain to him that which he does not understand; he can use them to check the fallibilities of his own memory. For reference, then, he will have to depend on libraries open to the public *and on his own.* There is no better way for a writer to spend money than on working books, for every one he buys will, in due course, save him hours of time. For many years, I myself have bought every reference work I could afford: general dictionaries, foreign-language dictionaries, specialized dictionaries—military, scientific, culinary, and God knows what. I have purchased almanacs, registers, guidebooks to unlikely places, histories, and texts and treatises on out-of-the-way subjects. I do not care if they're "outdated"—not if they're cheap enough. (A civilization probably greater, and certainly nobler, than our own could readily be founded on the 11th Edition of the Encyclopedia Britannica—which is a good idea for an sf story if you happen to be so minded.)

Books of your own are immediately available, either when you want to find out something or, occasionally, to browse in for ideas or for the germs of ideas. The public or school library, useful as it often is, is not really an adequate substitute. It takes longer to use; others compete with you for the book you want, or the reference librarian is too busy to attend to you, or he or she doesn't know enough about your area of inquiry to be of any help to you. Besides, it's never open when you wake up in the small hours filled with an idea that demands instant checking and immediate pursuit. On the other hand, your personal bookshelves can never be a complete substitute for access to a major library, and a really good general reference librarian is a pearl beyond price. Such librarians are by no means common; they must, like sf writers, aspire to universality; their map of the world, as reflected in the materials with which they deal, must be astoundingly complete. The sf writer should make it a point to get acquainted with the reference staff at whatever library he intends to use, to find out what they do and do not know, where they can be useful to him and where they more probably will fail. He should also familiarize himself with the mechanics of the inter-library loan system and with those library tools that enable one to locate hard-to-find books and periodicals.

Why is this so important? Because access to reference material, and knowing how to use it, can often save him from those errors which damage or destroy the believability and impact of his work. Errors of fact, words misused or even badly misspelled, errors inserted by a careless publisher—any of these can trip a reader up, spoiling the spontaneity of his experience. Even in mainstream fiction, which deals so largely with the already familiar, this is important; in sf, dealing with the unfamiliar and often the undreamed-of, it is far more so. It is not just a matter of getting all one's scientific (or other) data *right;* more often, it is simply avoiding any mention of dubious data that just may be *wrong*.

The delicate art of achieving believability consists very largely of not going into explicit detail except when it is absolutely necessary to do so and *never* doing so when your material is unfamiliar to you. Your reader may know much more than you do, and impressing him with your ignorance is no way to command his attention and build credibility. One error, if it is gross enough, can undermine the entire structure of a story.

Writers of historical fiction face this problem constantly (and so, of course, do sf writers of time-travel stories). Some years ago I read a novel based on the life of Will Adams, the first Englishman to come to Japan and the only Caucasian ever to become a samurai. Its author, a newspaperman, after mentioning the amount of research he had engaged in, opened his narrative with detailed accounts of Adams attending meetings of the Royal Society and the Hakluyt Society in the distinguished company of Sir Francis Drake, Richard Hakluyt, and Queen Elizabeth I. As the Royal Society was founded around 1660 and the Hakluyt Society not until well into the Nineteenth Century, and as it was not a time-travel novel, my interest in it perished instantly. Had the author taken the trouble to make a five-minute phone call to any competent reference librarian he would not have made the error and lost at least one reader.

Where unfamiliar and foreign names, backgrounds and situations, languages and dialects are concerned the writer should get his information from a reliable source, use it, then check the result with someone *thoroughly* familiar with the material, for it is only too easy to pick up a few seemingly accurate details and then, in ignorance, assemble them inaccurately. This is as true of science and technology as it is of cultural, historical, or geographical data. The rifle Frederick Forsyth used as a central element in his highly successful suspense novel *The Day of the Jackal* is a case in point. It is a technological absurdity: a barrel which, *with* its bolt action, is only eighteen inches long; a telescope sight; a silencer (of course!); two struts to form a skeleton stock—and every part light enough to be hidden inside the tubes of a metal crutch, the padded end of which became the butt plate. The cartridge was loaded with cordite (a propellant no longer used). For all this, Forsyth claimed an order of accuracy achieved only by heavy bench-rest target rifles, putting every bullet into something like a one-inch circle at around 150 yards. A two-foot circle would be stretching the probable actuality.

Forsyth writes well and tensely, but that one bad error made me read the book critically rather than spontaneously and enabled me to see its many flaws of plot and structure—episodes dragged in for sensation's sake and quite unnecessary to the story. This is not nitpicking; anyone at all familiar with rifles would have been put off by it, and there are a great many riflemen around. Generally good, the book still was not good enough to reestablish its believability.

There are stories, of course, good enough to survive errors which otherwise would ruin them. One of these is Norman Spinrad's delightful "A Thing of Beauty," from *Analog.* One of its two central characters is a multi-billionaire Japanese industrialist, very anxious to impress his wife's socially superior family with his taste and culture and very much the traditionalist. Norman introduces him wearing a "red silk kimono with a richly-brocaded black obi"—instead of the severe black kimono without a sash of any sort which is the traditional Japanese gentleman's formal attire. Naturally, the informed reader's first thought is "Hey, why's this guy in drag?"

The Challenge and the Opportunity

Again, all fiction deals with the adventure of being human—the adventure or the ordeal or the spiritual experience, call it what you will. Sf, very specially, deals with that adventure as our exercise of the scientific method is now shaping it or may shape it in the future. The sf writer cannot avoid man's problems; by the very nature of his craft, he must meet them head on. That is sf's challenge, and it is as big as the future of mankind. To make the most of it, each writer must develop his own individual universality and then, within that framework, take full advantage of his special knowledge and his special skills.

His opportunities are unlimited, but he must equip himself for the adventure.

NOTES

1. Notably James Gunn. See his chapter in *Science Fiction, Today and Tomorrow,* New York, Harper & Row, 1974.

2. In the preface to his *The Meaning of Culture,* New York, W.W. Norton & Co., 1929.

3. A good rule in choosing a teacher of writing is to find one who has written and published professionally.

4. To familiarize himself with the languages and themes of science fiction, the writer who has not grown up with the genre must first discover what his predecessors have imagined and created. By far his best introduction to the field —because of its scholarly thoroughness and because it presents so intimate a picture of how sf has developed thematically and visually—is James Gunn's monumental *Alternate Worlds: An Illustrated History of Science Fiction* (Prentice-Hall, Inc., Englewood Cliffs, New Jersey, 1975). This is a book that should be in every library.

5. Charles Panati, *Supersenses, Our Potential for Parasensory Experience,* Quadrangle/The New York Times Book Co., New York, 1974.

6. Readers unable to obtain a copy of the article can get copies of the viewgraphs shown during Dr. Forward's speech by writing to him at Hughes Research Laboratories, 3011 Malibu Canyon Road, Malibu, CA 90265. Also a 48-minute tape recording of the speech (with its title changed to "Phantasmal Physics") is available from The Center for Cassette Studies, 8110 Webb Avenue, N. Hollywood, CA 91605, for $14.95.

7. Charles Fort, *The Books of Charles Fort* (containing *The Book of the Damned, New Lands, Lo!,* and *Wild Talents*), Henry Holt, New York, 1941.

8. Randle Cotgrave's 1611 *Dictionarie of the French and English Tongues* gives fourteen different definitions for the word *livre,* a pound.

Reginald Bretnor

Reginald Bretnor was born in 1911 in Vladivostok, Siberia. His family moved to Japan in 1915, and he lived there until brought to the United States in January 1920.

He received a haphazard education in a number of private and public schools and in one or two colleges and has no degrees. During World War II he wrote propaganda to Japan and the Far East for the Office of War Information and afterward continued with the Department of State's OIICA until he resigned in February 1947. Since then he has been freelancing and is now living with his wife, Rosalie, in Oregon.

His fiction, much of it humor, has appeared in a wide variety of magazines: *Harper's, Esquire, Today's Woman,* a few academic quarterlies, the major sf magazines, *Ellery Queen's Mystery Magazine,* and so forth. Many of his stories have been anthologized.

His articles, on public affairs and military theory, have been published in such periodicals as the *Michigan Quarterly Review, Modern Age,* and the *Military Review;* and he is the author of *Decisive Warfare, a Study in Military Theory,* 1969 (Stackpole Books).

As editor, he has published *Modern Science Fiction: Its Meaning and Its Future,* 1953 (Coward-McCann), a now-standard critical symposium, for which he wrote the final chapter on "The Future of Science Fiction," and more recently *Science Fiction, Today and Tomorrow* (Harper & Row, 1974; Penguin, 1975), to which he contributed a chapter entitled "Science Fiction in the Age of Space."

He has lectured on science fiction, on writing generally, and on his special interests at colleges and other schools, to writers' organizations, and to more general audiences. He is also the author of the article on sf in two editions of the Encyclopaedia Britannica.

His interests include Japanese swords and related areas of Japanese art; antique and modern weapons (he is the inventor of an automatic mortar on which a U.S. patent has been issued); military and naval history and theory; parapsychology; people and their stories; the world at large; and the great adventure of the Age of Space. He is a member of several organizations that reflect these interests.

POUL ANDERSON

Star-flights and Fantasies:

Sagas Still to Come

Muse, tell of the keen-witted hero who wandered afar in the world after he plundered the holy and widely famed city of Troy. Many the men were whose towns he did guest and whose ways he did learn, and many the sorrows that smote him at sea as he strove for his life and to lead homeward his crewmen. But they were all doomed by their folly in eating the kine of the Sun-god Hyperion, perishing for it. O daughter of Zeus, howsoever you know of these matters, tell me.

Thus begins one of the oldest and greatest epics we have. We would be stretching words out of shape to call it an early piece of science fiction. But it lies at the root of a tradition to which a vast amount of science fiction belongs: the marvelous voyage. In like manner, many if not all war stories, including stories of future wars, stem from the *Iliad.* Beowulf is the archetype of the chieftain who delivers his people from monstrous enemies, be these demonic, man-made, or extraterrestrial. Although the tale of Gilgamesh lay too long lost to have had a comparable direct influence until recently, the seeker after immortality (or knowledge, or something else not to be found at home) is a figure equally pervasive.

No science fiction known to me is epic in

the sense of being written as a lengthy narrative poem. And only a small percentage is in the sense that it conveys a feeling of grandeur and heroism. Yet that part of the field seems worth discussing. In this age of narrowing frontiers upon earth and strangleholds upon the individual—this age of fantastically blossoming knowledge and capability, when the freedom of infinity is ours for the taking and nothing except ourselves holds us back—science fiction is almost uniquely well fitted to tell such stories and evoke such emotions.

Reginald Bretnor proposed the title of my essay. A meticulous semanticist, he must have borne in mind that epics, strictly speaking, scan, whereas sagas are prose narratives. However, the distinction is a bit arbitrary. Good prose has at least as much metrical structure as free verse does. The original sagas use considerable poetry, either as direct quotation or in close paraphrase. They were written down in medieval Iceland and Norway after being handed on orally through times that ranged from a few generations to hundreds of years. Some are fabulous, some historical. At their best, they are superb. That of Egil Skallagrimsson is among the finest biographical novels ever composed. Elsewhere we find passages splendidly stirring or, quite often, touching. The ideal held forth is far less frequently reckless bravado than it is endurance and common sense. The same is true of the major epics.

There are dull sections and entire works that are poor among both the sagas and the epics. The top-rate of either, though, have much in common. First and foremost, each tells a story. It is a story of mighty feats done by persons who, whatever their mortal failings, are not mean-spirited; and wonderful things happen.

Is this not true of a lot of the science fiction that we remember with pleasure? I think it is. Therefore I am going to use "epic" and "saga" loosely, interchangeably, in what follows. Both will refer to particular qualities of a work, rather than to formal organization of text.

Hence these words must cover a wide range. They do not connote mere slam-bang action; leave that to the boob tube. Lofty deeds need not be violent nor involve rescuing the universe. To take a real-life example, Fridtjof Nansen never fired a shot in anger and probably never struck a blow; he spent the end of his life forcing governments, by sheer moral suasion, to show some mercy to the hordes of refugees and starvelings they had created; but his career was epic if ever anybody's was. Turning back to literature, we can remark that Odysseus was only trying to get home and reclaim what was rightfully his. In the course of this, he did nothing other strong, able, courageous men could not have done. And heroism can be entirely of the spirit; remember his wife Penelope.

By and large, epical people are more interested in what they are doing and what they hope to do than in their own personalities. They are inner-directed but outward-oriented. This does not mean they are simple-minded. Jason, Moses, Igor, and Umslopogaas, to name just four, come through as quite complex characters. Ahab in *Moby Dick* is exceptional in that he doesn't enjoy life as thoroughly as circumstances allow. Even Shakespeare's Hamlet does; furthermore, this alleged dithering weakling—who actually has sound logical reasons for not acting impetuously—leaves behind him as gory a trail as any in drama. Macbeth, ravaged by remorse, does not whine about it and dies indomitable. Most epical characters, whether real or fictitious, live with huge gusto in a world they find wonderful. The marvels they encounter in it reflect those of their own minds and feelings.

The epic quality includes a certain high seriousness. This does not mean lack of humor. We need simply think of *Huckleberry Finn,* not to mention countless funny episodes elsewhere. But what happens in the story has genuine importance, whether to the protagonist alone or to his entire society. The whole world does. And the fundamentally tragic nature of existence is not glossed over. The narrative may have a happy ending, but there is no pretense that the survivors can live blandly ever after.

For its success, the epic is perhaps the most dependent on style of any kind of story. By "style" I mean "right choice of words," a matter unteachable and practically undefinable but instantly recognizable. I do not mean bombast or floridity (though these may have their function, especially in a comic interlude). The medieval sagas are, in fact, spare in their language, and Homer is more austere than his translators usually make him out to be. Yet in contrast, does not the manner of a Melville or a Doughty work equally well to convey stark sublimity and mystery?

Several of the original sagas incorporate what in effect are short stories, and several more are barely of novelette length in their own right. But as a rule, the largeness of epic themes requires elbow room. We shall mainly be discussing novels.

Largeness—diversity—marvels—seriousness, possibly leavened by humor, a conviction that life is worth living—attention turned outward to the surrounding world—the supposition that man can either bend fate, or can in his heart resist being bent by it—endurance—achievement—

a narrative that keeps moving—bold use of language—these are the hallmarks of epic and saga. They do not preclude values such as tenderness, compassion, awareness of beauty, or philosophical depth. The best of the tales we shall consider do contain elements like that. But those occur as well in stories of other kinds.

Nowadays the heroic traits are unfashionable in academe. Those professors and critics who still openly admire them are a minority who don't seem to have much influence. In most cases, if Melville, Twain, Conrad (Kipling is generally ignored) or a comparably oriented contemporary writer is studied at all, the study is of different elements in his work than these, *angst* or social protest or whatever. The opinion is dominant that a protagonist's principal activity should be introspection, and if life defeats him without any noticeable resistance on his part, we are told that that combines uncompromising realism with profound symbolism. Of recent years, a certain amount of science fiction has been based on this theory.

I am not sneering. In the hands of a talented writer—e.g., Herbert Gold or John Cheever—the method can be tremendously effective. Within science fiction, a few have made skillful use of it; Robert Silverberg comes immediately to mind. (I can't help wondering why he doesn't outright "go mainstream." He would sell far more books. But that's none of my business.) All literary forms are legitimate. We need them all, if we are to have any chance of covering the whole range of human experience.

In the confines of science fiction, too—confines which I hope will someday disappear, when books and magazines no longer bear category labels—obviously the epic is not and should not be the single species. The themes are numerous to which it is not suited. The heavy science or heavy political think-piece, the intensely personal small-scale event, the satire, the comedy or jape or farce, the mood-piece—these and many more are every bit as valid, with ancestries every bit as venerable.

Besides, far from being easy, the epical story is among the most difficult to write. At best, the failed saga becomes, in a famous phrase, mere adventures, like waves happening to an oyster. At worst, the author, attempting to strike a heroic pose, falls flat on his face into a puddle of steaming rodomontade. If certain of these efforts have nevertheless been popular, this suggests how hungry the reading public is for the genuine article. Likewise does the success of mainstream writers like Ernest Gann and Joseph Wambaugh: excellent craftsmen who accomplish everything they set out to do but whose work has little appeal to the professional critic.

However, some science fiction has been truly epical; while not equal to Homer, it bears a kinship which I don't think he would have disavowed. Let's look at a few examples, as well as at examples of works which, for varying reasons, don't belong among them. In the course of exploration, perhaps we can sharpen our concept of heroic fiction in general.

In his *Billion Year Spree,* Brian Aldiss maintains that the entire genre began with Mary Shelley's *Frankenstein.* I disagree. It seems to me that the origins are far more complex and diverse, going back to the seventeenth-century creation of scientific method and reaching full development under the inspiration of discovery and invention during the nineteenth; two distinct basic motifs or directions appeared whose primary sources were, respectively, Jules Verne and H. G. Wells. But whether *Frankenstein* be founder or harbinger, it sounds a Promethean note which was to be heard often again. The struggle, both exterior and interior, of both man and monster, is vividly enough realized to make this book at least a minor epic.

Verne might better be called Faustian, except that in his exuberant optimism he seldom or never shows any suspicion that Faust, mankind, will have a price to pay. Things generally go easily for his characters, and he conveys little sense of the hugeness and strangeness of the universe, even when he sends a crew around the moon. (Granted, NASA didn't either!) Only in *Twenty Thousand Leagues Under the Sea,* its descriptions of the ocean, its fights for survival, its powerful and enigmatic Captain Nemo, do we get something of an epic. And it is inconclusive. *The Mysterious Island* does not provide a very satisfactory sequel. Needless to say, this is no denigration of Verne, who had different pioneering to do. Chiefly from him rises that stream of science fiction which has the idea as hero and which celebrates man's triumphs of intelligence and will.

From Wells comes the second stream, wherein the emphasis is not on the idea or assumption *per se*—he outraged Verne by the frankly fantastic notions he used—but on the consequences to society or the individual. In him this emphasis was so strong as to forbid his writing a saga. Civilizations are described discursively; people are ordinary and unventuresome, except a few who are mad (e.g., in *The Island of Doctor Moreau*) or effortlessly perfect (e.g., in *Men Like Gods*). Again, I intend no put-down. Wells's realism was a very great gift to his successors. English-language science fiction has yet to see a better all-around writer, unless we count Kipling's three or four ventures into the field.

Being so good, Wells could not avoid giving us occasional glimpses of immensity. Although *The Time Machine* is close-focused, it does in passing convey—especially at the end—a feeling that ages have indeed passed inexorably by. But curiously, the epic quality is most present in certain of his short stories. Consider, as examples, "The Lord of the Dynamos," "A Dream of Armageddon," or "The Star." A quotation from the last of these will illustrate what I mean. A mathematician has calculated the orbit of the invading body and knows what destruction it will wreak.

"He looked at it as one might look into the eyes of a brave enemy. 'You may kill me,' he said after a silence. 'But I can hold you—and all the universe for that matter—in the grip of this little brain. I would not change. Even now.' "

About the same time, discoveries in the field of prehistory inspired two unquestionable epics: *La Guerre du Feu (The Fire War)* by J.-H. Rosny ainé and *Den Lange Rejse (The Long Journey)* by Johannes V. Jensen. Both concern the struggle of early man against nature and his fellow man, the mastery of fire and, more slowly, of superstitious dread; the Danish work, actually a series of books, continues through Columbus and the age of discovery. In America, Jack London tried his hand at the same theme, less successfully, as have others, notably Vardis Fisher. It is always dangerous to say that a certain field is exhausted. Some genius may come along and find what nobody else ever noticed. But for the present it does seem as if these writers used up the basic possibilities of the Eolithic and Paleolithic eras. In contrast, the possibilities that lie in the future are limited only by our own imaginations.

None is likely to surpass the imagination of Olaf Stapledon. In *Last and First Men* and *The Star Maker* he takes us through the whole of space and the whole of time and makes us feel we have really been to those uttermost bounds. He is not an outstanding stylist. And if an individual hero and a straight story line are requirements for an epic, these two books don't qualify; they may not even count as novels. But in awesomeness, magnificence of concept, tragic impact, they are unsurpassed.

Not to compare myself to him but to explain a little of his method, I would like to offer an anecdote. I was planning a yarn, *Tau Zero,* about a spaceship which was trapped into traveling closer and closer to the speed of light. In consequence, the laws of relativity made time inboard pass ever more slowly with respect to the rest of the universe, until at last the stars aged by millions of years while a crewman drew a breath; and thus the travelers outlived our cycle of the universe and saw a new cosmos reborn from the old. Now how could I hope to give a hint of the enormousness? Well, how had Stapledon done it? Studying him, I found he gets us used to one order of magnitude before moving on to the next; and each order occupies about as much wordage as the last. In mathematical terms, his progression is logarithmic. I followed his lead. My first chapter covered a few hours, my second a few days, and so on, the period increasing by approximately a factor of ten in each successive chapter. Many readers have told me how well it worked. But credit Stapledon. His books will be remembered far longer anyway.

For better or worse, the appearance of specialized magazines decisively influenced the evolution of science fiction. More accurately, the influence was for better and worse. Isolated from the rest of literature, authors were no longer subject to the rigors and challenges which a Hemingway or a Faulkner met; for a long while, with a few important exceptions, the standard of writing was abysmally low. At the same time, having a small but eagerly captive audience, the makers became free to develop ideas which—widely disseminated today—would doubtless then never have gotten past nonspecialist editors who neither knew nor cared about such things. These themes included several of epical scale.

But of course mere scale is not enough, neither necessary nor sufficient. With due respect for the entertainment value and for the precedents they set, stories by men like E. E. Smith or John Campbell in his superscientific aspect have nothing of the saga about them. We are *told* that the heroes cross thousands of light-years and subject to their wills entire planets and suns. The scope is more than godlike; it would have been beyond the comprehension of Zeus. But we are never really shown the events, let alone made to feel them and their meanings. This abstractness, combined with generally bald style and gee-whiz dialogue, leaves us emotionally on a level with the Rover Boys.

Campbell did far better in his Don A. Stuart persona, but with the arguable exception of "Who Goes There?" and, perhaps, "Blindness," these works of his arouse other moods than the heroic.

Had Stanley Weinbaum lived, he might well have brought forth a science fiction epic. "A Martian Odyssey," its sequel "Valley of Dreams," and *The Black Flame* have elements of it. Two early writers, happily still with us, who were not content to stay on a footing with the Lensmen were Edmond Hamilton and Jack Williamson. Of the former, P. Schuyler Miller has said, "Hamilton had understood the implications of the 'island universe' concept of cosmic structure before most astronomers did, and certainly before most of them accepted it" (*Analog,* July 1974). By imagining in detail and seeking words wherein to flesh his dreams, he has often touched on vastness, on man at strife against fate, and on doom bravely met. It is pleasant to be able to say the name of his wife, Leigh Brackett, and that she too remains active. As for Williamson, though his early "Legion" stories were mainly zap-zap, fun to read but little else, he has continued to grow and learn through a long career. His *Darker Than You Think* and *The Humanoids,* to name two of the best-known, count as true sagas, the first tragic, the second upbeat.

When Campbell took the helm of *Astounding,* the average quality of science fiction writing began a rise which has not yet stopped, while the peaks of it grew high indeed. By no means were all of those peaks epical. As I remarked before, there are plenty of different, equally worthy kinds of story. But let us consider several classics which can go under our present heading, and several which can't, and ask ourselves why.

Such masterworks of A. E. Van Vogt's as *Slan, The Weapon Makers,* and *World of $\overline{A}$* assuredly can. His detractors, of whom I am emphatically *not* one, have said harsh things about them, but that is beside the present point; we are here concerned strictly with the definition of what is or is not saga material. However, it is worth noting that, as far as I know, none of those detractors have ever even attempted anything epical. The trouble with most literary critics is that they confuse their personal tastes with the law and the prophets. Long may Van Vogt flourish.

Certain colleagues of his lead us into some interesting complexities. I might mention L. Ron Hubbard's *Final Blackout* as a very high-powered saga, then add what a complete failure his later rehash of it, *The End Is Not Yet,* turned out to be—partly because it was a mere rehash? In the romantic and sensuously realized world of *Fury,* in its driven protagonist Sam Harker, half hero and half monster, Henry Kuttner and his wife Catherine L. Moore created another memorable epic, under the pseudonym Lawrence O'Donnell; but they were also wry Lewis Padgett. Robert Heinlein's *Methuselah's Children* falls pretty clearly into our area and likewise *Orphans of the Sky;* but I don't feel that the rest of his work does, not even the hard-driving *The Door Into Summer* or the picaresque *Citizen of the Galaxy.* It seems to me excluded by its very virtues, whether being too leisurely (and fascinatingly) expository, too psychological, too satirical, or whatever. Similarly, of Fritz Leiber's writings, I would only describe as sagas his science fiction novels, *Gather, Darkness!* and *Destiny Times Three,* and, collectively, his swashbuckling fantasies about Fafhrd and the Gray Mouser. Everything else gives us different sorts of delights. True, *The Big Time* and *The Wanderer* have vast backgrounds, abundant suspense, lavish color and action; but the first is extremely concentrated, the second extremely wide-ranging, and neither has a definite protagonist. Analogues outside of science fiction might be *The Innocent Voyage* and *War and Peace.*

Isaac Asimov's Foundation series, taken as a whole, is a touchstone case. We find there the spaciousness and forward movement of an epic and encounter many wonderful things. On balance, though, I would not include it. My reasons may help make my definition clear. While numerous scenes are vividly brought to life, much of the work is devoted to ideas rather than emotions. Indeed, we get few emotional scenes, none of high intensity. The people are mainly of Wellsian ordinariness. Exceptions are Hari Seldon, whose gigantism is purely of the mind; the Mule, damned to ultimate futility; a couple of soldierly types whose efforts are likewise frustrated. The style of writing throughout is clear and clean but scarcely elevated. Asimov is always stimulating, but he himself may agree that he is not a maker of sagas. One might almost say he is too civilized.

One might say the same of L. Sprague de Camp. In such chromatic, exciting, and four-dimensionally convincing tales as *Lest Darkness Fall* or the Viagens series, there is still a sense of detachment or, better put, of intellectual self-awareness and ironic humor. Though irony is plentiful in the old epical works, not even in *Don Quixote* does it become this abundant. However, I admit my judgment turns more on atmosphere, on flavor (a flavor which I as a reader thoroughly enjoy), than on technical qualifications.

It does the same as regards Arthur C. Clarke. Evocative though novels like *Childhood's End, The City and the Stars,* and *2001* are, what they stir in me is different from what stirs at the books of Job* or Nehemiah, Mary Renault's *The King Must Die,* or the biography of Drake. Clarke's writing is poetic when he chooses, but it is a poetry more comparable to that of, let us say, Browning—just as Ray Bradbury may be compared to Swinburne—than to that of Kipling or Jeffers.

Among younger writers, I'd make a corresponding observation about Larry Niven. He can not only produce a stupendous vision, as in *Ringworld;* he can make us experience it, but we don't get quite the feeling about it that we would from a Hamilton or Van Vogt. We get more the thrill of a scientist—which is a valid emotion, too seldom dealt with in literature.

Today's highly technique-conscious newcomers and not-quite-so-newcomers generally produce finely crafted, sometimes brilliant miniatures. Roger Zelazny seeks more breadth. When he uses ancient myth, he is apt to be too elegantly mannered for the saga (and why shouldn't he be?), but an occasional tale like *Isle of the Dead* fits in very well. Samuel R. Delany has brought forth one readily identifiable epic, *Nova.* Ursula K. Le Guin has done it in both *The Left Hand of Darkness* and her Earthsea trilogy—and done it in spite of being as civilized and low-keyed (though extraordinarily subtle) as Clarke.

The late "Cordwainer Smith" was an epicmaker partly in the tradition of Stapledon. He did not reach as far through space-time—but then, the latter didn't always do so either, and I wonder how much of Sirius is in the former's half-human underpeople. Smith's writing has to be considered in its entirety. It all, or nearly all, belongs in a mosaic of which no part can do more than suggest the whole. But besides giving us this majestic overview and sense of miracle, in his compassionately rendered detail of individual lives he is also very much in the stream of Wells. In making the great and the small equally real, equally important, he was aided by his use of language, derived from the Chinese, in which he was fluent; somehow it combined clarity, strangeness, and music.

Nor is there any argument about how to classify novels like Frank Herbert's *Dune* and Gordon R. Dickson's *Dorsai!* But let me remind anyone who still confuses the saga with the simple adventure yarn that besides their amplitude, and beneath the exciting incidents, both these authors go deeper than ever Carlyle did into the nature and significance

**Job* is, of course, more a long lyric than a narrative; but the language and spirit are epical.

of the hero as savior. Whether he be a secular leader like Dickson's or a messiah like Herbert's, there is something cryptic, transhuman, about a man of this kind. We had better try to understand the phenomenon —for how many more overnight changes of the course of history can Earth survive? Or, maybe, what overnight changes do we need in order to survive? Far beyond the entertainment they give, we owe Herbert and Dickson a debt for the thoughts they provoke.

Superficially, Jack Vance appears quite different. His protagonists, never the least bit flamboyant in terms of their own cultures, always have limited objectives; he underplays their actions; he is as witty and ironic as de Camp, except for having a sharper bite; typically, a narrative of his ends not on a high but a subdued note. And yet I submit that he is not only among the three or four best writers currently doing science fiction of any sort; he is our foremost sagaman. The paradox will repay examination.

To be epical, a narrative need not take us to exotic places. But that helps and in fact happens more commonly than not. Vance is the absolute master of physical and cultural settings. His are as solidly timbered, logically plausible as de Camp's or Hal Clement's. At the same time they have the romance, the Faeriehood, of Lord Dunsany's. They and the people in them keep revealing facets that are wholly astonishing while being wholly believable—the masks worn in "The Moon Moth," the savage game played in *Trullion,* to pick two at random. His gift for bestowing names is unsurpassed. His style, precise and uncluttered, is also gorgeous. A quotation from *The Dragon Masters* should give, to those who aren't already familiar with him, a little of the savor:

> Phade [the minstrel-maiden] ran down the passageway which presently jointed Bird Walk, so called for the series of fabulous birds of lapis, gold, cinnabar, malachite and marcasite inlaid into the marble. Through an arcade of green and gray jade in spiral columns she passed out onto Kergan's Way, a natural defile which formed the main thoroughfare of Banbeck Village. Reaching the portal, she summoned a pair of lads from the fields. "Run to the brooder, find Joaz Banbeck! Hasten, bring him here; I must speak with him."

In their brooders men raise what they call dragons: descendants of captives from a hostile nonhuman race, bred through centuries into various types, formidable fighters, caninely loyal to their masters. Meanwhile the enemy has similarly been breeding humans. Few stories have had a more audacious concept, or told of such an Iliadic struggle—been Iliadic, too, in full and sympathetic portrayal of both sides.

The hero of *The Star King* is a quiet man but on an epic quest through the galaxy, seeking revenge upon the five outlaw lords who caused the slaughter of his family. With superlative richness, above a foundation of socioeconomic common sense which is far too rare in science fiction and which, again, persuades us that this universe of prodigies actually works, Vance unfolds event after event. They are not empty collisions. Besides glamour and suspense, pity and terror are in them and as chilling a study of the relationship between torturer and victim as I have ever seen anywhere. (On the infrequent occasions when he depicts cruelty, he makes everybody else in our field look tame. Perhaps his closest analogue outside it, in many more ways than this, is John D. MacDonald.) To date, the novel has had two sequels, each of which disposes of one more Demon Prince. Though as full of enchantments as the first, they have naturally not had the impact due to its sheer originality. In consequence, as of this writing the author has postponed the last two until he can develop something really climactic. The whole saga will be worth waiting for—but readers are getting mighty impatient!

I have discussed Vance at such length because his epical qualities are so strong that they overcome factors which put the tales of several other people into a different class. Thus he gives us an unequivocal example of what I am trying to establish and can therefore be my last subject.

Admittedly this means omitting quite a few fellow contributors and any consideration of whether or not any of their writings belong here. Alfred Bester, James Blish, A. Bertram Chandler, Hal Clement, Avram Davidson, Anne McCaffrey, and the late H. Beam Piper are among the more obvious possibilities in English, while in other language areas we might name "Francis Carsac," Ivan Efremov, Herbert Franke, "Charles Henneberg," and the Strugatsky brothers as a few of numerous candidates. Some works by some of these I would include, others not. But I hope I have explained my terms well enough that those who are interested can make their private evaluations.

I haven't touched except in passing on heroic fantasy, whose modern fountainheads are E. R. Eddison, J. R. R. Tolkien, and, on a less exalted plane, A. Merritt. But for present purposes, that doesn't require study. Whether good, bad, or indifferent, every story of this kind is a saga of sorts, by definition. Naturally, an archaic dream-world setting does not by itself make a fantasy heroic. James Branch Cabell never wrote in that vein and Dunsany seldom did; on the other hand, I would call Peter Beagle's gentle, half humorous and half lyrical *The Last Unicorn* at least a borderline epic because of its sustained narrative pace and purposeful characters. A more contemporary or realistic setting does not rule out great quests and conflicts in fantasy. Consider, say, various works by Charles Williams, C. S. Lewis, or the authors of several great books nominally for children. All in all, in this branch of literature such motifs and such treatment appear to be basic, though not exclusive, and certain to continue.

Let us therefore end by asking ourselves what the worth is of epical science fiction and what its prospects are.

The best of the tales mentioned will answer any question as to value. Sagas are not and should not be the whole of our field; but without them, it would soon become pretty thin stuff. These days, they are hard to find outside of it, straight fantasy, or literature labeled "juvenile." And are not those writers engaged in an honorable calling who deal in splendors, marvels, and adventure, hold up the ideals of courage, intelligence, and free will, celebrate life's magnificence in both joy and tragedy?

I think that as long as warm blood beats in human veins there will be readers who want these things. As said at the beginning, science fiction lends itself well to them. And it seems to me that of late, increasingly many writers, both new and old, are showing a spirit of outwardness. Never mind how academe reacts, and never mind about spotting a trend. As A. J. Budrys has put it, trends are for second-raters. What is alluring is the potentiality.

The age that Homer sang of was an age of upheaval, as were those of Rama, Arthur, Cuchulain, Njál, the Cid, Yoshitsune and Benkei. But these were also times of discovery, achievement as well as endurance, hope as well as horror; and they brought forth epics. Likewise did a seemingly more secure civilization, during that era of exploration and expansion around the globe now drawing to a close. We cannot be sure whether today's rampant chaos will overrun the world, or tyranny will, or liberty and justice prevail and our children reach the stars. At worst, our own epics, cast in our own future-oriented idiom, can help hearten us to fight on, stay alive, and pass down through the long darkness a heritage that folk will treasure when the dawn comes again. At best—

At best our sagas can help us appreciate another change going on around us, a fortunate one, the revolution in science and technology, human understanding and human capability. In the last few years the maps we had of reality have flamed away in our hands: cosmology, astronomy, physics, biology, psychology. We find that, like Odysseus, we have been standing on the shores of mystery. Like him, we are about to fare forth again. "To follow knowledge like a sinking star, / Beyond the utmost bound of human thought . . ." Is this not matter for many epics?

Science fiction cannot by itself change the world. But it can draw inspiration therefrom, and more and more nowadays it is doing so. I look forward to its future.

Poul Anderson

Poul Anderson was born in Pennsylvania in 1926 of Scandinavian parents (hence the spelling of the first name) and was raised in Texas and on a Minnesota farm, with intervals in Europe and the Washington, D.C., area. He graduated from the University of Minnesota in physics, with distinction, but having already sold some stories while in college (first significant publication in 1947), he decided to become a writer. Now a long-time resident, with wife and daughter, of the San Francisco Bay area; wife, Karen, occasionally writes, too.

He is the author of more than fifty books and two hundred-odd short pieces. Besides science fiction, they include fantasy, mystery, historical, juvenile, and here-and-now fiction; nonfiction; poetry, essays, translations, criticism, etc. Short stories and articles have appeared in places as various as the science fiction magazines, *Boys' Life, Playboy,* the Toronto *Star Weekly, National Review, Ellery Queen's,* and the defunct *Jack London's* magazine. Novels, nonfiction books, and short stories have appeared in fifteen foreign languages.

Former regional vice-president of Mystery Writers of America and former president of Science Fiction Writers of America.

Honors include: guest of honor, world science fiction convention of 1959, and several regional conventions; four Hugo awards and two Nebula awards for best sf novelette of the year; "Forry" Award of Los Angeles Science Fantasy Society; special issue (April 1972) of *The Magazine of Fantasy and Science Fiction;* Macmillan Cock Robin Award for best mystery novel; investiture in The Baker Street Irregulars, and twice winner of the Morley-Montgomery Prize for scholarship in Sherlock Holmes; Knight of Mark Twain. In the nonliterary field, knighthood in the Society for Creative Anachronism, for prowess in medieval combat.

Among Poul Anderson's more popular books are *Brain Wave, The High Crusade, The Enemy Stars, Three Hearts and Three Lions, The Broken Sword, Tau Zero.* Most recent novels are, as of now: *There Will Be Time, The People of the Wind, A Midsummer Tempest,* and *Fire Time* (a 1975 Hugo nominee).

HAL CLEMENT

Hard Sciences and Tough Technologies

There is no single way to incorporate scientific "realism" into a story; there are several approaches to the problem, including no doubt many which no one has thought of yet. I shall try to discuss the ones I do mention in some sort of order, but I disclaim any intent to produce a definitive classification, and I shall deliberately avoid giving names to any categories I may be moved to set up. I feel strongly that the more one knows of a subject, the more nearly impossible it becomes for him to supply unambiguous definitions and classifications in it. Any six-year-old will cheerfully tell you the difference between a plant and an animal, but no professional biologist would do so without numerous qualifications and exceptions. It has gotten to the point where I, who am reasonably well informed in astronomy, hesitate to produce a definition which will distinguish a star from a planet (see recent reports on Jupiter for the reason).

But back to using science in fiction. First, a writer may use the science as a mystery writer uses clues, solving the story problem or problems with the aid of scientific facts and, in effect, challenging the reader to beat him to the answer.

Second, a scientific or technological fact

may be needed to make possible a story situation that has occurred to the writer.

And finally, the science may "merely" provide general background, continually affecting actions, motives and problems of the characters but leaving the basic plot essentially "mainstream."

In all of these, the science may range from carefully worked-out, solidly based, accurate material, through sensational and poorly understood items expanded inaccurately from Sunday supplements and juvenile science books, down to sheerest gobbledygook worthy of the old high-pressure medicine-show salesman. Not only are there authors who work at all these levels; there are readers who are entertained and even impressed by them. Remember, *internal* consistency means more to the success of the storyteller than does consistency with the real world.

The classic example of the first variety, which I likened above to a mystery story, is seldom regarded as science fiction, though the author made his reputation as a science fiction writer. The story is Jules Verne's *Around the World in Eighty Days,* essentially an action-adventure tale through its entire length. The climax, however, depends on a scientific fact which should have been familiar to any educated adult of Verne's day (though many people a century later are still hard put to explain clearly why an International Date Line is a necessity). Verne called attention to the reading of Passepartout's watch, a perfectly adequate "clue," quite often enough to satisfy mystery-story standards.

The second category is sometimes supposed by the uninitiated to comprise all of science fiction. It does embrace the space travel and atomic energy stories which made up so much of the magazine contents from the late Twenties until after World War II. In my own childhood and for some time thereafter, my love for science fiction was frequently described even by my family and friends as attraction to "that Buck Rogers stuff" or to my "rocket ships and Martians." This is still a defensible way to refer to the genre, though the sophistication of the approach has increased with the passing decades. Buck Rogers walked around in his shirtsleeves on Mars and Jupiter, regardless of the actual conditions there; I worry about the conditions first and what sort of story they permit afterward. In fact, I still get my greatest fun out of making up solar systems and planets and working out the chemical, physical, meteorological, biological and other details which may later provide a story background.

In fact, in my case the story does not always get written—I am not a professional author. I have a fair supply of planets on hand if anyone needs them for a story and have been known to design worlds to order for friends.

The third type, in which the science is "merely" background, has become more popular in the last thirty years or so, largely as a result of the editorial policies and firmly expressed opinions of the late John W. Campbell. Robert Heinlein is possibly the best known, though far from the only, practitioner of this art (though he by no means confines himself to it).[1]

Throughout this discussion please keep the issue of consistency in mind—in fact, the two consistencies: with the "real" world and between different parts of the story itself (internal consistency). In literature other than science fiction or fantasy, one assumes that consistency with the "real" world is taken for granted—that the background is essentially the same as the one we live in. Even "mainstream" authors have been known to slip on this point, however.

For example, a well-known novel[2] has characters repeatedly lighting fires with the aid of a small boy's glasses. The boy, unfortunately, is repeatedly stated to be myopic (shortsighted). This cannot help jolting the reader who knows that the correcting lens for a myopic eye is concave and would spread out the sun's rays instead of concentrating them.

In rather similar vein, a mystery author lost me completely in a story that took place in and around an astronomical observatory.[3] My own training was in this field, and I quickly formed the opinion that the astronomer in the story was an impostor and that the real one must have been done away with somehow. I felt cheated when this turned out to be wrong.

But who and, perhaps more important, how many would know that a shortsighted person wears diverging lenses or would recognize unrealistic astronomical shop talk? This may not be a serious problem for most writers, but it is for the science fiction one. The non-science-fiction author has a comparatively easy row to hoe in this respect; his audience is seldom inclined to be highly critical about mere scientific slips. To me, it is rather amazing what some of them have gotten away with.

H. Rider Haggard was not only a famous writer but a good storyteller. He may have been covering up errors about Africa in *King Solomon's Mines,* but he had lived there and may have been correct about natives and their customs. Naturally, he was deliberately vague in his geography.

However, I was a little unconvinced about the medical details when one of the characters froze to death in this story, and I was seriously bothered by the three-hour total solar eclipse that occurred some three days after a full moon. Whether Haggard himself knew enough astronomy to realize these were impossibilities I don't know; the darkness of the eclipse was essential to the plot, and he may have been consciously betting that only an insignificant fraction of his readers would know any better; or he may, like Ray Bradbury, not have cared. In any case, he spoiled the realism of the story for me.

Science fiction writers have a much poorer chance of getting away with this sort of thing, and examples where they have failed to do so are numerous. Selecting a specific example here is not meant to be invidious; we all slip occasionally.

One such slip occurred in the series of stories generally known as the "Shaver Mystery," appearing in one of the magazines during the middle-to-late Forties. They were based on a modification of the Atlantis-Lemuria mythology; like others before and since, they assumed that much of human legend reflects the actual doings of ancient superscientific civilizations, some native to our planet and some visiting from elsewhere. The specific example I am bringing up involved taking a spaceship to the point between Earth and its moon where their gravitational pulls balanced out and there get vastly multiplied thrust from the rockets because the ship's *weight* would be essentially zero (nothing was said, as far as I can recall, about the weight of the rocket exhaust's also being zero).

It would have been perfectly legitimate for the author to build up the thesis that weight and mass are actually the same thing, if his story had really required it. He would have had to explain away, of course, however speciously, the evidence which says they are *not* the same and which more or less incidentally forms the basis of the mathematical rules that allow us to calculate spaceship orbits and predict eclipses, but he could have done it somehow.

He made no such effort, however, and left large numbers of science fiction fans with the impression that he didn't know what he was talking about. This is one of the science fiction writer's worst mistakes, especially when he is using the "Ms. Found in a Bottle" ploy—that is, the line that the story is a factual report of some incident that has been lost or concealed.

Such errors can be covered or otherwise rendered acceptable even to science fiction fans. Nelson Bond in his "Lancelot Biggs" stories made some pretty wild scientific statements.[4] At one point, for example, his characters have landed on a world whose *invisible* satellite has the property of trapping radio waves and causing messages to repeat themselves several times. This, it is claimed, is because the satellite is made of "pure, unadulterated galena, a colorless, transparent substance . . . a natural trap for radio transmission." Back in the early days of the Twentieth Century, galena was the substance used in the manufacture of experimental radio "crystal" sets.

It is hard to believe that Mr. Bond had never seen a sample of the black, shiny cubes of crystalline galena, or at least a picture of it. It is even harder to believe that he was unaware of the number of radio hams among the science fiction fans of the time. He was being deliberately funny—I haven't asked him but have no doubt of it—and making use of an artistic license as acceptable in science fiction as in any other form of storytelling. He was keeping up his *internal* consistency. One does not use this technique in a story that is portrayed as a factual report, of course; one risk involved is that some of one's less informed readers *will* take it seriously and saddle the embarrassed author with a semi-religious fan club, as happened to Mr. Shaver.

I have never been sure how seriously Shaver expected to be taken, but there was a rumor current at the time that the editor who bought the stories actually believed them. This is hard to credit, but people were in fact fooled by the Orson Welles *War of the Worlds* broadcast only a few years earlier.

Even science fiction is not immune to the temptation to use fast talk instead of careful reasoning. Gobbledygook was rather common in the early magazine days, and an interesting, if rather extreme, example was furnished by John Russell Fearn's two novels, *Liners of Time* and its sequel, *Zagribud.*[5] A quotation from the former illustrates the point nicely. The "good" scientist is explaining to the hero how his invisibility machine works. He claims that light alone will not make an object visible, since the light must be accompanied by radiant *heat* from the object; therefore stopping the radiant heat will automatically make anything invisible. He then refers to the blocking of light by crossed polarizers (he actually had a scientific fact here) and goes on to say:

> Now you have it. That curious quality which is supposed to be absorption of light is actually *radiation* of a wave-length. It is infinitesimally small, but

it has the power of turning light, if we can regard it for a moment as a *positive* state—like electricity—into a similar positive state. Hence, one repels the other, and the result is no light at all! Like repels like, of course. Now likewise it repels the radiant energy of any body, which is embodied in light, and is the *necessary addition* to light if light is to be made visible at all. . . .

This technique has two obvious advantages for a writer: the scope of his story is not constrained by mere facts; and a vocabulary can serve in place of scientific knowledge (as long as the words used have a scientific flavor—Dick Tracy's magnetic air car or Dr. Huer's gyro-cosmic relativator).

The disadvantage of the technique for writers in general and science fiction writers in particular is of course that it furnishes ammunition to intellectual snobs who can't admit that science fiction is a legitimate branch of the storyteller's art.

For obvious reasons, I regard the story in which the science has been carefully worked out in relation to the plot as much superior to the gobbledygook production, even granting that the latter does have a place in literature (humor, for example).

I also feel that the hard-science story is on a higher level than the "mainstream," though I admit that this claim is harder to support. The principal fact underlying this belief is that, in science fiction, the background facts are less familiar to the reader and must be worked into the body of the story clearly, early, and unobtrusively. This takes work—skilled and often hard work; and subjectively I share the attitude of the Boston drama critic who has admitted frankly that she greatly prefers plays in which it is evident that the playwright did some work before the curtain rose.

Fitting in the science has been a problem since the days of Verne and probably before. In the early magazines it was standard for the hero to have a dumb girl friend to whom everything had to be explained in detail. Since the author's scientific idea was commonly all there was to the story anyway, this was frequently sufficient, but it is no longer acceptable. Even coming up to the attitude of the present by shifting to a female hero with a stupid boy friend, or a virtuous pacifist explaining to a stupid colonel, remains a bit on the trite side. A major criterion of a good hard science fiction writer, such as Poul Anderson or Robert Heinlein or Isaac Asimov, is the way in which he solves this problem—

and the fact that he is not restricted to a single solution, as will easily be seen by the critical reader.

It follows that telling anyone how to write hard, or any other kind, of science fiction is not easy; there is no one way to do it, and there is no real substitute for a fairly large stock of scientific knowledge on the part of the author.

There are two rather general *approaches* to writing such a story which are quite easy to describe, however.

One is to have the scientific material, which—you hope—will inspire a story well in mind at the beginning, and then work up the plot to fit the science. This is essentially the mystery writer's technique, where the author knows who committed the murder and how from the beginning.

The other way is to have the story, complete with plot and major events, already in mind and then to find or invent scientific facts or situations that will permit these things to happen reasonably. In both approaches, the length of the intended story has a strong effect on what can be done and how easy it is to do it.

In a short story, it can be very difficult to present a nonstandard background clearly enough for the writer's purpose and to tie down tightly enough all the loose ends a new invention is likely to produce.

A full-length novel, on the other hand, while it does provide more opportunity for clear background development, also gives more opportunity for author's mistakes—read that "internal inconsistencies." These are very difficult to avoid when the background situation is deliberately strange. It is hard to avoid saying, or at least implying, "up" and "down" when relating a tale of a weightless environment. In Edgar Rice Burroughs' stories of timeless Pellucidar he did not always avoid slips such as "the winds tend to blow from north to south during one season of the outer earthly year." The "outer earthly" phrase almost had to be an afterthought, when Burroughs realized that he had slipped a time-based situation into a Pellucidar story. It was quite unreasonable; thermal conditions on the outer crust could have had no possible effect through the five-hundred-mile shell, with very peculiar composition and internal temperature, which Burroughs had established in the first book of the series. Again, I am not criticizing Burroughs, whose stories were entertaining if not very scientific; I am pointing out the difficulty of avoiding internal inconsistencies when one writes a long story with an unearthly or otherwise unusual background.

It can be done. In my opinion, one of the best examples is Robert Heinlein's *Beyond This Horizon.*[6] The mistakes, if any, are decidedly unobtrusive (I am covering for the fact that I didn't spot any). The basic scientific theme is the mastery of genetic manipulation, a possibility now giving some concern to our ethical thinkers (the story was written in the 1940s). Space travel is in the background, the problems of economics have been solved sufficiently to eliminate hunger, but there is still social snobbery—products of the gene selection techniques feel superior to the "control naturals." The author slipped in some controversial social notions, but he also did something that should serve as an example to fantasy as well as to hard science fiction writers. He gave a good, convincing description—no gobbledygook—of the techniques of gene selection used in the story. More important, he *spelled out their powers and limitations.* The writer of fantasy, using magic in his tale, frequently fails to do this, leaving the reader uncertain of what is and is not possible according to the current rules as he tries to guess what will happen next. This may not be important to the completely passive reader, but such readers are probably not too common among science fiction enthusiasts.

In the case of this story, Heinlein's care means that it has not become dated even by the subsequent discovery of the DNA structure and its genetic implications. It remains entertaining and thought-provoking.

It is not necessary to build a whole new culture, of course. A single discovery or invention will always have some impact on our everyday background, and that impact can make a story—short or long, depending on how far the ripples are followed.

Murray Leinster's "The Racketeer Ray" exemplifies this point.[7] The invention in this case was a sort of nonmaterial solenoid—a device that acted as though a spiral current-carrying coil were extending outward to an indefinite distance from the machine. This acted just as an ordinary coil of the same shape would have done, setting up a magnetic field along its axis and drawing ferromagnetic objects toward the device.

In the story, the inventor first used it for salvage, selling what he collected to finance his work. The police became interested when he recovered and sold a firearm that had been officially disposed of in the river. The criminal element then got the word and stole the machine. Exactly as could be predicted from its description, the device also tended to magnetize any steel in its path, so that while it did not pull cars off the road it stopped their engines, just as a strong magnetic field will stop a watch. It *did* snatch guns from the hands of pursuing police. It was a very convenient machine for criminals to possess, and the tricks for getting it back out of their hands made a very good story. Again, the science was worked out carefully, and as a result only the title has become dated. Forty years later, bank robbers are likely to be called "liberation fighters" rather than "racketeers."

In both these stories a single idea, perhaps not actually possible but at least basically scientific and related in straightforward fashion to what we "know," not only provided the seed for the tale but *guided its development*. This, I submit, is a major part of whatever makes "hard" science fiction what it is: the science provides not only the *inspiration* but the *discipline* for the writer's imagination.

Discipline is an unpopular concept with many people these days, suggesting the antithesis of liberty. Nevertheless it is necessary and need not be excessively restrictive even of a writer's ideas. Widely differing predictions can be based on the same bit of science or technology, as Larry Niven and I realized during the course of a conversation several years ago.

At this time, heart transplants in particular and organ donation in general were attracting great public interest. Larry had written several stories extrapolating on this theme, going into social consequences and, in particular, bringing up the possibility of "organlegging." It was dangerous for a traveler to check into a motel unless he knew the owner quite well; there was a good chance of winding up as a collection of spare parts on the black market. Political figures might use their position to insure their own longevity, at least as far as organ replacement could carry it.[8] Like that of genetic control, this question has more recently been the subject of serious debate on its ethical implications by doctors, politicians, and others not closely connected with science fiction. Larry had a good, reasonable, thought-provoking story basis.

It seemed to me, however, that another scientific fact with its resultant technology was likely to forestall the evolution of an organlegging culture. In the last few decades we have not only improved surgical technology enough to permit limb and organ transplants but have learned a great deal of fundamental biological and biochemical *science*. Specifically, the role of DNA (deoxyribonucleic acid) in the genetic process has become recognized and increasingly well understood. It seems to me that this knowledge should lead, in the fairly near future, to a technology that will allow us to grow a replacement heart or leg or liver from a sample of the *patient's own* tissue. It seems well established scientifically that the complete "blueprint" of an organism exists in each of its cells, or at least in each nucleated cell. It seems obvious that the creature's arms and eyes and kidneys did originally develop from a single cell containing that chemical plan and there seems nothing impossible about triggering a repetition of the process. If this actually is accomplished, we would bypass the present difficulty of rejection by the patient of a donated tissue or organ and would also forestall the social problem of organlegging which Larry used so effectively in his stories. I have used this notion in only one story so far,[9] but there is room for many more.

Neither Larry nor I is fighting about the matter; neither claims that he is the only true prophet; we simply recognize two possibilities. As a matter of fact, science fiction does not really claim to be a field of prophecy; that is for the mystics, in spite of the masthead on the Gernsback *Wonder Stories* of the '30s—"The Magazine of Prophetic Fiction." Both of us know we are extrapolating, both of us know enough physical science to recognize the unreliability of extrapolation, and both of us are fully aware of the myriad variables that would have to be evaluated and interrelated before anyone could possibly produce a reliable prediction of human society for even half a century ahead. (This is why the physical sciences are so much easier than the social ones; why it is so much easier to put a man on the moon than to cure war or poverty.)

Trends can be guessed at, of course. Some factors, such as decreasing natural resources, must carry a great deal of weight in any such guesses; but even these can lead to a wide variety of futures. There are many ways, different but not always mutually exclusive, of attacking the problems offered by this decrease. There are a multitude of possible degrees of success which can attend each of these methods. Each difference corresponds not to a different future but to a different *set* of futures, since the decrease of natural resources is not the only general problem facing mankind.

Apparently minor bits of scientific fact may lead to technologies, or merely to understandings and insights, which will have profound and rapid effects on human life. The understanding of solid-state physical chemistry which led to our present semiconductor technology—transistors and chip circuits—is an example. Robert Heinlein, for all his knowledge and imaginations, didn't quite hit this. In one story[10] the ballistic calculator doing the orbit work for a maneuvering asteroid was referred to as "three tons of thinking metal." Later on[11] he did point out that machines which were to last indefinitely should have no moving parts larger than electrons and implied a no-moving-parts calculator of unspecified size; but this was about the year 2150. The fact is that nearly two centuries earlier we have a computer quite capable of handling the general run of orbit problems, with the volume of a suitcase (or less, perhaps; I'm a couple of years out of date in this).

But we can balance this example with one which puts Robert Heinlein ahead of reality. In our space activities it has been found that working in space suits is very difficult because the interior pressure tends to keep the arms and legs extended. Bending them requires that the wearer compress the air in his suit, which takes effort. Heinlein pointed out this fact in one of the stories mentioned above[10] and had the joints of the space suits he described made with an accordion-pleated structure which bent without changing the internal volume. Maybe this is actually harder to design and execute than it sounds, but one wonders why the real space suits weren't made this way.

There seems, in other words, no way to tell what is "reasonable" extrapolation (after all, if there were, it would be extrapolation too!). Science fiction writers can only use their own knowledge to the best of their imaginative ability.

A few decades ago there was a "gap" in the electromagnetic spectrum between the shortest radio and longest infra-red ("heat") waves. Writers endowed the radiation in this gap with strange and wonderful powers, such as usefulness in a mechanical educator[12] or as repulsion rays.[13] There was no scientific reason to expect any such properties; Maxwell's equation had been with us for nearly a century, describing the general properties of electromagnetic waves quite nicely, and not even the more recent quantum mechanics offered a real excuse for what was being done. The writers could be, and sometimes were, laughed at.

Similarly, the elements then missing from the chemists' periodic table, #43, #85, and #87, were used by authors in need of special materials with equal lack of justification and in the face of similar ridicule from the scientific purists. (I am not bragging. I was, and still tend to be, one of those stuffy purists.)

On the other hand, those same scientific snobs would never have accepted as a prediction the now well-known fact that accumulating large quantities of the isotope Uranium 235 in one spot could have such drastic effects as it does, nor would they have accepted as a reasonable idea the semiconducting properties of germanium and silicon mentioned a page or two back. *Now,* of course, it is easy and fairly safe to predict that we will be using doped diamond in such devices before too long.

This leaves much of the machinery invented by science fiction writers in a sort of limbo. Jack Williamson's "geodynes"—electromagnetic geodesic deflectors[14]—and other devices for traveling faster than light: are they valid extrapolation or wishful thinking? Is there any way to tell? Does it make any difference what kind of science fiction is involved?

To the last question, apparently no. Everything said through most of this chapter has applied to all the categories I suggested back near the start, except the gobbledygook subclass. The categories seem to be more useful for librarians and critics than for writers and even readers. The last two have to decide in every case what is acceptably "real" science and what is fantasy; what is convincing extrapolation and what is the sort of wish-fulfillment that makes a story just another fairy tale.

I can give only a subjective answer to this. There are a few scientific "laws" I feel strongly about and some others which I do not; but sitting back and examining myself, I am forced to admit that the distinction rests on rather unscientific, or at least nonobjective, grounds.

I do believe in the Law of Conservation of Mass-Energy. I was as stuffily critical as any of the old purists mentioned earlier when Lin Carter powered one of his Lemurian aircraft with a double-spring motor, one half of which rewound the other while also driving the ship.[15] The fact that the steady-state cosmology favored by a number of famous and competent astrophysicists during the '50s and '60s demanded the abandonment or modification of that particular law did not seem a real excuse for Mr. Carter.

On the other hand, I tend to treat quite cavalierly the implication contained in the theories of relativity that no material object or signal can exceed the speed of light. Here, too, there are competent professionals (physicists, not writers, I mean) who have their doubts about relativity; but I cannot honestly quote them as my excuse. The fact is, I like to lay the scenarios of my stories on non-Earthly planets of my own devising. We know too much about the planets of our own solar system to let me use them very freely for this purpose, so I have to set up elsewhere. This forces me to assume faster-than-light travel for many of the stories. Furthermore, I *want* to believe that there is some way of getting to the stars. (As a moderate supporter of women's lib, a strong objector to racial discrimination, and an ardent anti-smoker I am embarrassed to find myself so deeply committed to a double standard; but none of us is perfect.) Anyhow, this particular bit of non-science has of course been widely accepted as legitimate in the field of even hard science fiction.

Jack Williamson's "geodynes," mentioned above, *sound* good. They use the same verbalisms as are commonly employed in trying to explain relativity without mathematics. They were, as far as I can recall, the first major science fiction usage of the so-called "space warp," a term which has since been inflated almost to the meaninglessness of the four-letter words in an "adult" novel.

E. E. Smith's "inertialess" drive[16] was justified, he said, by a brief reference to the possibility in a work on theoretical chemistry. Its implication that mass can be divorced from inertia implies an error in relativity and to that extent is internally consistent, but critics have pointed out associated problems which Dr. Smith failed to mention. It is hard to see, for example, how inertialess atoms in a living body could collide in order to carry on the body's essential chemical operations.

We are at best in a gray area where a piece of artistic license legitimate from the storyteller's viewpoint is much more dubious from the side of the scientific purist.

Another such area is that which has been variously called "parapsychology," "paraphysics," and "psionics." I am aware that the bodies of alleged phenomena covered by these terms are not quite identical, but the terms themselves seem never to have been defined precisely enough to make distinction worth the trouble. They include telepathy, clairvoyance, telekinesis, prediction, and other things which tend to overlap into the realms of the mystic.

There is no disputing that these are legitimate areas for scientific investigation and certainly for science fiction, too. A good deal of careful and competent research has indeed already been performed. Unfortunately, a great deal of sheer mysticism has also been uttered without the control and self-criticism that are supposed to characterize science. By the time the reports from either source have gone through two or three relays of journalism it becomes very difficult to judge the validity of any statement on the subject.

No scientist would claim that our present picture of the "real" world is complete, and the fact that most psionic phenomena fail to fit the detailed physical picture is not a conclusive argument against their reality. In any case, psionics appears quite legitimately in science fiction.

When using "psionics."

When an author uses it, however, he should remember the consistency criteria; he must take the same precautions as when he is frankly using magic and writing a fantasy story. He must, that is, set up the rules and limitations early enough in the story to be fair to his readers—to let them assimilate the nonstandard background in time. The new magic power, or the new rule of psionics, appearing just in time to get the hero out of trouble is irritating to the reader.

Admittedly, the new invention can be equally so; but if the science has been well and accurately worked in, the invention *may* have been predictable—and therefore fair play.

A final (for this chapter) example of a field that has furnished plots for science fiction at all levels of hardness, and is of rather dubious "hardness" itself, is what might be called either the Atlantis theme or the Chariot-of-the-Gods syndrome. This is the notion that there have been highly scientific ancient civilizations on this planet, either originating here (Atlantis) or arriving from other worlds (Chariot).

As with psionics, this is essentially impossible to *dis*prove. As with psionics, it will take more thoughtful and properly controlled research to *prove* than anyone has so far given the question. As with psionics, the attitudes of many people toward the subject are of religious intensity. Arguments tend to be evaluated emotionally and very, very subjectively.

One of the favorite points stressed by supporters of the notion is the claim that all our ancient legends and myths must have originated in historical fact. In its most literal implication, this is an insult to the imagination of every storytelling human being since the first cave man came home to explain to his wife how the dinner got away.

Granted, everything we imagine is based *in some fashion* on things we have seen, or heard, or been told, or otherwise have had fed to us; but the connection will usually be far too distant and tenuous, and involve the combination of far too many unrelated experiences, to justify any firm conclusion on—say—what Ezekiel's wheel really was. The possibilities are almost literally infinite.

It *may* have been a spaceship. This suggestion has some traceable connection with "reality" as we know it, but it may be little if any closer to the truth than the explanation of Homer Nearing's Professor Ransom[17] in *The Hermeneutical Doughnut*, which was pure humorous gobbledygook.

To say that the wheel *was* such and such a thing for purposes of science fiction is legitimate storytelling. To say that it "must have been" that or anything else, as a serious scholarly claim, is apt to reflect heavily against a writer's intellectual power—or his intellectual honesty.

To summarize: "Hard" science fiction is a recognizable field within a field; it is enjoyed largely by people who take their own scientific knowledge seriously; writing it therefore demands on the part of the author a fair amount of scientific knowledge and ability (partially replaceable by good research facilities and informed friends whose brains can be picked); and the worst mistake a hard science fiction writer can make, aside from failing to tell an entertaining story, is to write something that makes him look ignorant. He can disagree with accepted science, but he'd better have an impressive-sounding excuse.

And for the excuse, he'd better have clearly in mind just what sort of audience he is trying to impress.

NOTES

1. Heinlein, Robert. The stories of this author actually represent all the categories, except the gobbledygook subclass. One which might best represent the "background" type is *Star Beast,* originally appearing in the May through July 1954 issues of the *Magazine of Fantasy and Science Fiction,* titled *Star Lummox.* It has since been reprinted in several hard cover and paperback editions.

2. Golding, William. *Lord of the Flies,* New York, Coward, McCann & Geoghegan, 1954, 1962.

3. Taylor, Phoebe Atwood. This story appeared in a collection of three of her Asey Mayo stories *Asey Mayo Trio* about 1945; I have tried without success to get hold of a copy. Many of the Asey Mayo stories were reissued by Norton in the last few years; I don't know whether the *Trio* was among them.

4. Bond, Nelson. *Lancelot Biggs, Spaceman.* This is a collection of short stories, most originally appearing individually in magazines, tied together and published as a single book by Doubleday in 1950.

5. Fearn, John Russell. *Liners of Time, Amazing Stories,* May–August 1935; *Zagribud, Amazing Stories,* December 1937–April 1938. The first story was also published in hard covers by The World's Work (1913) Ltd, Kingswood, Surrey, in 1947.

6. Heinlein, Robert. *Beyond This Horizon, Astounding Stories,* April, May 1942; reprinted in hard covers by Fantasy Press in 1948. Paperback editions have appeared more recently.

7. Leinster, Murray. "The Racketeer Ray," *Amazing Stories,* February 1932.

8. Niven, Larry. *A Gift from Earth.* Ballantine, 1968. This is only one of several Niven stories using the "organlegging" theme.

9. Clement, Hal. "The Mechanic," *Analog,* September 1966. Also included in the collection *Small Changes,* Doubleday, 1969.

10. Heinlein, Robert. "Misfit," *Astounding,* November 1939; reprinted in various anthologies, the most recent *The Past Through Tomorrow,* Berkley, 1975.

11. Heinlein, Robert. *Methuselah's Children.* Original version in *Astounding,* July–September 1941; reprinted frequently in somewhat longer form; most recently in *The Past Through Tomorrow.*

12. Smith, Edward Elmer. *Skylark Three, Amazing Stories,* August–October 1930. Like most of Smith's work, this has been frequently reprinted, and paperback editions are probably still available.

13. Hamilton, Edmond. *The Universe Wreckers, Amazing Stories,* May–July 1930.

14. Williamson, Jack. *The Legion of Space* series included the title story (*Astounding,* April–September 1934); *The Cometeers, Astounding,* May–August 1936; and *One Against the Legion, Astounding,* April–June 1939. All have been extensively reissued. All use the "geodyne" and advancements thereon.

15. Carter, Lin. *Thongor of Lemuria.* Ace, 1966.

16. Smith, Edward Elmer. The "Lensman" series by this author, starting with *Triplanetary* and going through *First Lensman, Galactic Patrol, Grey Lensman, Second-Stage Lensman,* and *Children of the Lens,* takes place in a universe where the natives of a planet called Arisia are in conflict with the forces of evil, the Eddorians. Interstellar travel is accomplished by the "inertialess drive." The stories appeared originally, not in chronological sequence, as magazine serials during the '30s and '40s; they were published in hard cover by Fantasy Press a few years later (and are now collector's items) and have reappeared in recent years in paperback.

17. Nearing, Homer. *The Sinister Researches of C. P. Ransom,* Doubleday, 1954. A collection of stories, most of them originally published in magazines, based on the humorous gobbledygook approach. I am not belittling it; I found it quite entertaining and have reread it several times.

Hal Clement (Harry Clement Stubbs)

Born in Somerville, Massachusetts, in 1922, Hal Clement attended public schools in Arlington and Cambridge and received a B.S. in astronomy from Harvard in 1943. He served with the 8th AAF in World War II, flying thirty-five missions over German-occupied Europe as copilot and pilot in B-24 bombers, and after the war he obtained his M.Ed. at Boston University. He then taught high-school science and math for four years until recalled with his Air Force Reserve unit for two years in 1951—but he did not go overseas this time. He returned to his teaching position at Milton Academy, Massachusetts, in 1953, and is still there but has since acquired an M.S. in chemistry. He is still in the Air Force Reserve, working in an information unit, with the rank of colonel.

Sold first story to *Astounding Science Fiction* magazine while a sophomore at Harvard and has produced a small but fairly steady flow of science fiction ever since. He has also done a number of scientific articles in various publications, generally under his real name (Harry C. Stubbs).

He is a member or has been of such scientific organizations as AAAS, New England Association of Chemistry Teachers, Bond Astronomical Society, and the Meteoritical Society. He was a charter member of New England Science Fiction Association and for two years has served on the Nebula Awards Committee of Science Fiction Writers of America.

Married since 1952 to the former Mary Myers of Atlantic City, New Jersey, he has one son in college, one about to go to college, and one junior-high-school-age daughter.

Iceworld, 1953 (Gnome)
Needle, 1953 (Doubleday)
Mission of Gravity, 1954 (Doubleday)
Cycle of Fire, 1957 (Ballantine)
Close to Critical, 1959 (Ballantine)
Natives of Space, 1965 (Ballantine), 3 novelettes
Small Changes, 1969 (Doubleday)
First Flights to the Moon, 1970 (Doubleday)
Star Light, 1971 (Ballantine)

NORMAN SPINRAD

Rubber Sciences

Science fiction and politics are, in theory, arts of the possible, just as fantasy and religion are arts of the impossible. In actual practice, however, politics usually turns out to be the art of the all-too-probable, whereas science fiction usually turns out not to give much of a damn about probability at all. In fact, a case could be made that the more improbable science fiction is, the better it is as science fiction. Until it crosses the line between improbability and impossibility and becomes fantasy.

This, then, will be a chapter about precisely that murky area between "hard science fiction" and "hard fantasy" in which most science fiction writers work most of the time.

Indeed, it's rather difficult to come up with a definition of "hard science fiction" that doesn't end up being somewhat self-contradictory. "Hard scientific content" in science fiction is usually defined (at those rare moments when anybody bothers to define it at all) as known scientific fact. "Hard science fiction," then, is science fiction written around known scientific facts or at least not-unproven theories generated by "real" scientists. But is it? All fiction is lies—if it weren't, it would be biography, history, or reportage. Science fiction or speculative fiction is a form in which at least one element of the reality in which the imaginary characters move is also imaginary. Not *impossible* but not a fixture in the universe of the writer and reader either. The speculative element, it's usually called. Where does that leave "hard science fiction"? If there is no speculative element, it isn't science fiction; and if there is a speculative element in the so-called scientific background, we're then into measuring "degree of hardness" on some kind of technological peter-meter.

Larry Niven, for example, is generally considered a writer of "hard science fiction." J. G. Ballard is not. Niven's stories are full of two-headed aliens, telepathic powers, various flavors of time-travel, galactic cataclysms, hyper-drives, tractor beams, and so forth. Most of Ballard's novels have been rather tight extrapolations of a world drastically altered by one reasonably plausible meteorological change, and even his later more stylistically dense works don't ask the reader to swallow very many scientific improbabilities whole. Hal Clement's alien creatures are part of the hard science fiction canon, but Cordwainer Smith's Underpeople are not. Aficionados of hard science fiction accept Poul Anderson's medieval space cultures without a murmur but eschew the future worlds of Mack Reynolds which are worked out with a much more sophisticated and rigorous knowledge of economics and politics.

On the other hand, it's easy enough to recognize the diametric opposite of hard science fiction—full-bore space opera, which is really straight fantasy in science fiction drag. Jockstrap-clad superheroes swinging their swords through hyperspacial extensions of time-probability worlds while planets ricochet off the cushions of the cosmic pool table in three-corner bank shots from the übercues of beings from the 27th dimension with a perverted lust for brass-bound boobs and human pain, opposed only by our blaster-armed hero, his positronic robot horse Trigger, and the Galactic Overmind, who in reality is Lamont Cranston, playboy energy creature from the center of the sun. We've all read that one, and too many of us have written it as well.

But somewhere between the Scylla of Jungian archetype opera and the Charybdis of the kind of rigid Gernsbackian "scientifiction" that is hardly written anymore lies the great main current of science fiction. Including, I would submit, most of what is called "hard science fiction."

Indeed, if there is any meaningful definition of hard science fiction at all, it is that science fiction which convinces the reader that its scientific content is as sound, metallic, and conservative as a Swiss franc. It's really a matter of technique more than content, a technique explored elsewhere in this book.

Here we will discuss other techniques for achieving the same basic end: an illusion of verisimilitude around imaginary content. Isn't that what science fiction is all about?

Having to some extent pooh-poohed the possibility of writing real science fiction based on real scientific fact, I should hasten to point out that scientific illiteracy is by no means a prime qualification for a science fiction writer. In fact, the kind of science fiction I'm going to talk about probably requires a firmer grounding in the *Weltanschauung*, philosophy, history, and psychology of science and technology than what is usually called hard science fiction.

After all, a reasonably intelligent writer can read a piece in *Time* about quasars, black holes, organ transplants, or the latest model space capsule and write a story with this material as trappings or setting. No different from reading a good book about the American West or Timbuktu and setting a story there.

But when you really head for the wild blue yonder there are no road maps or almanacs to crib from. When you get down to essences, descriptive knowledge is not enough—you must really understand. And that, of course, is a deeply scientific attitude in itself.

When you're writing about tomorrow's technology, it's enough to be accurate, to more or less faithfully describe the gizmos, theories, and discoveries that scientists and engineers are speculating about in their own magazines and bull-sessions. But when you're writing about scientific discoveries, technological innovations, scientific theories or even whole new sciences that you've made up yourself, you can't rely on accuracy to give the reader a sense of verisimilitude. There's nothing anywhere in the reader's world or your own for you to describe accurately.

Instead, you must be *plausible,* which is a bem of a different color.

To give an example of what I'm herein calling "Rubber Science" as opposed to straightforward pseudoscientific doubletalk, let us consider the granddaddy of them all, FTL, hyperspace, overdrive, spaceships exceeding the speed of light.

As we all know (we *do* all know, don't we?), in our current Einsteinian picture of the universe, a mass traveling at the speed of light becomes infinite, and it would therefore take an infinite amount of energy to accelerate it to that speed and a transfinite amount of energy to accelerate it beyond that speed. Which is why faster-than-light travel is theoretically impossible within Einsteinian parameters.

Which may be tidy for cosmologists and astrophysicists but which is a pain in the neck to science fiction writers. The literary necessity for faster-than-light travel is all too obvious. Without it, we could have no stories of galactic empires, not much anthropological science fiction, few pictures of alien cultures or *outré* planets, a dearth of first-contact stories —in short, science fiction writers would be pretty much confined to our own solar system. Of course many fine stories have been written about just this light-speed limitation problem, but science fiction is the literature of multiplex realities, and to confine it within a strict relativistic straitjacket would simply be literarily unacceptable.

Thus hyperspace. Or overdrive. Or whatever it takes to get our literary spaceships from star to star in literarily usable time. Given FTL as a story necessity, the question then becomes how do you get the reader to accept it smoothly, how do you make what is currently a scientific impossibility seem plausible?

One obvious and frequently successful method is simply to ignore the problem. "He switched on the hyperdrive and five minutes later they arrived at Epsilon Bootes." After all, if you're writing a story set in the present, you can have your hero drive from Hollywood to Pasadena without pausing to explain the internal-combustion engine.

However, if you choose this method, you must really be consistent. If you're not going to offer an explanation of hyperdrive, then you'd better not explain any other futuristic technology in your story, because what you're really doing is writing from the viewpoint of the people in your future time. And you'd better not have any element of your plot dependent on the hyperdrive. "He switched on the hyperdrive and five minutes later they arrived at Epsilon Bootes, beating out the space pirates by a good twelve parsecs due to the superior juxtaposition of their frammis-warp to the space-time matrix" is dirty pool.

Also, even if you're not explaining your hyperdrive, you still have to make the rest of your universe consistent with known scientific facts unless you want to point a big red finger to the fact that you're not explaining it because you're an ignoramus. Further, even an unexplained hyperdrive must operate according to at least internally self-consistent rules. It can go from anywhere to anywhere in five minutes, or it can propel a ship at a hundred times the speed of light, but not both interchangeably. The point is that you want the hyperdrive to seem scientifically plausible whether you attempt to explain how it works or not, which means that the logic of its operation must seem reasonable, must *feel* scientifically correct. Internal consistency is a necessity no matter how much or how little you choose to explain. Rule One of the Rubber Sciences.

Of course it's more of a challenge to try to actually explain your hyperdrive. Moreover, if you do explain the thing consistently and establish its parameters at the outset, you *can* use its workings and properties for later plot points. If, for example, you establish that a larger mass moves faster in hyperdrive than a smaller one, you can have your hero's ship beat the space pirates to Epsilon Bootes by dragging a small asteroid into hyperspace with it. But this property of hyperdrive must have been established long before it is used, otherwise it becomes the equivalent of "With a superhuman effort, he leapt out of the pit." Rule Two of the Rubber Sciences: any pseudoscientific fact or principle that is going to be used for plot purposes must be planted in the reader's mind near the beginning of the story and long before it surfaces as a plot element.

Okay, so rather than gloss it over, you're going to invent a hyperdrive. Right away you are faced with a fundamental choice. Current best scientific knowledge says that faster-than-light travel is impossible, so you must either come up with a "bugger factor" in Einsteinian relativity or forthrightly state that by the 25th Century Glockenspiel proved that Einstein was wrong.

I wrote a story called "Outward Bound" using the first method, and it worked well enough at least to convince John W. Campbell, Jr. Here I accepted Einsteinian relativity and had a theoretical mathematician talk about "transfinite substitutions in Einstein's equations.

". . . if you accept the Special Theory of Relativity, the reason that the speed of light cannot be exceeded is that mass is infinite at the speed of light, hence it would take an infinite force to accelerate it to that speed.

"*But*, if there were a drive whose thrust was a function of the mass it was accelerating, then, as mass increased, thrust would increase, and at the speed of light, theoretically, where mass was infinite, *thrust* would also be infinite. And if the thrust-mass equation involved a suitable exponential function . . . thrust could become transfinite.

"Making it possible to go faster than light!"

What kind of drive has a thrust which is an exponential function of the mass it is accelerating? Are you kidding? If I knew that one, I'd be writing my Nobel acceptance speech, not this chapter.

Rule Three of the Rubber Sciences: you are not Albert Einstein—know when to *stop* explaining.

Here I have pointed to a possible hole in relativity through which an FTL ship might sneak, but I have not succumbed to the hubris of trying seriously to design the actual hyperdrive. I've contented myself with establishing a theoretical basis for the thing in something like the Einsteinian universe, so that later on the artifact will seem plausible. The same principle applies to tachyon drives, black hole gates between the stars, and other "bugger factors" in relativity. If you think you can explain the whole thing from bugger factor to actual hardware, you may find yourself in a funny farm having long conversations about it with Napoleon.

Then there is the alternative: simply postulating a future cosmological viewpoint that supersedes Einsteinian relativity. *Simple?* Yes and no. Einstein, after all, didn't knock Newton into a cocked hat; he created a new cosmological paradigm of which Newtonian physics was a still-valid special case. That's the way sciences seem to evolve, at least at this late date. You can't simply state that in 2394 A.D. Glockenspiel showed that magic in fact worked and that in the 25th Century faster-than-light starships zip through the ether on ectoplasm. If you want a new cosmological paradigm, you must construct it along lines consistent with the way sciences evolve. The chance that 20th-Century physics will later be shown to have been a complete crock is nil. You have to try something like the notion that our four-space universe is really a bubble in five-space, or that black holes are hyperspacial tunnels between points in our own continuum, or that objective time can somehow be contracted as well as subjective time—paradigms that *contain* Einsteinian relativity but transcend it, rather than contending that it's all pure baloney.

Rule Four of the Rubber Sciences: when creating a new science or a new master-theory for an established science, pay attention to how sciences evolve; don't just wave your magic wand and produce magic with scientific mumbo-jumbo trappings.

I've spent all this time on faster-than-light drives because they are surely the most pervasive example of Rubber Science in science fiction and because they most easily and clearly illustrate many of the basic rules. But FTL, most often, is an example of first-order Rubber Science:

something you create for plot or setting purposes. Beyond lies a higher order of Rubber Science—scientific speculation about the nature of the universe, life, culture, and the mind of man.

No doubt the best example of a "science fiction science" that we have is one that strictly speaking was never a fictional science at all: Scientology. But since Scientology is the creation of L. Ron Hubbard, a full-time science fiction writer at the time he created it, since the history of the Scientology movement reads like a science fiction novel, and since Scientology so beautifully illustrates so many of the principles of Rubber Science creation, it's still worthwhile to consider it for a moment.

Basically, Scientology is a kind of crossbreed of simple Freudian psychology with even simpler computer theory. "Traumas" become "engrams" and "neuroses" become "engram chains." Instead of "complete abreaction" as the ultimate goal, we have the "state of clear," in which all engrams have been cleared from the mind, much as old programs are cleared from a computer. Instead of a patient free-associating or relating his dreams on a couch to an "analyst," we have an "auditor" running a "clearing program" and the patient clutching the handles of an "E-meter." The E-meter, or Engram-meter (actually a simple skin galvanometer, a piece of a lie detector), supposedly tells the auditor when his question has hit an "engram." He then bores in until the E-meter shows him that the engram has been "cleared" or eliminated and continues to run his program until all such engrams are cleared.

For the purposes of this chapter, the question of whether or not Scientology actually works in the real world is irrelevant. The point is that it would surely work beautifully in a story. It has plausibility, and it does raise some interesting speculations on the workings of the human mind.

From whence this plausibility? For one thing, Scientology is based on two existing sciences, psychoanalysis and computer theory. The new Rubber Science is created by interfacing two existing sciences which had not been cross-disciplined before. This gives it some genuine content, which not only creates plausibility but even raises true validity as a genuine askable question.

Isaac Asimov did much the same thing when he created "psychohistory" for his *Foundation* series; here the interfaced sciences were history and statistics. Various writers have done it with "psionics," most often by interfacing psychic research with brain physiology and/or bioelectronics. I myself have done it with pharmacology and various psychological sciences and produced things like "psychedelic pediatrics" and "psychedelic design." I've also (in a nonfiction piece) interfaced pharmacology, brain physiology, systems analysis, psychology, holography, and a handful of other existing disciplines and created "psychesomics," the science of the mind-matter interface itself.

Rule Five of the Rubber Sciences: interfacing two or more existing sciences will generate a plausible (if not necessarily valid) new science.

Another lesson in Rubber Science plausibility that can be gleaned from Scientology is the use of terminology, or, if you will, jargon. Fiction, after all, is word magic, and a well-crafted system of magic words in itself has a certain intrinsic reality, as witness law, religion, philosophy, criticism, and advertising. Too often, the coined words in science fiction stories exist in isolation, both from the actual Rubber Science material to which they refer and from each other. In Scientology we can see how it *should* be done. Words like "engram," "clear," and "auditor" all have both specific meaning pertaining to specific elements of the pseudoscience and metaphorical overtones relating the word system to the general body of human knowledge. They can be put together or qualified in ways that extend their meanings in a reasonably self-evident manner. Once "engram" is explained, "engram-chain" has real meaning; once the state of "clear" is explained, "clearing program" becomes self-explanatory. The terminology holds together as a system, which lends plausibility to the Rubber Science as a system.

How much more solid Scientology seems than fuzzy Van Vogtian psionics or even Asimovian robotics! One can discuss it beyond the bounds of Hubbard's books and in Hubbard's own terminology. Some psychotherapists have even picked up "engram" and apply the concept to other psychological systems. Rule Six of the Rubber Sciences: systematize your terminology and relate it to the rest of human knowledge by choosing some of the words for their metaphorical resonance in the reader's mind.

Finally, notice how Hubbard has given plausibility to a "soft" Rubber Science by inventing a piece of hardware, the E-meter, which solidifies the whole system with the new reality of a functioning apparatus. In terms of plausibility, it really doesn't matter that the E-meter is nothing but a very crude lie-detector. If Hubbard had opted for the use of real lie-detectors (technically superior in every way to the E-meter for the very purpose for which the E-meter was designed) he would have lost the credibility effect of inventing an apparatus intrinsic to his own pseudo-science. "New science" is so identified in people's minds with "inventions" that you almost can't have one without the other. Rule Seven of the Rubber Sciences: solidify your pseudo-science with believable hardware.

Now that we've seen how to give plausibility to an invented science, we can approach the whole question of genuine speculative scientific content. For in its highest form, the Rubber Science in science fiction can, on occasion, actually contribute to the dialectic of scientific evolution; it can come very close, sometimes, to being the real thing.

This is one reason, I would contend, why truly great science fiction transcends other great literature. Science fiction has the potential not merely to describe existing realities, not merely to imagine nonexistent realities, but actually to *create* realities. It can have extra-literary extensions into the real world.

Consider science fiction, for a moment, not as a branch of literature but as a style of consciousness, a philosophy of the nature of reality, a series of camera-angles on the universe.

Like fantasy, science fiction describes currently nonexistent realities, but unlike fantasy, it does not *require* the reader's suspension of disbelief, it seeks to *create* it. It does this by relating the invented reality to the reader's own reality logically. It seeks to create new worlds that are logical evolutionary extensions of the world the writer and reader both share. It assumes the responsibility for taking the reader from *here* to *there.*

Often, in conscientiously written science fiction, this means that the writer works out a great many evolutionary steps that the reader never sees. For instance, my own novella, "Riding the Torch." This story is set entirely in a far future in which the last remnant of humanity lives in a great fleet of interstellar ships. Each ship is built around a hydrogen ramscoop fusion torch, which not only propels it but provides it with virtually unlimited internal power and with raw material from the interstellar medium. The culture of this story has unlimited energy and unlimited raw materials, which, combined with the ability to transmute matter almost totally, gives it the power to create just about anything it wants to. Further, full-sensory computer transceivers implanted in the people's brains give them, among many other things, the power to live in any subjective reality they choose.

"Riding the Torch" is set entirely in this future society and told entirely from the viewpoint of characters in the ship culture, but in order to give it the solidity I wanted, I found that I had to work out for myself a capsule history of how mankind got from *here* to *there*, technologically, as well as politically and socially.

Thus I had to contemplate such things as how the earth might become uninhabitable, the development of fusion technology in deep space, matter transformation, the psychology and artistic implications of the computer-brain link, and so forth. All this just for one story—the "homework" that was done before I wrote the first word of the actual novella, material the reader never saw, took up many pages.

Science fiction writers do this sort of thing all the time. They are psychically at home in the future. Even the term "*the* future" is an oversimplification of the science fiction consciousness, for (with the exception of some writers who get bogged down in setting all of their stories in the same consistent future) science fiction writers contemplate *different* futures every time they set out to write a new story. They are at home not merely in "the" future but in multiplex futures. They have assimilated the multiplex nature of reality, the new realities that radiate outward from the nexus of every possible space-time event. The consciousness of science fiction is a transformational consciousness; the logic of science fiction is the logic of perpetual flux.

I would submit that there are few minds outside of science fiction who fully assimilate this type of consciousness and virtually no other intellectual community or discipline that shares it communally. Futurology, which comes closest, is a pale shadow of science fiction; indeed it is probably a new science that science fiction actually created.

In addition, science fiction writers are the original "generalists" or "synergists." To create plausible pictures of future sciences and technologies, science fiction writers must have some familiarity with all of the physical sciences. To create pictures of imagined other planets, they must know some astrophysics, meteorology, geology, ecology, and biology. To create future or alien cultures, they must be able to think sociologically, anthropologically, and psychologically. A little perception of the cultural evolution of art and religion comes in handy too.

Not merely must science fiction writers have some knowledge in all of these areas, what they deal with is precisely the interaction of all these factors to create a total natural, technological, and cultural environment. This is exactly the kind of thinking that "synergists" like Buckminster Fuller "specialize" in.

But science fiction writers go far beyond the synergists, for they are not scientists, they are literary artists, and their proper primary concern is the human heart. When science fiction truly succeeds, all the multiple factors that go to make up a total natural, technological, and cultural environment are brought home to living, loving, suffering characters, to the territory of the soul, and we have a truly visionary exploration of man as a physical and psychic creature of the universe.

Science fiction writers, as much as anyone, and probably more so, are engaged in visionary contemplation of man's total being in the total reality of the universe. It is therefore not always entirely vain for them to create imaginary new paradigms and dare to consider that they may eventually prove to be not only plausible but valid.

Scientists, after all, are tied to a logical process that forces them to prove the validity of every conjecture they make, whereas science fiction writers can examine any alternative reality of which they can conceive in physical and psychic detail. We can do just about anything we please. We can be "wrong" as much as we want to and still be "right."

So why not use this instrument to the fullest and deepest extent possible and seriously contemplate the universe within and without us? Why not carry the Rubber Sciences beyond mere verisimilitude-creating techniques? The literary methods science fiction has developed to give speculation plausibility free science fiction writers to make any conjecture they like and still maintain literary verisimilitude.

What I'm saying, in short, is that sometimes the Rubber Sciences can turn out to be not so rubber at all in the end. Rule Eight of the Rubber Sciences: you can use the Rubber Sciences as tools for genuine intellectual exploration of the unknown.

We have, after all, been right upon occasion, not only in mere details but also in insight.

Decades before the best-seller *Body Language,* A. E. Van Vogt had created a pseudoscience which is to "body language" as nuclear physics is to chemistry. Here the concept of reading emotional states from body postures was carried to a near-telepathic conclusion. Van Vogt's adept could virtually read actual thoughts from body postures and facial expressions and structures. Science has not yet fulfilled Van Vogt's vision, but what has been accomplished was preceded by decades by his insight, and furthermore what Van Vogt described was the distilled essence of such a future science. Not merely a lucky prediction but a true visionary flash.

It was science fiction writers who first speculated about antimatter physics. The now-existent science of "xenobiology" comes straight from science fiction (including the name of the science itself), and even most of its current theoretical speculations can be found repeated over and over again in decades of science fiction stories. And the translation of "xenology" from science fiction to reality awaits only the discovery of another sentient race upon which to practice this already-developed science.

Sometimes our Rubber Science fantasies turn out to be valid, true, useful in the real world. So finally we should also consider how to dream truer dreams if we are to exploit the Rubber Sciences fully in the creation of literary art.

But science fiction writers should always bear in mind that they are creating visions, not science. Science fiction writers are literary artists, not scientists. Upon occasion, scientists have proven the validity of some of these visions, or been inspired by them. That is *their* function, not that of the science fiction writer. Indeed, for science fiction writers to worry about the validity of their visions would be to straitjacket them needlessly.

What science fiction writers should concentrate on in this area is the further development of their visionary consciousness. One of the keys to this is not to get too hung up on the "science" in "science fiction writer." As I've tried to show in this chapter, most of the so-called science content in science fiction is really literary techniques and scientific logic, not actual fact. What is generally considered "hard science fiction" is not so much more rigor in scientific speculation as a common and rather limiting attitude toward the material and to the visionary faculty.

Larry Niven, Hal Clement, Murray Leinster, John W. Campbell, Jr., among others, are generally considered hard science fiction writers. In addition, certain works of writers like Poul Anderson, James Blish, Lester del Rey, Isaac Asimov, and Arthur C. Clarke are also considered hard science fiction. What do these works of "hard science fiction" have in common?

For one thing, there is what can only be described as the hard science fiction "feel." One has a sense of hard black vacuum and cold pinpoint stars, a universe filled with hard-edged metallic artifacts and a reality whose rules are all of a piece, fixed, seamless, and invariant. The same feel you get watching *Destination Moon,* most of *2001,* or an Apollo launch. The same feel you get looking at a Chesley Bonestell painting. All hard science fiction stories seem somehow to take place in the same essential reality, no matter the differences in superficial detail, and that reality is the hard-edged, materialistic, deterministic reality of a structured and filled-in scientific *Weltanschauung* which admits of no fuzziness in locus, no blank spots, no indeterminacy, no multiplexity—more Newtonian than Einsteinian.

Secondly, hard science fiction seldom if ever focuses its attention on its characters, and when it does, there is little genuine inner life portrayed. One thing hard science fiction emphatically is *not* is the literature of the interaction between altered external environments and altered inner psychic states. Almost without exception, the characters in hard science fiction stories have mid-20th-Century consciousness, no matter how far out their bodies are in space and time.

All this is not necessarily to put down hard science fiction. Many fine stories have been written within these narrow parameters and have even drawn a kind of creative tension from their very narrowness. What I am pointing out is that these *are* narrow parameters for visionary speculation, that hard science fiction basically confines itself to a single reality and a very narrow range of consciousness in its characters.

The proof of this is that many writers of hard science fiction also write more "rubbery" stuff, and it is often their best work. The Arthur C. Clarke of *A Fall of Moondust* is certainly not the Clarke of *Childhood's End.* The Frank Herbert of *The Dragon in the Sea* is not the Herbert of *Dune.* The Isaac Asimov of the early robot stories is not the Asimov of *The Caves of Steel* or *The Naked Sun.*

No one can seriously contend that Clarke wrote a visionary novel like *Childhood's End* because he couldn't write the hard stuff, nor that Frank Herbert wrote a visionary novel like *Dune* because he couldn't write *The Dragon in the Sea.* Rather, these writers assimilated the hard science parameters without being imprisoned by them and transcended them, producing works with the same sort of clarity but set in much more complex realities and dealing with speculatively evolved consciousness.

This is what I mean by developing the visionary consciousness of science fiction; visionary consciousness is, after all, the crown of the

Rubber Sciences. In the last half of the 20th Century, technological innovations, alterations in man's external environment, have proceeded at an ever-accelerating rate. The result has been rapid and fissioning evolution in human consciousness itself, for consciousness is the interface between internal and external realities. This process is not going to stop. We have entered a state of permanent and ongoing transformational evolution. Our consciousness and our technological environment have entered into a feedback relationship which virtually guarantees permanent ongoing evolution of human consciousness.

Examples:

Birth-control pills free female sexuality from previous biological restraints, leading to the "sexual revolution," leading to the feminist movement, leading to altered female consciousness, leading to altered male-female relationships, leading to altered male consciousness, leading to . . . what?

Television brings a war into our living rooms, leading to altered perception of what war really is, leading to an altered consciousness in fighting-age men which enjoins them from participating in killing, leading to a peace movement and an all-professional army, leading to altered geopolitical realities, leading to further changes in human consciousness.

The space program gives us visual images of the Earth as seen as a whole from the outside, leading to the perception of "spaceship Earth," leading to a new ecological awareness, leading to new attitudes toward technology itself, which will lead to new kinds of technology, which will further change our consciousnesses.

Organ transplants force us to contemplate new definitions of death, which must create new definitions of life and a new consciousness of aging, which will alter subtly our entire perceptions of what it is to be human.

It is precisely this area where the Rubber Science of visionary consciousness can be used to enrich science fiction—the ever-evolving interface between the total environment and human consciousness which it has always been science fiction's peculiar genius, at its best, to explore.

The ultimate Rubber Science is the science of the nature of reality itself. There has always been a narrow but rich vein of science fiction that has delved into this area of ultimate sentient concern. A. E. Van Vogt was doing it in the 1930s, 1940s, and 1950s. We have had the profound cosmological and evolutionary visions of Olaf Stapledon. Robert A. Heinlein's *Stranger in a Strange Land* was so successful in this area that it helped to spawn a new style of consciousness in the real world. Writers like Gregory Benford, Frank Herbert, Cordwainer Smith, and Damon Knight have mined this ore from time to time. Perhaps the pinnacle of this strain of science fiction has been the work of Philip K. Dick, who manages to unite the most convoluted of metaphysical speculations with a deep and immediate humanity and an unusual empathic warmth toward his characters.

How can writers of science fiction expand their skills in this area?

One way is to realize that there are now new fields of knowledge with which one should familiarize oneself. Just as the science fiction writers of the 1950s added the "soft sciences" of psychology, sociology, anthropology, and economics to their spheres of interest, the science fiction writers of today should be looking into psychopharmacology, Eastern and Western systems of consciousness alteration, media analysis, perceptual psychology, systems analysis, the social and internal psychology of life-styles, and, if you will, psychedelia.

Personally, I have found Marshall McLuhan's *Understanding Media* the single most consciousness-expanding book of the decade, not so much for its often questionable content but for the entirely new perceptions on the relation between internal and external reality that it generates. Feminist literature, while frequently wrongheaded, does open up whole new areas for further speculation. And there are some books about consciousness itself which feed the head, like *The Steersman's Handbook* by L. Clark Stevens and some of the works of Buckminster Fuller.

Of course much of this material is very rubbery science indeed, but such is always the state of the frontiers of human knowledge, and the frontiers and beyond have always been the natural province of the science fiction writer. Further, the generalist grounding of science fiction writers should enable them to evaluate this sort of thing with a clear and open eye.

As for writing about evolving human consciousness, what this takes, more than anything, is the willingness to look within, to try to put your own consciousness in the strange fictional psychic spaces you're trying to write about. To empathize with states of being that may not now exist.

Fortunately, science fiction gives writers the best possible training for doing this—we try to write about the interior worlds of sapient aliens, don't we? If science fiction writers can penetrate the souls of hypothetical silicon-based quadrisexual octopoids from Sirius, surely they can penetrate the psychic spaces of 25th-Century man, of cyborgs linked to computer banks, of communal consciousnesses, hive minds, Eastern mystics, takers of imaginary drugs, and yes, why not, true psychic supermen. Even women.

Above all, science fiction writers should never lose sight of the fact that what they are writing is literature, not science; that, more than anyone else, they are the poets of the future, the seers of human destiny. Hard science, soft science, or rubber are tools of the trade, means to the end of visionary insight and artistic creation. They should never be mistaken for the end itself.

Norman Spinrad

Norman Spinrad was born in New York City on September 15, 1940, and has lived in New York, Los Angeles, San Francisco and London. He has been a full-time writer since 1965. His novels include:

Bug Jack Barron, a speculative novel about television, immortality, and Presidential politics, a Hugo and Nebula nominee. (He has also written a screenplay based on the book.)

The Iron Dream, which was a National Book Award nominee and won the Prix Apollo in France.

Passing Through the Flame ("The Last Hollywood Novel"), a novel about modern Hollywood, Berkley-Putnam, 1975.

His short stories have appeared in *Playboy, New Worlds, Knight,* and about a dozen other magazines, have been reprinted in about three dozen anthologies, and have been collected in two volumes, *The Last Hurrah of the Golden Horde* and *No Direction Home* (Pocket Books, 1975).

His fiction has been translated into French, Italian, Spanish, German, Danish, Portuguese, Dutch, Russian and Polish.

In addition to fiction, he has written extensively on politics, media, and economics; some of these pieces have been collected in the book *Fragments of America.* He has also written on scientific subjects and food. He has written for television, been a film critic for two years, consulted on film editing, and was a contributing editor for the Los Angeles *Free Press* and the Los Angeles *Staff.*

He is the editor of two anthologies of science fiction stories, *The New Tomorrows* and *Modern Science Fiction.*

In addition to his writings, Norman Spinrad has been Vice-President of the Science Fiction Writers of America, a literary agent, has lectured on science fiction, general fiction, and politics at colleges and high schools, has guested on radio and television shows, and had his own radio interview-and-phone-in show in Los Angeles.

The Parameters of Creativity

ALAN E. NOURSE

Extrapolations and Quantum Jumps

For all of the peculiar distinctiveness which we have come to associate with science fiction or science fantasy, the construction of a successful science fiction story depends on certain factors that are common to any kind of fiction at all, as well as other factors that are unique to science fiction and to science fiction alone. Among the factors that good science fiction must share with any kind of fiction are such critical features as *premise, conflict* and *characterization*, and of all these perhaps the most critical is *premise*.

In his book *The Art of Dramatic Writing*[1] the playwright and director Lajos Egri has long since pointed out that any successful fiction story—or any other work of dramatic writing, for that matter—must above all have a well-formulated premise. Call it what you will—*theme, thesis, root idea, goal, driving force*—the premise of a dramatic work is essentially a proposition to be proved, a basis for argument, an idea leading to a conclusion, and it must form the basic foundation for any story if the work is to be dramatically whole. Without such an underlying premise no situation however intriguing, no characters however brilliantly drawn, no emotions however compassionately portrayed, and no conflict however dramatically staged can amount to very much, for the story will lack point and direction.

In the greatest of dramatic works the premise can often be identified and stated in a simple sentence. In *Romeo and Juliet,* for example, the premise is clear from the beginning of the play: *Great Love defies even death.* In Ibsen's *Ghosts* it is shown that *the sins of the fathers are visited on the children;* in *Macbeth,* that *ruthless ambition leads to its own destruction;* and in *Othello* that *jealousy destroys itself and the object of its love.* And premise is as vital to good science fiction or fantasy as it is to any other form of dramatic writing. Thus in John Campbell's "Who Goes There?" it was shown beyond any question that *things are not always what they appear to be;* in Tolkien's *Ring* trilogy that *the forces of good can ultimately overcome the forces of evil, but only at a price;* and in Asimov's *Nightfall* that *blind superstition can overcome reason and lead to disaster.* Even the works of such experimental, nonlinear or symbolic writers as Aldiss, Ballard, Disch, Sallis or Ellison, at their best, reveal powerful premises. At one Milford Conference for science fiction writers some years ago a story was presented in which the hero/anti-hero was pursued, trapped and, ultimately, devoured by a giant refrigerator. Whatever else might be said about this story, the author's premise was clear: that *man can be destroyed by uncontrolled technology.*

Hardly less important than premise are two other major factors: *character* and *conflict.* It is the heart blood of science fiction to deal with the impact of science in the past, present and future upon human lives, minds and emotions. Such impact can only be successfully dramatized when the impactees—the human beings involved in the story—are drawn as full, rich and believable people with lives, minds and emotions capable of receiving the impact and reflecting its results. The characters must seem real enough to involve the reader deeply in their fictional lives, either through empathy or antipathy. They must seem believable enough in their origins, their behavior and their reactions that the reader is forced to say, "Yes, that would happen; yes, that action is consistent; yes, that result is inevitable."

But in modern fiction rich, real and believable characters cannot adequately be drawn simply by telling about them. They must be *shown in action,* revealed by the things they think or do, portrayed in the process of moving or being moved, and the great common denominator in such character revelations—indeed, the great common denominator in all real-life human behavior—is *conflict.* It matters little what form the conflict may take so long as it arises logically from the characters' minds, emotions and circumstances and is resolved by the characters' actions and reactions, revealing the "true" nature of those characters all the while. If the conflict is between two or more characters, each character involved is revealed. If it is between one character and a society, both the character and the society are revealed; if between a character and his environment, both character and environment are revealed; and if the conflict is internal—the character in conflict with himself—then two or more different facets of the same character will be revealed. In any case, the character revelation through conflict can be highly dramatic because conflict in its very nature is dramatic; and the resolution of the conflict or conflicts, consistent with the actions the characters as they have been revealed *must take,* will support or prove the guiding premise of the work. The end result is a work that will delight, excite, entertain, amuse, instruct, caution or chill the reader, but above all it will *satisfy* him, stir his emotions and, ideally, leave him with more to think about than he brought with him to the first page of the story.

These factors of premise, character and conflict are as vital to the impact of *The Martian Chronicles* as to *The Merchant of Venice,* as critical to the success of *A Canticle for Liebowitz* as to *The Godfather,* and any attempt to structure a science fiction story without any one of them, simply because it is a science fiction story, is doomed to failure. But in certain other areas science fiction stands uniquely and unmistakably alone, especially in such areas as originality of idea, selection of incident, depiction of situation and development of background. It is these areas that distinguish science fiction as a singularly imaginative and speculative literature—indeed, more than any other genre, a *literature of ideas.*

In considering these areas it is important to realize that there are few rigid conventions in science fiction or fantasy as regards time, place, circumstances or setting. Good science fiction stories can (and have) been written from the viewpoint of a primitive cave man in the Stone Ages of human prehistory, against a background of ancient Rome, or concerned with events in Scandinavian mythology. They can (and have) been laid in the immediate present of today, in the near past or near future of yesterday or tomorrow, or in the almost unimaginably distant future of millennia hence. Yet whatever the time, place or circumstances of a given story, virtually all science fiction stories share in common a device that is not ordinarily found in any other literary genre: the construction of incident, situation and background through the use of *extrapolation.*

We can determine the impact of yesterday's scientific advancements or today's scientific achievements on human lives by virtue of simple observation, research and analysis. But how do we predict the impact of tomorrow's science on human lives? Some might say that we can't because the nature of tomorrow's science is not yet known—yet science fiction writers have been doing this for years, often with singularly startling, enlightening or fascinating results simply by inferring or projecting that which is not known on the basis of what is already known —in short, by extrapolating from the known present to an as-yet-unknown but cleverly imagined and carefully reasoned future.

Myriads of examples can be found from among the scores of recently published science fiction novels. Consider the following:

1. In one widely popular novel set in the very immediate future (that is, in the future only a few years hence) a space capsule scoops up an alien virus from the near reaches of space around the earth and then inadvertently crashes, releasing a deadly viral plague on a small southwestern town.[2] The plague is temporarily confined only due to the happy accident that (a) space authorities know the location of the crashed vehicle and (b) the crash point is a desert village that can be effectively isolated from the rest of the country at least for a time. The bulk of the story involves the race against time and the utilization of (then) ultramodern laboratory and medical techniques to find a way to wipe out the virus before the virus wipes out mankind. The impact of this particular novel was enhanced not a little by virtue of the fact that it was published precisely at the time that man's landings on the moon were about to be attempted, and a great many biomedical authorities were alarmed at what they regarded as grossly inadequate precautions taken to guard against inadvertently bringing an alien virus entity back home with the spacemen.

2. In a totally different kind of novel the story is laid, far in the future, on a planet so unspeakably arid and hostile as to make the Sahara seem a Garden of Eden by comparison, and concerns itself with characters who must learn by hard and painful stages the necessity of living in harmony with the ecology of an apparently unlivable planet rather than attempting to live *on* the planet through exploitation of its scanty and ultimately finite resources.[3]

3. In another novel, set in the early 21st Century, government has

imposed a massive health-control program throughout the nation, centering on sterilization and eugenic manipulation as a means not only of population control but as a guideline to health care and delivery as well, engendering a widespread and totally illegal black market in medical care.[4] In this black market renegade physicians team up with procurers of medical and surgical supplies to carry on clandestine medical practices outside the pale of government control. The story concerns the activities of one such physician and his "bladerunner" when faced with the emergence of a deadly epidemic that the government health-control program is helpless to deal with by virtue of its own oppressive nature and rules.

4. In yet another novel, set in a far-distant future, over three trillion human beings on earth live crowded into enormous and hive-like underground cities.[5] For reasons that evolve with the story, these overcrowded half-humans have been bred to be physically tiny, soft and defenseless, sexually neuter unless stimulated by hormones, nurtured and clothed and totally controlled by machines, and rewarded for good work by being taken on hunting trips to the surface where they and their omnipresent machines would hunt down the few "wild" human creatures that still clung to a feral fugitive existence outside the hives.

It would be hard to imagine four more dissimilar science fiction novels than those noted above, yet all have one distinctive feature in common. All utilize extrapolation in delineating the central idea, in selection of background detail, in development of story situation and in choice of incident. And in each case it is extrapolation that determines the basically science fictional nature of the novel.

In the first case, for example, we know—just as the author knows—that there has not yet been a single example of a virus or any other kind of organism identified anywhere that we have thus far searched in our solar system excepting on the surface of the earth and within its atmosphere. On the other hand, we also know something of the nature of viruses. We know that they are composed of tiny packets of nucleic acid surrounded by coatings of protein, that in and of themselves they are essentially inert and lifeless sub-living entities but that they have the capacity to parasitize the living cells of higher organisms, to replicate themselves within those cells, and to cause serious, even fatal, disease in the process. Further, we know that the introduction of a new virus —a newly mutated form, for example—can wreak havoc in a population that is unprotected by specific immune defenses: witness the worldwide epidemic of Asian flu that struck in the 1950s. Finally, we know that viruses in their inert state are remarkably hardy and might very conceivably be carried with the dust of interplanetary or interstellar space over unimaginable distances over unimaginable periods of time.

With such a basis of solid knowledge, it is perfectly reasonable to imagine that an alien virus might indeed be brought home by one of our space probes and might indeed have the potential for causing a devastating worldwide epidemic. It is also perfectly reasonable to suppose that if such were to happen, our medical research resources would be strained to the limit to contain and control such a disaster and that many research weapons now only in the developmental or experimental stages might by then (in the near future) be available in the struggle.

Thus we see that *The Andromeda Strain* utilizes a very limited degree of extrapolation in certain very limited areas in near future time to develop what is essentially a cautionary tale pointing out certain potential biomedical dangers in our present and projected space programs and suggesting that preventive measures should be reconsidered and strengthened to provide common-sense protection against a very possible form of "alien invasion." The author clearly started with a question: "What would happen if . . . ?" and then carried his answer to one possible logical conclusion that he explored in detail in his story. The answer could just as well have been that the alien virus could have proved to be a purely botanical pan-parasite that left animal cells untouched but wiped all plant life off the face of the earth—but that, of course, would have been a different story. It could equally as well have been that *nothing at all would happen* because no earthly organisms happened to contain any cells that the virus was able to parasitize—but that would have resulted in no story at all. As it was, the author chose an extrapolation that served his dramatic needs, provided a wealth of background detail, situation and incident for his fictional purposes, and, above all, *enabled him to voice the warning he wanted to voice* through the device of the novel. He did not have to reach far, nor strain his readers' credulity in the least; indeed, the impact of the novel was far greater set as it was in the very near future—in fact, *in the immediate tomorrow*—than if it had been set sometime in the middle of the 22nd Century. Everything in the novel *except* the necessary minor extrapolations was deliberately kept as close to home as possible. Whether NASA authorities heard or heeded the author's warnings is another question altogether; indeed, we have yet to find out. But *the warning was voiced,* widely and with startling impact upon a multitude of readers.

In his fascinating novel *Dune* author Frank Herbert went much, much farther afield with his extrapolations in order to achieve an even more striking impact. The author's basic premise was very much wedded to the here and now: he was saying, in essence, "*With the aid of technology, and with faithful attention to fundamental principles of ecology, the desert regions of earth could be made to flower and fruit.*" But no novel dealing with a modern-day ecologist working in the Libyan desert today could possibly have presented this premise with the unforgettable impact with which it was presented in *Dune.* Herbert developed the background, situation and incident of his novel by extrapolating a surrogate Sahara on a planetwide scale and then extending that concept of a totally desert planet to an extreme that made the most arid of earthly deserts seem positively friendly by comparison. The planet Arrakis (set in the far future but never clearly identified as to time or place) was portrayed as a desert hell, almost totally bereft of water, populated by hideous and exotic desert monsters, totally forbidding, barren, bleak—a veritable cloaca of the universe in its aridity and hostility to life-as-we-know-it. And yet it was populated by very real, living, breathing and understandable human beings leading fully active and not-at-all-so-intolerable lives there. Indeed, the only ones who found the planet truly intolerable were those newcomers who did not understand it and could not or would not learn to live in harmony with the planet's nature rather than merely seeking to exploit it.

The real richness of the novel, however, arose largely from the fact that the author's creative imagination reached much farther than this superficial, bare-bones image of a desert planet. In logical and exquisite detail he extrapolated the culture of the natives of this planet, the workings of their society, their mythologies, their human natures, their aspirations, and their physical capabilities, drawing largely upon what is known of earthly desert cultures and then carrying that knowledge much further. He extrapolated the planet's geography, its physical features, its native flora and fauna (including a creature that could never have evolved anywhere except on an arid planet since it was destroyed by contact with water), in every instance drawing upon what is known of desert areas on earth and carrying that knowledge to an extreme. He imagined a compellingly logical reason that political and economical control of such a hell-hole might be of enormous value to the rulers of richer and greener planets, avoiding the more obvious clichés which might come to mind and extrapolating instead from what is known of the economics of earthly narcotic drug traffic—but even here the extrapolation is intriguingly complex in detail, for the desired narcotic end product in the novel is deeply and logically interrelated with all facets of the natural ecology of this desert planet, so that to destroy the ecology of the planet by exploiting it would be to destroy the fantastically valuable end product—precisely the ecological conundrum we face here on earth today! As an example of the extremes of extrapolative detail with which the novel is filled, there was the matter of the everyday dress of the natives of this desert planet. We know that desert peoples on earth wear flowing headdresses to protect their heads and necks from the sun and heavy, often even woolen, robes to insulate their bodies from the heat. We also know that they tend to settle (or, in the cases of nomadic tribes, at least congregate) around oases where water, if not plentiful, at least is present. But in *Dune* the planet Arrakis was so intensely arid that there was virtually no free surface water at all—no oases, except in rare instances in which they had been created by the determined application of sound ecological principles. But how, then, could human beings survive at all? Obviously, only by painstaking conservation and recycling of each individual's own body water. But how to do that and still allow the individual to move about, travel, work, carry on his daily life? Herbert's solution was the invention of the so-called "stillsuit" worn by the natives of Arrakis: close-fitting, micro-insulated suits covering the entire body except the eyes and nose, capable of collecting perspired, exhaled and excreted moisture, distilling and purifying it, and then providing for convenient reuse. Only a dust mask covered the nose, but the natives of this planet were conditioned through lifelong habit and necessity always to inhale through the nose and exhale through the mouth (*into* the stillsuit); always to dig in and rest in the shade during the day and travel only at night; and always to carry as much water as possible *inside* their bodies simply by drinking large quantities of the recycled water at a time rather than spacing it out a sip at a time—easier and less energy-wasting than to carry a surplus supply on one's back! Indeed there was no facet of water-and-energy conservation under desert conditions that the author of this novel did not consider, explore and carry to a logical extreme in his story, utilizing both known technology extended to meet his story's needs and as-yet-undeveloped, yet logically probable, technology imaginatively created for specific purposes, given the conditions and the needs of the people in the story.

It was just such imaginative, logical and detailed extrapolation that lent *Dune* its spellbinding fascination and thrust it head and shoulders above other science fiction novels of its time, just as it was the singularly intriguing degree of extrapolation that lent Alfred Bester's *The Demolished Man* a comparable stature in an earlier era. Both authors had the talent, and spent the necessary time and care, to "imagine in greater detail than their readers," as the late science fiction editor John W. Campbell often expressed it. In *Dune* every detail is meticulously thought out, elegantly accounted for; there are no holes, no disturbing omissions or *non sequiturs;* every detail *fits,* and in the end, every detail proves necessary. The end result is a powerful work of fiction with a vitally important premise compellingly demonstrated, and if certain of the characters seem unidimensional and some of the conflict seems stagy and awkward, it does not matter, because the reader, in his fascination, willingly abides these minor flaws.

Thus extrapolation can provide the imaginative substance of the good science fiction story, the matrix within which the characters and conflicts are developed and the premises fulfilled. But extrapolation need not be limited to scientific or technologic matters. It can equally well be applied to social, religious, psychological or political ideas or institutions. In everyday life we see the social evolution of a culture in terms of continuing ferment and change, with one idea leading to another and new social needs appearing as old social needs are recognized, met and resolved. Any reasonable and logically supportable extrapolation of current social trends into future patterns can be acceptable in science fiction; the same can be said of the extrapolation of future political patterns.

In fact it is in such areas as these that science fiction can find some of the most fertile ground for truly creative imaginative speculation—yet it is here also that writers fail most frequently and fall short of what might potentially be achieved. There is a razor's edge at which a science fiction story based on social or political extrapolation can cease to be an imaginative and entertaining story and become a social or political tract. In no other area do control, balance and sensitivity play a larger role in the success or failure of a story. One can properly ask a reader to consider, agree with, perhaps even espouse a social or political premise deeply embedded in a truly imaginative and entertaining story in which the premise is the logical, perhaps seemingly inescapable outgrowth of a compellingly thought-out and presented extrapolation. One cannot clothe a political discourse or a social plea, however worthy, in a cobweb of a story and expect the reader to be anything but irritated. In short, extrapolation in these areas must be even-handed and must above all provide only background, situation and incident against which the characters act out their conflicts. The extrapolation must not be allowed to become the story or all is lost.

Precisely such a problem arose in planning and writing my recent novel *The Bladerunner*, in which I sought to explore the possible impact upon future medical care in this country of certain medico-political trends that are already discernible in our society today. Considering the steadily growing social and political pressure toward some form of federalized medical care that is already present today, it was not hard to extrapolate an all-inclusive, cradle-to-grave socialized medical program legislated in the not-too-distant future, recognizing certain of the benefits that could accrue with such a program but also recognizing certain of the evils that also might accrue and have to be dealt with somehow: over-utilization, astronomically spiraling costs, an ever-increasing population of aging people receiving a disproportionately large fraction of available medical care while paying a disproportionately small portion of the cost, and an ever-increasing tax burden upon a steadily decreasing population of young, healthy and productive members of society.

At the same time, considering the continuing threat of overpopulation we face today, it was not difficult to imagine a point in future time when it would become politically expedient to deal with problems of a massively top-heavy socialized medical program not by cutting back on benefits available to a powerful and vocal majority of aging people but by instituting strenuous eugenic controls designed to reduce demand for health care and control overpopulation at the same time. Extrapolating a step further, it was possible to imagine a system evolving in which the "free" (i.e., federally provided) health care would be available only to individuals willing to submit to sterilization as a direct and rigid prerequisite: a popular (and thus politically feasible) plan among the aging population but an onerous repression to the young adults who were, by and large, supporting the system. Finally, considering the distaste with which most physicians view impending socialized medical controls in this country today, it seemed not unreasonable to extrapolate a steadily decreasing number of recruits into medical training and a growing and desperate need to program and computerize medical services to the maximum extent possible so as to use the time of such physicians as there were with the greatest possible efficiency. From that point, for example, it is not difficult to imagine a surgeon being forced through political, professional and economic pressures to spend a large portion of his time programming computerized servo-mechanisms—robots—to perform surgical procedures of increasing complexity in order that, sometime in the future, a single surgeon might be able to monitor a dozen simultaneous robot-performed operations in the amount of time that would be required for him to perform one such operation himself.

The problem in planning such a background for a science fiction novel was not to find the social, political and medical trends for extrapolation but rather to avoid turning such a story into a single-minded harangue on the evils of socialized medicine, eugenics controls and computerization of medical care. Valid social needs had to be recognized; valid benefits of socialized and computerized programs had also to be pointed out. Human feelings had to be explored, not only feelings of those people in the society who required medical care but the feelings of the physicians providing it as well and indeed the feelings of those engaged in the illegal medical underground which inevitably would arise in the face of such a repressive health-control program. It was necessary to take a position quite clearly neither for nor against socialized medicine, to handle the extrapolated background as even-handedly as possible, and to explore the potentials opened up by that extrapolation as broadly and honestly as possible. Ultimately the success or the failure of the novel had to rest not only on the strength of the story developed against the extrapolated background but almost as much on the degree to which an even-handed, multidimensional balance was achieved in the background portrayal.

Finally, the novel *Half Past Human*, by T. J. Bass, illustrates yet another aspect of extrapolation that can be used to strengthen the impact and enrich the fascination of a science fiction novel. So far we have considered extrapolation only as a smooth, logical and imaginative extension into the future of current trends of scientific progress, technological advancement, social development or political evolution. But this limited view overlooks a fundamental and easily demonstrable fact: that progress and change, whether in scientific advancement or in social development, are not by any means always evolutionary in nature, unfolding in smooth, orderly, step-by-step and potentially predictable fashion. In fact some of the most staggering social changes and some of the most fundamental scientific advances have occurred not by evolutionary stages but in quantum jumps as a result of sudden and convulsive, even revolutionary, social or political upheaval, or as a result of abrupt, totally unexpected and unpredictable scientific breakthroughs. The Industrial Revolution in England brought social and political change by evolutionary stages, but there was nothing remotely evolutionary about the French Revolution in the 1700s, or the explosion of Bolshevism in Russia in the 1900s. The social and political history of the world has been shaken repeatedly by the occurrence of a wild and unpredictable variable—the emergence of a Christ or a Hitler, a Lenin or a Mohammed. Scientific progress has repeatedly been revolutionized by the emergence of a Galileo or a da Vinci, a Newton or an Einstein—or by the invention of such a simple and revolutionary device as the transistor.

From the very beginning science fiction writers have quite legitimately extrapolated such quantum jumps in developing their stories. For example, a long succession of excellent science fiction novels, ranging from Van Vogt's *Slan* through Asimov's *Foundation* novels to multitudes of more contemporary works have turned upon the emergence of full-blown extrasensory perception of one sort or another as a human "wild talent" either in a single critical individual or in a segment of the race. Alfred Bester used psychokinesis as the extrasensory breakthrough —the extrapolatory quantum jump—on which *The Stars My Destination* was based. Unconscious extrasensory interference with the laws of probability played an important role in my own novel *The Mercy Men*. Ursula Le Guin employed such an extrapolatory quantum jump in conceiving the androgynous sexual nature of the people native to her ice-shrouded planet in *The Left Hand of Darkness*. Yet another common quantum jump, still used successfully in science fiction, is a story involving time travel—a fictional "technological achievement" which, so far as we know today, is now and (probably) forever impossible. The same may be said for the story involving faster-than-light travel. In these cases the authors make no attempt to explain the "hows" of the technological achievement involved, or else employ pure science fictional gobbledygook as an "explanation." This is generally unnecessary. One assumes that the achievement exists; the reader suspends his disbelief in order to accept the impossible as a for-granted premise; and the author can win if the story based on that premise is clever enough, interesting enough, intriguing enough, and (otherwise) believable enough.

In *Half Past Human* Bass used both evolutionary extrapolation and quantum-jump extrapolation with equally stunning effect. He postulated an earth of the future in which every available inch of the surface of the planet was required, and used, for cultivation of food, with the human population living in huge, underground hive-like cities. Certainly one can reach such an end point by imagining stepwise changes over a prolonged evolutionary chain of events and at the same time come up with a wealth of corollary detail—for example, the logical notion that virtually all surface-living flora and fauna would ultimately be wiped out to make room for the cultivation of cereal grains and that the planting, cultivation and harvesting would ultimately be done by robot machines controlled by remote control from the hive cities. One might also imagine quite logically that such meat protein as was available to the population would be supplied largely by reprocessing protein salvaged from humans who had died.

The quantum jump, however, came in imagining in great detail the nature of the humans populating the hives: a race of people who had been genetically engineered to be uniformly tiny in size, able through genetic engineering to subsist on 25 percent of the hemoglobin that normal human beings of today require for respiration, conditioned through inactive, sedentary existences and the pressures of sheer numbers to be soft, weak-muscled, dull-minded, utterly dependent on computer maintenance, sexually neuter except when specifically stimulated for reproductive purposes—a dim, half-living subrace of once-humans, at first quite repugnant to the reader, yet ultimately made appealingly human and empathetic in their few remaining recognizably human characteristics, thanks to the author's skill in character portrayal. These creatures, changed so radically from the human forms that we are accustomed to, by means of massive application of a technology which is barely emerging today as a recognizable science, represent far too great a reach to be considered evolutionary extrapolation—yet the reasons for the changes are so compelling and the fictional reality of the changed world so believable that the reader readily accepts the quantum jump.

In short, extrapolations and quantum jumps are both devices that can be used freely in the construction of science fiction stories and indeed often provide the very richness and fascination that make the story unique and memorable. Such devices cannot replace a soundly thought-out premise, believable characterization and suspenseful conflict in a successful story; the tale which is all background, situation and extrapolatory incident will invariably fail for lack of the more vital basic ingredients. But given those ingredients extrapolations and quantum jumps can and do provide the qualities that distinguish good science fiction from other literary forms and contribute a richness of idea and a source of fascination that ultimately makes good science fiction so singularly stimulating and compelling.

NOTES

1. Egri, Lajos. *The Art of Dramatic Writing.* New York, Simon and Schuster, 1946.

2. Crichton, Michael. *The Andromeda Strain.* New York, Alfred A. Knopf, 1969.

3. Herbert, Frank. *Dune.* Philadelphia, Shulton, 1965.

4. Nourse, Alan E. *The Bladerunner.* New York, David McKay, 1974.

5. Bass, T. J. *Half Past Human.* New York, Ballantine, 1971.

Alan E. Nourse, M.D.

Alan E. Nourse was born in Des Moines, Iowa, in 1928 and spent his childhood in Iowa, New York, and New Jersey. After graduating from high school, he started his premedical studies at Rutgers in 1945, but these were interrupted by two years in the Navy's hospital corps. In 1948, he returned to Rutgers, where he received his B.S. in 1951, and was admitted to the University of Pennsylvania School of Medicine. After getting his M.D. in 1955, he interned in Seattle and then devoted two years to freelance writing before entering general practice at North Bend, Washington, in 1958. In 1963, he returned to full-time writing.

His first national publication was a short story, "High Threshold," published in *Astounding* in 1951, and this was followed by some sixty sf stories and novelettes which appeared in virtually all the magazines of the time. In addition, he published a short novel, *A Man Obsessed* (Ace Books, 1954), and wrote *The Invaders Are Coming* (also for Ace) in collaboration. His writing, at the time, helped to pay for his medical education, and of course still reflects a strong medical orientation.

Nourse has published fiction and nonfiction in a great many magazines: *Saturday Evening Post, Playboy, Argosy, Ellery Queen's Mystery Magazine, Better Homes and Gardens, Boy's Life,* and so forth.

He lives in North Bend with his wife and four children and also maintains a writing retreat in eastern Washington, where much of his work is done. His hobbies include reading, fishing, hunting, and back-pack hiking in the mountains.

NONFICTION

Nine Planets: Astronomy for the Space Age, 1960 and 1970 (Harper & Row) and 1962 (Pyramid Books)

The Management of a Medical Practice, 1962 (Lippincott); with Geoffrey Marks

So You Want To Be a Doctor, 1964 (Harper & Row); one of a series all for the same publisher, including *So You Want to Be a Lawyer; a Scientist; a Nurse; an Engineer; a Physicist; a Chemist; a Surgeon; an Architect,* several of which were collaborations, (various dates)

Universe, Earth and Atom: The Story of Physics, 1969 (Harper & Row)

Venus and Mercury: A First Book, 1972 (Franklin Watts)
The Ladies' Home Journal Family Medical Guide, 1973 (Harper & Row)
The Outdoorsman's Medical Guide, 1974 (Harper & Row)
The Backyard Astronomer, 1973 (Franklin Watts)

SCIENCE FICTION AND JUVENILE FICTION

Trouble on Titan, 1954 (Holt, Rinehart & Winston), 1964 (Lancer Books)
A Man Obsessed, 1954 (Ace Books)
Junior Intern, 1955 (Harper & Row)
Rocket to Limbo, 1958 (Ace Books), and 1957 (McKay)
Scavengers in Space, 1958 (McKay), and 1960 (Ace)
The Invaders Are Coming, 1959 (Ace), with J. A. Meyer
Star Surgeon, 1960 (McKay)
Raiders from the Rings, 1963 (McKay)
The Universe Between, 1965 (McKay)
PSI High and Others, 1967 (McKay)
The Mercy Men, 1968 (McKay)

SHORT-STORY COLLECTIONS

Tiger by the Tail and Other Science Fiction Stories, 1960 (McKay)
The Counterfeit Man: More Science Fiction Stories, 1965 (McKay)
Rx for Tomorrow: Tales of Science Fiction, Fantasy and Medicine, 1971 (McKay)

THEODORE STURGEON

Future Writers in a Future World

Science fiction (hereinafter sf) is essentially extrapolative fiction, and extrapolating into the future is a legitimate function for it but is not all that sf does nor all it can do. Extrapolation can proceed in any direction, and sf writers can be expected to write, and readers to read, narratives of the past and of the present and of environments simply *other;* and that *other* includes not only an infinity of exterior environments but the dictum with which humanity in general, and sf writers in particular, are becoming increasingly aware: that there is more room in inner space than in outer space.

Much more.

Therefore my first reaction to this assignment—and, I confess, my own knee-jerk reflex!—was Migod, Science Fiction Is Prediction and I am being asked to Predict. Prediction is not a quicksand into which I willingly wade.

But . . . what price honest intent? If I am to write of, and write to, sf writers of today and tomorrow, there is no way to pretend that I am not writing about the future. And heaven help me, there is no way to do this without attempting yet again to define sf, what it is and what it does. Like virtually every other practitioner, I have my own modifications of every other definition ever proclaimed (except Damon Knight's, who said, "Sf is what you happen to be pointing at when you are talking about it").

Further, it is not possible to discuss intelligently the nature of future sf without examining the nascence of the thinking, the statements, the (if you like) messages of future sf—that is to say, where will they get their ideas?

To understand anything I state herein, you must understand where I am when I state it, so here I go again, taking (analogically) that one hot fudge sundae, that one li'l ol' drink, that one drag from the new carton—having devoutly sworn off. I shall define sf. I shall tell where we get our ideas from. I shall predict.

Just this once . . .

Good writing in any category depends upon two factors: matter and manner. What you say in writing sf is the science part; how you say it is the fiction part. Excellence in manner, to the exclusion or minification of matter, will sell your stories and might even get you the reputation of being a good writer. It will never get you known as a great or important one, however, because if you get through by gloss and polish alone, or almost alone, you may be remembered but you won't leave anything behind. Soap bubbles are like that.

Preoccupation with matter to the exclusion of, or minification of, manner will in all likelihood be the greatest obstacle you will encounter in selling your stories at all. People who like to read fiction—the ones, you see, who keep publishers alive and well—react badly to getting tracts and manuals for their fiction money. (It isn't that they don't like tracts and manuals; they just don't like paying for them when they are misrepresented as fiction.)

In teaching, reviewing, and enjoying sf, my emphasis is always on the fiction. This is not at all because I think that the fiction in science fiction is more important than the science in science fiction. Far from it. It is because I like writers to be read and remembered and (when they can) to move people and shake them; to ignite, to increase their ability to share their visions and their joy and their terror, as well as their knowledge. It is possible to write a story that will be a peak event, that will change the very life and thought of the ultimate expert on the structure of secondary pheasant-feathers, but since such experts are a submicroscopic minority in the population, the chances are not great that the story will have much effect on anyone else.

One should write one's fiction carefully and consciously *to* someone, as one writes a letter; and the selection of that someone is the single most important skill that a writer can develop. See to it that he or she is someone who is open to the kind of vision you want to share and not someone with a close and tiny specialization. Never make it someone who knows more than you do (about facts, about life), someone you don't know and are trying to impress. Make it someone you do know, someone you know well, and as you write, *watch that face.* Watch for round-eyed, open-mouthed fascination, watch for laughter, watch for astonishment, watch for tears. Watch for detachment, watch for yawns, watch for incomprehension, watch for sleep. There is this wonderful thing to be said about this technique: never in life will you have such an audience, for, on realizing that he fell asleep three thousand words ago, you can rip out the three thousand words and he will return to exactly the burst of laughter you provoked at that time; and he will return to it three times, or three hundred, as you go back and try, try again.

I must change the metaphor for a moment. Unless the writer is one who can produce a masterpiece, and having gratified himself by the activity, throw the manuscript into the fire unread by anyone else (and I have never met one of those), he must be a communicator. Visualize a radio transmitter on a mountainside, pumping watts and kilowatts into the atmosphere. It will be worse than useless if there are no receivers in the valley. It will be of relative unimportance, for all its perfection and power, if there is only one receiver, or two. It will, however, be a significant force if it reaches hundreds, or hundreds of thousands. Hence it behooves the transmitter to broadcast material to which his audience can readily tune.

To what things are readers—most readers, many readers—attuned? Why, to those things closest to the personal experience of each. And what are those things?

Love, and pain, and greed, and laughter, and hope, and above all loneliness.

Now if you feel that you have something of significance to say about secondary pheasant-feathers, encase it in these, and you will get through. For fiction is *people*—people interacting with people, ideas acting on people, hardware acting on people. Even stories with no people in them at all, like Murray Leinster's astonishing "The Wabbler," so personify the protagonist/artifact, and so underline the effect on humanity of such a device, that they follow this precept.

So again I say: fiction is not the most important part of science fiction but is the carrier, the vehicle, for the science in science fiction, which cannot and will not carry itself. This is true for us now; it will be equally true for you in the future.

In speaking of the science in science fiction, one confronts the question of defining the entire field. I can only tell you what works for me, and modestly point to my array of pennants and obeisances to show that indeed it works well. As "everybody" knows, and as any good dictionary will point out, science is the arrangement, classification, and retrieval of data, and, by experiment, the rationalization of hypothesis into theory and of theory into law.

To which I apply an ardent "Poppycock!" and, for my working definition of sf, repair to etymology, to discover that the root word, the Latin *scientia,* means none of the above. It means, solely and simply, "knowledge." To me, sf has always been "Knowledge Fiction," and by this definition I have comfortably been able to avoid taking sides in sf's turbulent controversies about whether or not extrasensory perception, or the psychology of ritual magic, or dadaistic prose, or experimental narrative, or sex, ought or ought not to be admitted to the club. For all that, my requirement of what is or is not sf is hard-edged and most rigorous. If the science—knowledge—aspect of the story can be extracted from the narrative and still leave a cohesive fiction, then it is the cowboy story made to occur on Mars instead of in Arizona and I'll have no part of it. In all other ways I surf contentedly on the crests of New Waves and Old.

There is one more thing to be said of sf in the Twentieth and forthcoming Centuries. Because it habituates its people—writers, editors, and readers—to other worlds (in the broadest, deepest connotations of that phrase), to alternates and alternatives, to probabilities, possibilities, probable possibilities and improbable certainties, to results and resultants, to thought and thoughts of a magnitude and freedom exceeded only by poetry—*science fiction is the only possible pill against future shock.*

All right.

Where do we get our ideas?

Or in the present context of future writers and writing: where will you get your ideas?

To that great synthesist Isaac Asimov we owe the observation that there are only three kinds of sf, though they may be mixed and mingled in the same story: "What if . . . ," "If only . . ." and "If this goes on. . . ." The first injects the unusual into a more or less stable situation. The second is a wish-fulfillment kind of thing: if men could fly; if no one could tell lies; and so on. The third has to do with whatever bothers you in the here and now, or, by analogy, what bothers the people in a future or other place—things like gun control, nude beaches, the welfare state, malpractice insurance. Take it from here and run as far as you like. It helps if you believe in something—if you really give a damn. If you don't there's a between-the-lines something you can't eradicate and no editor can fix. It's the something young children instantly divine and reject when a writer "writes down" to them. There's a lot of difference between ignorance—that is, the lack of knowledge—and stupidity, which a good many writers seem not to have discovered but about which any five-year-old can tell you with his first squirm. *Life* magazine was saying the same thing in the super-secret form-book given to new editors in their orientation phase. "Never underestimate the reader's intelligence," said the book, and "Never overestimate his information." Sage advice indeed, especially for the sf writer. If you write about important things—and I don't mean things important only to you, like pheasant-feathers, but things that touch us all (or might, or will, if this goes on . . .)—then you just can't write down. One thinks of Joanna Russ's brilliant polemic *The Female Man;* you may feel she is writing to enemies, but not for a moment is she speaking to idiots. And so much of Heinlein compels, not so much for the polished milling of the nuts-and-bolts science and engineering in his work but for the urgency of his caring.

What, then, will you be caring about in the decades ahead?

Love, and pain, and greed, and laughter, and hope, and loneliness, of course. And these will occur in the context of such changes as the world has never before seen.

"The good is getting better," said a beautiful Hollywood mystic I once knew, "and the bad is getting worse; and that is the name of Armageddon." We have freedoms of life-styles, of speech and art and behavior, that would have been unthinkable ten or even five years ago, concurrent with growing encroachments of government and industry. Said Will

Rogers: "Your freedom to swing your fists ends where my nose begins." A lot of freedom-swingers seem to have lost their flywheels, as it were, and an increasing number of the noses are attached to clubs and guns. The tension shows every likelihood of reaching a point where just one incident—a bombing, an assassination, perhaps even something far less if the tension is great enough—and the fabric will rip. There could then be turmoil and its certain reaction: an iron regimentation "for the greater good" backed by weapons and techniques that simply cannot be opposed.

And that could last for centuries.

Write about that. Not about how it begins; it has already begun. Write about life in the new dark. Write about the new dawn afterward and how it comes about.

If you do it well enough, maybe you can stop it.

A marvelous mix of "what if . . ." and "if only . . ." is the "alternate history" story. A perfect example is Ward Moore's *Bring the Jubilee,* a beautifully written and scholarly narrative in which the South has won the Civ—excuse me—the War Between the States. And a true *tour de force* is Norman Spinrad's extraordinary *The Iron Dream.* In this novel, an author, who had emigrated from Germany as a teenager and who had become a pulp magazine illustrator, produced this explosively violent, dreadfully written novel of pure-blooded heroes and their conquest of hybrid subhumans. Aside from exaggerated *machismo* and phallic symbolism, the story contains no sex, no characterization, nothing but bloody conquest and ethnic superiority. The author's name is Adolf Hitler, his novel is titled *Lords of the Swastika,* and it is followed by a splendidly articulate, scholarly appreciation by one Homer Whipple, who thumbnails Hitler's biography (describing his death from tertiary syphilis some six weeks after the book was written) and ponders the personal and historical influences which have produced such an effusion as this book. It filters in to the reader that Mr. Whipple is writing in a world in which (if I remember correctly) World War I was won by the Kaiser and there was a subsequent atomic war in the early Fifties; Mr. Whipple dates his contribution in 1957. So you see, you begin in your own here-and-now, are flung into Author Hitler's mad universe, and are made to realize that it was created by Hitler in Mr. Whipple's, which is vastly different from ours; all in all, a unique and ingenious tapestry of narrative threads, quite impossible to any other convention than that of speculative fiction, and generously yielding a harvest of many different fruits; for a story like this casts light—sometimes a baleful one—on our own history, in fact and as recorded, which are very often two different things. Further, this kind of narrative evokes an interest and often a detailed study of history, an unfailingly enriching activity.

Ward Moore and Norman Spinrad did not invent this alternate history trick. Vladimir Nabokov's *Ada* takes place in a world in which the Allies lost the war. In the 'Forties, L. Sprague de Camp wrote a lovely yarn about a contemporary American flung back in time and trapped there, imbued with the obsession that he must and could prevent the Dark Ages. It was called *Lest Darkness Fall.* Poul Anderson has written, and continues to write, dozens of fine swashbuckling stories about Goths and Huns, Mongols and ancient Greeks, some of them mixed with myth and fantasy, some with quasi-technological time-travel, but all pivoting on the historical record. One must mention Mark Twain's *A Connecticut Yankee,* of course; and I remember my very first stage play, to which I was dragged not quite kicking and screaming and which I found fascinating and unforgettable; it was called *If Booth Had Missed* and dealt with an America in which Lincoln lived through the Reconstruction period. (He got shot anyhow.)

The important thing for a writer to remember in tackling this kind of thing is that, since history, real or imagined or real and interpreted in some new way, is indeed the pivot, then the reader must be informed, somehow or other, of which history (and whose idea of history) it is that you're writing about. There is a caution to be made here:

It is easy for a writer—especially a good writer—to fall into the trap of assuming that his readers are as interested in history as he is and that they know as much of it as he does. There is adequate and profound reason for this. Almost the very definition of a good writer is that, aside from the gloss of his skills with language, he is interested in people—in their motives, their feelings, the extraordinary differences in choices of action which one person or another may take, given the same stimulus. This is, of course, the very definition of the true historian and of the writer who follows his bent. History is full of surprises and perplexities, and the impulse to cast a fictional net around the murder of the two little princes in the Tower, or the real reasons for Leon Czolgocz's lethal bullet (oh, you thought L. H. Oswald was this century's only "insane sole Presidential assassin," did you?)—that impulse is well-nigh irresistible.

"Any answer is not necessarily the only answer," said that jovial,

Jovian iconoclast Charles Fort (a deep-plunging observation I should like to see tattooed on the backs of the hands of rigorous scientists everywhere) and writers of neo-, pseudo-, quasi-, future-, alternative-, and speculative fiction are readily hooked by it. That a President decided not to run for another term is a simple historical fact. That he gave his reasons is documented, in the files and retrievable. That these may not have been the only reasons, or not the real ones, is, to the writer bitten by the history bug, a big red button wired to an infinity of what-ifs.

All of which is a continuation of this cautionary passage. If you are going to write about the past, and frame your narrative with known events and people, you research carelessly at your peril. All of your readers are not careless, and if you place an arquebus out of its period, or blotting paper before it replaced dry sand, you will most certainly be caught at it. It would be a rotten shame to have your reader, in the midst of some fascinating convolution in the fate of empires, stopped cold because you used buttons instead of hooks.

The injection of "what if . . . ?" into historical themes is especially provocative. Not long before this writing, I attended a hang-gliding championship. I was amazed and fascinated by these tiny silent kites—minimal aeronautics, an absolute symbol of my long-held conviction that true basics are never complex. The amazement stemmed from a certain obsession I have had since early high-school days with the history of aviation and the realization that it had to go from the intricate fragilities of Lilienthal and Chanute through the clean lines of the skin-stressed monoplanes to these breathless nylon butterflies, where, in design, the whole thing should have begun. And *could* have begun! Leonardo failed in achieving powered flight for lack of the right power plant, which in his time was beyond his technological reach. Not so the hang-glider, which was within a craftsman's grasp hundreds and even thousands of years ago. Like the dewdrop hanging to a spiderweb which no shepherd ever recognized as a lens; like the wooden propeller which any boy can whittle in five minutes—and no boy ever did—the hang-glider was available, and could have carried clouds of spearmen off the lower slopes of the Alps, in the vanguard of Hannibal's hordes—and think of what *that* would have done to history! All it lacked was the one observant eye, the one minuscule explosion in one man's mind. (And by the way, no law has been passed to prevent the same thing from happening tonight or tomorrow . . . happening to you.)

In writing about writing about history, I must share with you a conversation I had with one of the finest, gentlest, and most powerful minds I have ever encountered, that of Richard McKenna, shortly before his death. "You can change the past," he declared and went on to equate a human life with an artist's work-in-progress, and suggested that perhaps the canvas was smeared with muddy bits, revolting dark swirls, splashes of that which was inappropriate, clashing, inartistic; and how the artist, with a clear eye for what was already there, with careful design, could include all of that—covering up nothing—in a masterpiece, beginning right now, in such a way that every shadow would give boldness and reality to a new light, every ugliness set off and give prominence to a new beauty. McKenna, whose vast and wise tolerance was a miracle, would, because of this, never judge a life until it was finished, any more than he would presume to judge an unfinished painting. Now, there's a challenge for a writer! Present the real world, in all its grit and ugliness, past and present, and—covering up nothing—so design its future that you change its past into something lovely.

In the matter of history in speculative fiction, then: Do your homework. Make real history real, no matter what injections you make into it. Make fictional histories—alternates, probables, futures—viable and credible. And populate them with real people with real motivations, have them feel real triumph, real pain, real love, and above all loneliness—even as real people have felt these things in the real world.

Here's another scenario for the future writer. We have doomsayers who are preoccupied with pollution of the atmosphere and the death of the oceans. We are fairly warned that if we do not correct our habits, then it isn't merely that we'll have to breathe dirtier and dirtier air; we may not have enough air! Then there are those whose legitimate terror lies in the possibility of nuclear war, and this one needs no elaboration. Then there are the mutations we have produced by our synthesized antibiotics and the likelihood of new strains of bacteria and viruses which might defy anything we can devise against them. Already we have had plague-spots of Newcastle disease in poultry and equine encephalitis for which the only practical treatment is to slaughter the infected and quarantine the exposed, and proponents of this horror point at the statistical certainty that our sophisticated therapies will produce a mutated strain that will give us humans an incurable plague. A startling amount of documentation has appeared concerning the cumulative effects of fluoridated water, insecticides, and freon from aerosols, all promising a rising incidence of cancer and other diseases. There are others.

The point worth making by making such a catalogue is one apparently overlooked, not only by the general public but by each of the abovementioned doom-criers: that none of the hells they describe need necessarily "win" over the others, despite publicity and partisanship; that they are not mutually exclusive, and that they could well and truly happen all at once. If one clings to the idea that a well-formed sf story might be effective in raising public awareness to one or another of these nightmares, and create a counterforce, one may cling also to the idea that a superbly crafted story might serve to slow or stop them all.

Write that one.

A current preoccupation is with the "energy crisis," about which there is an appalling lack of truly basic thinking. Such thinking at once dictates the simple solution: get rid of the fossil fuels, all of them, altogether. Horrified cries that such a move would bring to a halt the greatest technological structure the world has ever seen can be silenced by pointing out that methanol—wood alcohol—and its source methane can be produced simply and cheaply by treatment of solid waste. Los Angeles alone produces enough solid waste to supply electricity to every city and town west of the Rockies from Canada to Mexico. Seattle and St. Louis are already tapping this rich source to power their fleets of vehicles and to generate electricity. And if we must mine something, let's mine the vast areas of landfill into which we have dumped incalculable amounts of treasure in the form of organic material and recoverable metals for decades.

Given an equivalent refinery capacity, methanol could be produced more cheaply than gasoline. You can pour up to 25 percent of it into a 1975 automobile and get improved performance with a cleaner engine with less pollution, with virtually no adjustment of the carburetion or anything else. With slight modification you could go to 50 percent or more with still further improvement. Why, then, do we see so little effort in this direction?

Truly basic thinking leads us to the obvious: there is more money to be made by the use of fossil fuels than any alternatives. Wind and water power, geothermal and atomic energy, and especially solar and pure hydrogen devices can all give us cleaner power, but not with the kind of profit margins offered by coal and oil. The truly basic thinker does not moralize; he confronts. So down here near the source of the trouble (which is where basic, simple solutions usually live) we find the element of greed.

Greed should, I think, be removed from the roster of sins and be welcomed into the diadem of virtues, where it can be proudly and openly worn. It has almost worked its way up there anyway. And by the studied manipulation of greed we can not only move the earth; we may find a way to save it. If it's methanol we want instead of gasoline, the clear-sighted effort we should be making is not only to make methanol cheaper to buy but also, purposefully and energetically, to make it more profitable to the producers. If this means heavy taxation not only on gasoline but on all the means for its production from wellhead to cracking plant, and tax abeyance or forgiveness on all the means for making and distributing methanol, that is only one of several ways of bringing about our goal. Turning greed into an acknowledged virtue, at the current stage of our moral evolution, would bring about a rule of thumb that would save our bodies and in the long run might save our souls: make it profitable to be good and costly to be bad. That means hard-cash profitable and not virtue being its own reward.

I mean these specifics to lead to simple basics. You need not write about methanol, therefore. Write about pragmatic morality. Write about greed.

A discussion of methanol from solid waste leads to one of the simplest and most basic of all laws: *no organism can live in an environment of its own waste products.* The production of civilization's life blood directly from its wastes might seem to abrogate this most basic of all biological laws. Yet the abrogation of natural law is one of the most avid activities of the naked ape. We'll whip the laws of gravity yet; see if we don't. We'll beat aging and weather and Einstein's "c," I'm convinced of it. It is in our nature to abrogate such laws. The prime example is what we have done to *Only the fittest survive.* We have broken that law within our own species (partly by redefining "fittest," but we also break it in other ways). Ponder this carefully: wolves and eagles and other such prey on strays, on the sick, on the old. When we go out to hunt bighorns or elk, or fish for trout, or shoot wild turkeys, which ones do we get in our sights? Why, the best, the biggest, the swiftest and strongest. I cannot, because of my human bias, completely condemn what we do to our own gene pool, because Richard Wagner was a sort of gnome and Nicola Tesla was one walking birth-defect, and your strict eugenicist would have drowned both at birth. But the cool destruction of the best of other species, leaving the weak and the laggard to degrade their genes, makes one pray to God that there is no divine justice.

The spastic and irregular spurts of our social evolution have produced something everybody knows which is probably not so: namely, that to achieve the millennium we must survive a disaster. Millennialists (the term is Michael Barkun's, in a fine provocative book titled *Disaster and the Millennium*) seem sometimes not only to picture and promote their special idea of the millennium to come, when the lion lies down with the lamb and all human folly is obsolete, but also to promote the disaster that is to bring it about. Or at least to welcome it. Or perhaps simply to let it happen, to make no effort to avert it. My own profound conviction is that a millennial situation can be brought about with a disaster. (I must interject here one observation of Barkun's, however: that there can be cases wherein the disaster *is* the millennium!) Post-doom stories are a drug on the sf market and have been for a long time. I'd like you, or someone like you, to write about a man who by his own conscious efforts avoids disaster and by that act brings the millennium.

Do bear in mind that despite the wishful thinking of utopians, any lasting and worthwhile millennium cannot be static, regulated, pyramidal. Its Rule One must be life-oriented and recognize that life is change, and all human law has its season and the season will pass. Stasis is death, which is why utopias, be they by Plato or More, or Joanna Russ, have hidden in them the characteristics of the necropolis.

Where do you get your ideas? You look around you. You say "What if . . ." and "If only . . ." and "If this goes on . . ."

You take someone you know well, someone who through and through *is* something—cobbler, philosopher, high-jumper, lover, whatever—and you plonk him down in a situation in which he may not be that. Now watch him wiggle. Watch him, perhaps, succeed anyway.

You read, very carefully, Paragraph Two of the Fourteenth Amendment to the U. S. Constitution, which has been in force for 115 years (at this writing) and *which has never been invoked!* I'll say no more about it here. Do your own research. I'm convinced that here is one of the wildest stories that could ever be told. Suppose, just for example, that through this route a case could be made that the Income Tax is unconstitutional because a significant number of congressmen were not qualified to vote on it, and the Government has to give all the money back!

You develop a highly intelligent alien species which in the course of its development is female until it bears, male until it fathers, neuter throughout a long maturity. Now write for us its love poetry.

You inject into education, from kindergarten on, a profound involvement of youth in the matter of old-age planning and see what happens.

You alter some basic human characteristic (it need not be a major one) to suit the environment on an alien planet so that a colony can survive. You watch the growth of a civilization composed of individuals so altered, and see how the conventions, traditions, mores develop. You then drop some of these people back here on good old Terra.

And whatever your idea or statement, gimmick, gadget or message, you will (to be read) encase it in love, and pain, and greed, and laughter, and hope, and above all loneliness.

You will be writing in a very different intellectual environment from that in which my contemporaries developed. Sf was the pornography of its day. My stepfather located my stash of 1935 *Amazings* and tore them to postage-stamp-sized pieces and made me clean them up. *Astounding* and *Planet Stories* were found by irate schoolteachers hidden between the covers of geography books, with the principal's office and home chastisement the consequences. In 1965 there were two college courses in sf; in 1975, including those in secondary schools, close to 700. Academia has discovered us with a special joy, for we are a mother-lode to the "publish or perish" fraternity, and they are writing bushel lots of papers, mostly in dead seriousness, interlaced with Eng. Lit. technicalities and inexcusable invasions into the authors' most intimate motivations and having titles like "The Exemplification of the Nietzschean Superman in the Works of Clifford W. Simak." We have become, in sum, respectable, and the aspect of sf is vitally changed.

For one thing, it has ceased to be the membership-club, the pure-structured "in" thing it once was. Nabokov, Pynchon, Lessing, Golding, William Burroughs and others write it unabashedly (without calling it sf) and it is regarded as mainstream. This is one of the reasons it is so difficult to define. Serious critics still, by and large, refuse to take it seriously when it is called sf and written by people who survived in its ghetto. But sf, as such, does indeed survive and will continue, for only poetry is so horizonless, so rich in invention and possibility, and so potent to move and to shake.

Theodore Sturgeon

Theodore Sturgeon was born on Staten Island, New York, in 1918. He started writing during the three years he spent at sea after attending Penn State Nautical School; he sold his first sf story, "The Ether Breathers," to John W. Campbell's *Astounding* in 1939, and by that time he had already published forty or more stories in different fields as well as some poetry. Once launched in sf, he produced a long string of memorable short stories and is celebrated (with Heinlein, del Rey, Asimov, and others) as one of the creators of science fiction as it is today. His stories appeared in all the leading sf magazines, and in 1947 one of them, "Bianca's Hands," won a $1,000 prize from the English *Argosy* (Graham Greene taking the second prize).

Sturgeon's first collection, *Without Sorcery,* appeared in 1948. Then, when *Galaxy* was founded, he began writing for it the psychologically oriented stories which culminated in his novel *More Than Human,* winner of the International Fantasy Award. Since then he has been accorded innumerable other honors, including both the Hugo and Nebula Awards for "Slow Sculpture," a *Galaxy* story. He has written TV scripts for *Star Trek* and other shows, is preparing a new sf television series, and is married to TV personality Wina Sturgeon. He continues to produce his incomparable novels and short stories. A master of characterization and style, he has been called (by Damon Knight) "the most accomplished technician the field has produced, bar none." His dominant theme is love, which he has examined in all its imaginable possibilities and permutations.

Besides all this, he is a singularly acute and perceptive critic, with the rare ability to illuminate that which he discusses, and has reviewed books for *National Review, The New York Times,* and *Galaxy.*

Without Sorcery, 1948 (Prime Press), with introduction by Ray Bradbury
E Pluribus Unicorn, 1953 (Abelard Press)
More Than Human, 1953 (Farrar, Straus & Young)
A Way Home, 1955, selected and with introduction by Groff Conklin (Funk & Wagnalls)
Caviar, 1955 (Ballantine)
I, Libertine, 1956 (Ballantine); under pseudonym Frederick R. Ewing
A Touch of Strange, 1958 (Doubleday)
The Cosmic Rape, 1958 (Dell)

Aliens 4, 1959 (Avon)
Beyond, 1960 (Avon)
Venus Plus X, 1960 (Pyramid)
Voyage to the Bottom of the Sea, 1961 (Pyramid)
Some of Your Blood, 1961 (Ballantine)
Sturgeon Is Alive and Well, 1971 (Putnam)
The Worlds of Theodore Sturgeon, 1972 (Ace)
Sturgeon's West, 1973 (Doubleday)

JERRY POURNELLE

The Construction of Believable Societies

Construction of believable societies is not craft but art; there are no simple formulae. It remains one of the most important tasks the science fiction writer must face. A believable society is one which gives believable motives to the story's characters. It is therefore impossible to write science fiction without giving attention to social order.

Although one can write science fiction without knowing much about physical or biological sciences, sloppy technical workmanship is likely to produce failure. Certainly the more the writer knows about science and technology, the more likely that his story will succeed. Some writers habitually fudge on scientific knowledge and make their stories hang together through sheer strength of language, but even they would write better stories if they knew more of what they are talking about.

This is even more true of the social sciences. There are stories with no attention paid to the social structure in which the story takes place. Some of these succeed, but they would be better if the writer had given more attention to his sociological details. Indeed, the writer may be totally ignorant of technology and get away with it, but he cannot even write a story without assuming some kind of social order. He may think he has done so. He may totally ignore social details and concentrate on technology; but he must, consciously or otherwise, have in mind some idea of the social background of his characters.

This is so because fiction is about people. They may be human or alien, but they will yet be people; and they must act from believable motives. We can state as a rule of thumb that no story can be believable unless there is behind it a social background that makes the characters act in believable ways. Of course some stories are not meant to be believable, thus escaping this rule, and of these more later; but the mass of science fiction is not like that. Most sf is intended to be realistic—that is, the author and reader believe the story might happen, although it probably will not.

Now characters may have to do bizarre things to make the story work; and the more bizarre the actions, the more careful must be their explanation. That explanation requires some examination and presentation of the society that produced the character. Even madness cannot escape some limits: the ways men[1] go mad are in large part determined by their backgrounds and upbringing.

In a word, I am saying that development of social order is as important as any other aspect of science fiction. Now no one would argue were I to say this about historical fiction. In historicals we expect the author to embed the characters in their times; we expect to see what motivates them.

Characters in historicals act from one of two classes of motive: (1) motivations similar to those which work in our own society, and (2) those peculiar to those times.

It will be as true for sf as for historicals. Of the second class of motive we can note that, without explication of the social factors that produce them, the story will be incomprehensible. Of the first we have two further subdivisions: (1) motives that are timeless, universal, stemming from the nature of man, and (2) those arising from social institutions similar to our own.

The historical fictioneer cannot ignore these questions. Still less, then, can the science fiction writer who cannot even turn to a history book but must invent his own. Only writers who concentrate on contemporary characters in contemporary society can omit study of the character's social order, and then only because he absorbs its influences through his pores; the motivations that compel his characters will at least tug on their author, and thus he has some understanding of them. This cannot be true of the science fiction writer.

The point seems obvious, but let us take an illustration. "The Cold Equations" is rightly acclaimed as the epitome of the hard science story. Its major focus is the pitiless universe that gives the characters no choices and makes the tragic ending inevitable. Nothing could be further from a "sociological" story.

And yet the social factors are vital. Economics: if fuel were cheap, the situation could not have come about. The victim of the universe's inattention is a young girl, naïve, who arouses in the reader all the protective instincts engendered by Western civilization; were the society of the story one in which young girls were expendable, the ending would have been the same but the effect on the characters would not: it would not have been, for them, a tragedy at all. And in one scene the girl communicates with her brother; were family ties not important, that scene would not work.

I trust the point is made. If "The Cold Equations" thoroughly depends on unstated but vital social conditions, how much more so must stories without that emphasis on hard sciences?

Given the obvious importance of social order to science fiction, it is amazing that of all the thousands of sf stories in print there are so few memorable social orders. It can be argued that one of science fiction's most important tasks—other than entertaiment—is the exploration of human societies and examination of ways human institutions might respond to changes in technology, population, or even the passing of time. It is surprising, then, that so few sf writers set about creating social orders in any systematic way.

Writers will take great pains to get the orbits of their planets in the right places; to ensure that their alien sun is at the proper temperature and mass; to work out local gravity, atmospheric conditions, tides, etc.; and then, almost as an afterthought, dash off the social background of the story. This can often produce ludicrous results.

Harry Harrison is a fine writer who has done a number of deservedly popular works; but consider for a moment his *Ethical Engineer,* one of the "Deathworld" novels. He shows us a hunter-gatherer society in which every man's hand is against his neighbor. Those who do not rule are slaves. The masters have neither friends, nor allies, nor faithful dogs, nor watchful robots. Even their women are slaves and are treated as such except for the moments when they share the master's bed. Every member of the band lives only to kill the master and take his place. These small groups spend their lives wandering about a barren land searching for roots. On occasion one master will try to poison another; the motive for the attempt is not clear, but presumably in order to take over his neighbor's slaves.

This is ludicrous. It is obviously unstable: how is it to perpetuate itself? How are children to be born, and who is to care for them? Given that children somehow manage to live, does a master enslave his own sons? What is to prevent what seems the obvious course, one master organizing a clan? Given cooperation and trust, he can arm some of his followers; conquest of his solitary neighbors would follow inevitably. No need to break a butterfly on the wheel; my point is that Harrison, in order to illustrate a political point, has attempted to present what never was and never could be as reality. In another part of his novel he shows us a society of unrestrained and brutal *laissez-faire* capitalism. It is no more believable than his hunter-gatherers. Granted that Harrison hopes to bring us a political message and heap scorn upon advocates of *laissez-faire;* but would not his message have been more effective if he had made his straw men viable?

Now it is obvious that authors do not always intend their social orders to be taken seriously. Satire is a legitimate art form in science fiction as elsewhere. So is allegory. Harlan Ellison is famous for stories which are filled with internal contradictions. His antithetical societies are highly exaggerated. No one would suppose, for example, that the middle-class survivors in the underground city of Ellison's "A Boy and His Dog" would *really* live that way, or that the Rovers would last for more than a generation if that. Ellison writes in large part to arouse emotions, and he does that skillfully; those who can bring that off can ignore the kind of critique given here.

Similarly, some stories are written for humor and little else. Sheckley and Goulart delight in surrealistic stories in which quite literally incredible things happen. Such stories are perfectly legitimate but, like Ellison's allegories, are not the subject of this essay. We can note that there are far more attempts at humor than successes and get on with a discussion of realistic science fiction.

We should also note that some of the most effective social criticism succeeds *because* it is realistic. *Brave New World* and *1984* are frightening precisely because they are believable, and they endure in a way that most allegorical works never will. There is evidently considerable value in knowing how to construct believable societies.

Moreover, even writers who intend always to employ surrealism and satire would do well to know more of how social orders are constructed. The best surrealist painters are excellent draftsmen. So are the best abstract painters. If an artist cannot put a line where it must be, his painting will fail; and if a writer cannot construct societies which give his characters believable motives, his satires are unlikely to be very successful.

The Social "Sciences"

Einstein was once asked why physicists were able to produce weapons and technology that men seemed unable to control. His reply was that physics is far easier than political science.

He was fairly obviously right. Physics is easier to learn if only because physicists are agreed on *something;* social "scientists" cannot even agree on the nature of their subject matter.[2] There are any number of basic reference works that a writer can use to assure himself that his technology and hard science will be "standard" and agreed upon. When he turns to works on the nature of man and society he finds only confusion. C. Northcote Parkinson comments:[3]

> In the field of politics we have not yet reached the point at which scientific progress began. We are still (literally) at the stage of reading Aristotle. What is worse, we are still telling each other the eternal principles of political theory. One theorist will say 'The history of all known society . . . has been the history of class struggles.' Another will reply as firmly that representative government is 'the ideal type of the most perfect polity.' A third will cry that the general will is always right, and a fourth will assert that the dictatorship of the proletariat is bound to come. A fifth will intone his conviction that all men are born equal, only to be shouted down by a sixth who will have it that men are everywhere in chains. Government, we are assured by a seventh, is instituted to secure for men their right to life, liberty, and the pursuit of happiness. At all times, shouts the eighth, the principles of democracy have brought people to ruin. The place of the hero, growls the ninth, is with the stars of heaven. As soon as the people are brought to silence, concludes the tenth (hopefully) their voice is most distinctly heard. . . . [We note] a score of these eternal principles, founded for the most part on nothing.

What is the writer to make of all this? When he turns to the experts, he finds only contradictions. If he asks advice from a dozen social theorists he will likely get two dozen (or more) opinions. Is it then better to ignore all this drivel and construct our own future societies?

Perhaps; and of course no writer can help doing so anyway. We all of us have our own theories of the nature of man and society, and we cannot avoid reflections of them in our work. Even so, unless a writer is steeped in real study of real societies, he would do well to avoid making up his social orders out of whole cloth. It simply will not do to go about picking up bits and pieces from this theory and that, tossing them into the story at random, and calling the result a social order. The result is as likely to be appetizing as would be a pudding made by the same procedure.

The Art of Social Criticism

Philosophers of science are forever searching for definitions of their subject matter. One of the better ones is: "Science is public. If you cannot write down your results and send them to a competent colleague in the full expectation that if he employs the same procedures he will obtain those same results, it is not science at all."[4] We may note problems with this definition and still find it useful; and in those terms there is no "social science" at all. There is simply no way that we can agree on what constitutes a viable society, or even agree that such have ever existed.

Thus we find that construction of a believable fictional society, like the description of believable characters, is an art. There is no simple formula. For planetary motions we can turn to Kepler's Laws, but for social orders we have nothing even remotely similar. Yet the task must be accomplished; how?

In a sense there is no answer. Writers who cannot learn to create believable characters should probably look for another line of work. Writers who cannot learn to create believable societies should stay out of the sf genre. Yet, of course, there are some approaches that may be valuable and that can be taught. They are like characterization tips: such bits of advice as "Decide what your character did on his twelfth birthday." Some writers employ the device, some don't, and some do when they think of it or when they're stuck and have nothing better to do.

The same is true of the advice given below: it works for some people and may not for you. The important thing is to be aware that creation of believable social orders is vital to most good science fiction.

In building a fictional social order you cannot escape being a social critic. Critic is probably the wrong choice of words, but I find no better. In the sense in which I mean it, critic does not necessarily imply criticism; it might also imply appreciation. Although there is not so much of that kind of sf now as there has sometimes been, it is possible to write stories that show just how well off we are in comparison to where we might easily get to.[5]

In any event this is an art, not a teachable science or even a skill; but that does not imply that there is nothing to learn about it.

The first task, then, is to ask ourselves certain questions about our future society. The ones discussed below seem important to me; I think there are many ways of asking them, but I doubt they can be ignored. The answers assumed to the questions may not be as important as that the questions were asked.

The Nature of Man

Just how much of human behavior is determined by society, and how much is innate? There is no agreed answer to this. The nature-nurture controversy rages in every discipline of social science. Thus there is a broad range within which the writer may choose, and it does not much matter which position he takes; but it does matter a great deal that he takes a position and stays with it.

Whatever is assumed it will not relieve us of the task of constructing a social order. Even the most ardent defender of heredity and instinct as prime movers of human action must admit that societies are important in developing character. However, the social order constructed will be dependent on what was assumed about nature-nurture.

Take as an example the territorial drive. Is this absolute and unchangeable? Many psychiatrists would have it so, as would theorists like Robert Ardrey. Take away man's chances to possess territory of his own, and man becomes irrationally aggressive. Wars and violence result. Peace is possible only if there be some substitute for war. (Richardson's study of the statistics of deadly quarrels, one of the few truly scientific studies of aggression, suggests strongly that whether by duel, murder, or war the proportion of people killed by violence does not change much over the centuries.)

Of course an opposite view can be taken; education may change man's drive for territory, and the term "rootless" becomes meaningless. The view that the writer takes on this question must profoundly influence the society he invents.

This is as good a place as any to point out that social assumptions are not independent. It is no good taking different theories at random. One can, for example, hardly be a good Marxist and assume that instinct plays much part in human behavior. Marxism demands that human nature be malleable; that after the Revolution all human values can be reconstructed. "Bourgeois sentimentality" and ethics are temporary phenomena and will vanish when the Revolution makes all things new. Territorial imperatives are eradicable if they exist at all. Incidentally, this need for a theory of malleable human behavior is the primary reason that Lysenko was and is so important in Soviet biology; Mendelian genetics is very nearly incompatible with good Marxist theory.

Now quite a good story can be built around the assumption that an imposed social order is contrary to the nature of man. The society is not viable unless held in place by force; but it might last a long time, and the internal conflicts in it could produce some great scenes. Even if the story has nothing to do with the coming downfall of the social order, the background could make the plot far more interesting. Poul Anderson has done this many times with telling effect.

A question allied to the first is: how perfectible is man? The traditional Judeo-Christian view is that man is flawed; he cannot perfect himself, and thus can never create a perfect social order. This leads to such observations as Acton's dictum that "Power corrupts; absolute power corrupts absolutely." It leads to the "checks and balances" of the U. S. Constitution and the theory of the Framers that government must be limited because "all men will pursue their interests." The opposite view has produced two opposing political schools: Communists and anarchists. The former believe that man can be perfected through creation of the perfect society; the latter believe that man will perfect himself only when the restraints of society are removed.

Closely allied to this question is: what are governments for? There are many possible views, but two important ones are Jefferson's—that governments are instituted to secure basic rights for all men; and that of the Book of Common Prayer, which states that Christian rulers should "truly and impartially administer justice, to the punishment of wickedness and vice, and the maintenance of true religion and virtue."[6]

Fairly obviously a government which attempts to punish wickedness and vice can easily become a tyranny and will probably be seen as one by some of its subjects; less obvious but equally certain is that disagreement over basic rights can cause men to see Jefferson's variety as no more than democratic despotism in which the mass attempts to plunder the industrious.

My point is that all these questions are related. One can assume any position one likes and write a believable story; but having taken a position on one question, one is forced into compatible positions on the others.

Of course, it is possible to delude oneself into thinking that he has avoided having to take a view on the nature of man. One can, for example, write a story about an isolated man far from other humans and give him as motive the conquest of nature. That should do the trick.

Of course it does not. What is Conrad's "Heart of Darkness" but such a story? Kurtz might have been another Schweitzer. Which of the two men is the more likely? Has Kurtz become what he is because he too is a victim of "society," or is this what man will be if he does not ask and receive divine grace?

The problem becomes even more acute when several people interact in the story. Do they come from families, or has the family in our future society been abolished? If the latter, by whom were they raised? If modern psychiatry can explain much delinquent behavior on the grounds that the criminal "came from a broken home," what will be the effect of having no homes to be broken? Or is modern psychiatry drivel?

The War Between the Sexes

Assume an expedition to a far place and a straight adventure story about what is encountered there. Can we escape the background of the characters?

Is the crew all male, all female or coed? If all of one sex, there must be a reason; given present trends, it is unlikely. If coed, how do the sexes relate? Do families and stable ties exist? Does marriage? Is casual recreational sex the norm? If so, how does this affect the relationship between man and woman? What has happened to romantic love?

Some writers are fond of saying that romantic love was invented in the Middle Ages, which is nonsense: Jacob did not toil fourteen years for Rachel simply because he wanted to marry into a powerful family. (He managed that in only seven years when he got Leah.) It is true enough that Classical Greek writers as often as not considered romantic love a curse, and Sicilians today talk about "the thunderbolt" as something to be avoided; but the all-consuming passion of one man for one particular woman (or vice versa) is hardly new in either history or literature. If we invent a society without families or stable ties, how is this sort of thing to be handled in our stories?

More to the point, as the women's-rights movement advances, what happens to the ancient tradition of "women and children first to the lifeboat"?

Note that we cannot escape these questions even if their answers do not directly affect the plot. The nature of the sexes and their interaction is in fact part of the whole question of the nature of man; but in recent times it has assumed a peculiar importance. Writers who take the wrong view here may find themselves the subjects of vituperative reviews. Some have been driven by fear to avoid the problem, and for those who succeed this may be the wisest course; but a scrupulously honest writer cannot avoid the problem of human sexual bimorphism.

Are the women in our stories of the future different from the women we know? Does our future society have legal equality for women? How do "equal" women act? How, for that matter, do men act in a society in which they must compete with women at every level? Will those women be like those men?[7]

Most species exhibit sexual bimorphism. Sometimes it is extreme: angler fish, praying mantis, black widow spider. Nearly all have behavioral as well as physiological differentiation between sexes. Many have very different roles, particularly with respect to the young. Response to infants is highly sex dependent in most chordates; will this be true for mankind in the future, or is it in man, unlike in other mammals, merely a cultural phenomenon to be erased by education?

Nor is this independent of some of our earlier questions. It would be a skillful writer indeed who could assume strong instinctual behavior in humans and at the same time ignore psychological sexual bimorphism. Obviously there is room for a number of stories on this theme: how compatible is enforced sexual equivalence with human nature?

Technology

We cannot divorce technology from sociology. Is there cheap and plentiful energy in our social order of the future? Then it can hardly operate from an economy of real scarcity; if there is scarcity it must be imposed. Even in the midst of plenty the characters may be motivated by greed; today's riches are tomorrow's poverty. And of course as the state imposes material equality on men it gathers power to itself, so that there is great inequality of power.

"Nothing is beyond the dreams of avarice" and thus men may compete long after every conceivable biological need has been fulfilled—as indeed they do now. Still, precisely what is it the characters want?[8] It is true enough that most millionaires work harder than most bookkeepers, but what happens when everyone has available to him what millionaires have now? (It is hardly necessary to point out that in the U. S. nearly everyone does have what the aristocracy of the past had: changes of clothing, comparatively cheap travel, many hours of leisure each week, not only enough to eat but some variety in their meals even in mid-winter, as well as TV, telephone, good mail service, rapid travel over dozens to hundreds of miles, penicillin, and good teeth past the age of thirty-five, none of which even the wealthiest king could have a hundred years ago.)

Obviously much more could be said about the interaction of technology and society. Some consider this the essence of science fiction, and several volumes could be written on the subject. Here we can only call attention to its importance.

Sovereignty, Authority, and Obedience

Most people obey the laws and not merely through fear of the police. Well-ordered states are legitimate and rule through authority. This can go to extremes: in the old Roman Republic there were no state agents; the commands of the state were enforced by the citizens themselves without recourse to police. Something of this has survived to this day in the form of the *posse comitatus.*

What gives states authority and causes its subjects to obey, indeed to take its commands as something almost mystical? Because in many times and places reverence for "The Law" has been a prime motive for human action.[9]

There is no rational answer. It is easy to show by reason that it is to every man's best interest that there be governments; but there is no rational argument to show that one kind of government is better than another, or that this man should rule and not that one. Legitimacy rests upon myth. This does not make it less powerful; in fact, myth is generally far more efficient as motivator than ever was reason.

Myths of legitimacy include: this man rules because he is the Chosen of God; because he is the son of a certain father; because he has been chosen by a group which has the right to make the choice; because he has been chosen by 50 percent-plus-one citizens; because he has been chosen "by the people" as their glorious leader; because he is the wisest and best of the people; etc. None of these myths is particularly compelling except to those who believe them. None answers the question of why this group should choose.[10] Is it seriously thought that 50 percent-plus-one will always be correct? Then why have democracies voted themselves fools for governors and policies that lead to disaster? That "the people's choice" as leader is infallible and thereby embodies their will? Then how could the Duces and Führers have led their people to disaster despite their enormous popularity on plebiscite? And so forth.

The point here is that nearly any myth of legitimacy will do, and many have done. True, we feel that the times are enlightened now, and as history is one long tale of progress toward democracy we will never again return to any other myth; but this is silly on the face of it. Fewer people live under democracy now than in 1932. Plebiscitory dictatorship by individuals or a party appears to be the characteristic form of the 20th Century as democracy was of the 19th. A glance at history will show that it has all happened before and usually ends in monarchy, as indeed India may already have done.

Of course many writers choose stories about rebellion and revolution. They construct social orders against which men will—and should—rebel.

This is not as easy as it looks. Skillful writers may get away with the straw-man dictatorships that were so common in *Astounding* during John Campbell's "liberation theme" period, but they can hardly believe in them or expect others to. Police states certainly are real enough, but they are not simple. Why, for example, do the police obey? Particularly in the fascist America beloved by many sf writers: what motivates the defenders of the public order? If nothing, then the society falls—and quickly. If no one loves it, it will not last an hour. Heinlein knew this well enough, which is why his "If This Goes On . . . ," published in 1940 and describing the unlikely dictatorship of a fundamentalist religious sect, has even today a credibility that the host of McCarthy-era fascist-Amerika stories never had.

To which someone will reply that we live today in a fascist Amerika, only most of us do not realize it, and thus prove the point I have been trying to make. Incidentally I do not concede *their* point; I merely point out that social orders generally have at least the passive support of most of their citizens and must have the active support of at least the police —who, incidentally, cannot be the incompetent buffoons who so often appear in science fiction stories.

Decadence is another popular theme in science fiction. It is not often understood. The sort of backwater autocracy that exists through fear and whose purpose is the enrichment of the leader is relatively rare in the modern world. Even the classic examples—Spain and Portugal—are seen to be exceptions now that their autocrats are losing their grip.

Decadence generally results when a society or people has run out of myth; that is, when their myths of legitimacy included certain goals, and those goals have been fulfilled. If no new myths and goals come to take their place, the society will stumble along, sometimes for generations, sometimes for only a brief moment; and it will fall for lack of defenders. Some would say that the Western democracies have reached that stage: they have civilized the heathen to the point at which the heathen has thrown them out; they have enfranchised everyone who conceivably might be enfranchised; they have instituted basic minimum wages, subsistence allowances, and the like; eliminated gross inequalities; and now find that there is nothing left to do. True, not all the goals have been met 100 percent, but what is left to do is so small in comparison to what has been done that few can now believe finishing the job will bring about the millennium. Thus there is a lack of enthusiastic supporters; the goals are to be carried out by paid civil servants; and heroes are not needed.[11]

One need not accept this as a valid picture of Western liberal democracy to see its relevance in constructing stories of decadent societies.

The problem in a decadent society is to find motives for its police and army. If proper motives are not found, there is usually a brief resort to mercenaries. Mercenaries have two defects: either they are not effective in the defense of the society, or they are all too effective and, having nothing but contempt for their non-warrior "masters," decide to rob the paymaster. They have, after all, a monopoly of organized force; they have the usual opinions warriors hold for cowards or those they see as cowards; and they are encouraged to believe material goods are the only coin in which they can be paid. Often, of course, they rob the paymaster and take control of the society, only to fall to another warrior outfit, thus exhibiting both defects at once. Of course the military will have its own myths: they rule in the name of "national honor." Both ancient and modern history are full of examples of this. Incidentally, John Stuart Mill, who loved freedom no less than any man, remarked that a people sufficiently decadent should think themselves fortunate to find an honorable military ruler: Charlemagne, Akbar, Mustafa Kemal might be preferable to some domestic demagogues.[12]

My point is that nearly any social order will, in time, become decadent, or at least history strongly suggests this. Monarchy, aristocracy, oligarchy, republic, democracy, egalitarian plebiscitory democracy, dictatorship, Bonapartist empire, and back to monarchy; such as happened in the past in regular succession. True, we may today be so wise that it cannot happen to us; but the speculative fiction writer has a fruitful field to draw on if he wishes to vary his social orders.

Conclusion

There is no magic formula for construction of a believable social order; there is not even agreement among theorists as to what constitutes a viable social order, or whether in fact such a thing ever has or could exist. Any number of social orders have been ardently defended in the past, and no single one has ever been universally accepted. If one seeks the "natural state" of man, history suggests that it is some form of empire which expands until it absorbs everything but an empire similar to and as strong as itself; but this is suggestion only, and certainly there have been exceptions lasting for many generations.

A writer may choose almost any social order he pleases; it does not matter which from the view of "science" or "realism." Having chosen it, though, he has lost part of his freedom. Each of these systems has an internal logic. Each has its characteristic myths. The writer must become familiar with them.

This means study. No writer would consider doing a story about black holes without taking pains to find out what black holes are and how they behave; why, then, should writers expect to be able to create believable social orders without giving some study to the subject?

Often, too, the writer hopes to be advocate. He is not merely describing a society; he hopes his readers will find it congenial, will perhaps adopt its myths as their own and work either to keep it (if they have it now) or establish it. In so doing he is tempted to show his opponents as a pack of fools. This is a mistake. The writer who does this is preaching to the choir; he will make few converts because few who do not think as he does will find him convincing. Better would be to devote some study to the opposition as well, so that readers would find it believable; then show its flaws if that be his purpose.

What I am here advocating is that science fiction writers understand what they're talking about. That will require some study; and more importantly, it will require that they give the subject some thought. In constructing social orders of the future as in many other aspects of science fiction, the writer's questions will be more important than the answers he assumes.

NOTES

1. With apologies to feminist readers, I find the habitual use of "he/she," "his or her," "person," and the like both tedious and inelegant. Obviously both characters and the authors who write about them can as easily be women as men.

2. I have several advanced degrees in social science. My view may be wrong, but please do not ascribe it to unfamiliarity with the material.

3. C. Northcote Parkinson, *The Evolution of Political Thought.* New York: Viking Press (Compass Books), 1964. This book is highly recommended as a good introduction to political theory for writers.

4. Gustav Bergmann, lecture given at the University of Iowa, Iowa City, 1953.

5. Perhaps one explanation for the near universal alienation of intellectuals from the societies in which they live is that they often have the same relationship to statesmen and political leaders that drama critics have to playwrights.

6. These views are not mutually exclusive, of course; the Framers would, many of them, have heard the Book of Common Prayer communion service nearly every week of their lives. It is a matter of emphasis rather than exclusion.

7. Joan Vinge in an essay in the fanzine *Notes from the Chemistry Department, #13* (Box CC, East Texas Station, Commerce, Texas) addresses this problem and concludes that men and women in future societies will be very much alike. She points to characters in Le Guin's *The Dispossessed* as examples of "truly human beings" who are not blinded by sexist limitations. With respect I disagree for reasons given in the same issue of *Notes,* but it is certainly one possible view.

8. Many observers would suggest that power is all that is left to compete for when there is material equality; and that power is an addictive wine indeed. See, for example, C. S. Lewis, *The Abolition of Man,* New York, Macmillan, 1965. See also Wilhelm Roepke, *A Humane Economy,* Chicago, Regnery, 1960.

9. The best discussion of this is probably the twin works *Power* and *Sovereignty* by Bertrand de Jouvenal, available from the University of Chicago Press.

10. In addition to "the people" or some defined but large sub-set thereof, groups which choose leaders have been: an aristocratic council; the Senate of Rome; Presidium of the Communist Party; College of Cardinals; the officer corps; etc.

11. Revolutionary movements produce heroes because they have their myths. Western democracy is in dire need of heroic defenders and has found many in time of need; but oddly enough, few come from the ranks of the socialist intellectuals who have produced our modern welfare states. Even during the Spanish Civil War, where the issues were thought to be clear, the only socialist intellectual of note to go to the lines was George Orwell; and the British Labor Party was unable to fill a company of volunteers. The *Communists,* of course, did far better.

12. To class honor among political myths is not to imply contempt for honor as a value, nor to denigrate the men motivated by honor.

Jerry Pournelle, Ph.D.

Jerry Pournelle is science editor of *Galaxy* magazine and a full-time writer of both fiction and nonfiction. His monthly column in *Galaxy,* "A Step Farther Out," discusses new developments in science and technology, including energy, computers, ships for man in space, basic principles of space flight, Velikovsky, flying saucers, and the terraforming of Venus. He is author of more than a score of science fiction stories that have appeared in *Analog, Galaxy,* and other magazines.

His nonfiction article "America's Looming Energy Crisis" was published in *American Legion* magazine in 1971 and has since been reprinted in several hundred thousand copies for distribution by both private and publicly owned power companies.

He holds advanced degrees in operations research, mathematics, psychology, and political science and worked in the aerospace industry for over ten years. He was Chief of the Experimental Stress Project in the Boeing Human Factors Laboratories and a delegate to the aerospace industries space requirements council. He also served as a space scientist and manager of special studies for other aerospace firms.

He has been a successful political manager in both city and national elections and has served as Executive Assistant to the Mayor of Los Angeles. A former professor, he now writes full time and has been president of the Science Fiction Writers of America as well as chairman of the SFWA Grievance Committee.

His works include *A Spaceship for the King* (serialized in *Analog* and published by DAW Books); co-author with Larry Niven of the Hugo-nominated *The Mote in God's Eye* (Simon and Schuster; Pocket Books), and *Inferno* (serialized in *Galaxy;* to be published by Simon and Schuster). With Stefan Possony he is co-author of *The Strategy of Technology* (Dunellen, 1970).

He was the first winner of the John W. Campbell, Jr., Award for the best new science fiction writer of the year. His works have five times been nominated for the Hugo.

Dr. Pournelle lives in Southern California with his wife, four sons, one dog, and no cats. He is an ardent sailor, backpacker, and general outdoorsman.

FRANK HERBERT

Men on Other Planets

They're human.

You surmise this from the descriptions. They're bipedal. They have two arms with conventional hands. The head is in the right place with chin, mouth, nose, eyes, hair on top, visible ears. But they may be both male and female in one body, shifting from one sex to the other at the behest of strange chemistry (Ursula Le Guin's *The Left Hand of Darkness*) or they merely assume human shape for disguise (Jack Vance's *Star King*).

From *Star Trek*'s Spock through the Wellsian cannibals at the end of time, these humanoids stalk the worlds of imagination. They walk on other planets, in space craft or on an earth so changed that you would not recognize it without a program. Then again, it may be your earth, but changed only in ways which accent trends visible all around you—*Brave New World, 1984, 20,000 Leagues Under the Sea, Childhood's End* . . .

What price a glimpse of tomorrow?

Where does fiction end and fact begin? When is it another world?

In a real sense, Joshua Slocum is a man on another planet. He lives out a recurrent human fantasy in chosen isolation. That isolation aboard his tiny sloop, *Spray,* is so different from the ordinary lives of most humans it might as well be on the black side of a planet circling a star in the Draco Cluster.

When we put our fictional men on fictional planets, we are dealing with a phenomenon that has surpassed in popularity the onetime front runner, detective mysteries. Why, in this particular age, have we singled out science as the guilty party (or the hero) instead of the butler?

Whodunit?

We all did. But why?

When you begin to glimpse an answer to that question, you begin to understand the craft behind this genre. Cyrano de Bergerac understood this when he turned from a real life of sword and sorcery to send a fictional hero to the moon. Certainly most who practice the craft of science fiction today understand the problem.

At one level, to put humans on another planet requires that you make alien places and people understandable to contemporary readers. (Let posterity take care of itself in this regard; there'll probably be academics around who can translate us for *their* contemporaries.) You begin by creating an understandable human/humanoid/sentient in an alien culture and right there, even though you may not intend it, you will reflect in some way the current human condition on Planet Earth.

Your Time Machine will have the appearance of a horse-drawn sleigh. Your hero will go to the moon on a lighter-than-air balloon or be fired there from a gigantic cannon. It's interesting to speculate how the writers a hundred years from now will make this same comparison looking back at our obsession with rockets. No matter how hard we try, we cannot entirely escape our times. Some small point will drift into print and leave its mark. *Player Piano,* although a landmark in its day, already is rather quaintly out of date. We may be past *1984* already.

Yet the science fiction phenomenon remains and the *why* begs an answer. It is not in stick-figure characters playing at Cosmic Mechanic or Rover Boys on Pluto; it is not in our time-bound curiosities. You won't find the answer there. But you will find it in those penetrating accuracies which glitter on Captain Nemo's control panel, in Cleve Cartmill's devastating prediction about the manufacture of atomic weapons, in Arthur C. Clarke's almost casual revelation of Telstar twenty years before the launching, and even in my own 1952 warning *(Under Pressure)* about the coming crisis in fossil fuels. It's in all of these: in Samuel R. Delany's *Babel-17.* It's the solid sense of character reality in such creations as Harold Shea (L. Sprague de Camp's *The Incomplete En-*

chanter) or Isaac Edward Leibowitz (Walter M. Miller, Jr., *A Canticle for Leibowitz*).

Star Trek's control-room drama may have opened doors for people with misconceptions about science fiction, or for those who had never been immersed in it previously, but this is not where the current popularity rests, nor does it explain the fascination of putting humans into other futures, other planets, other cultures.

No, we have other things going for us.

First, we are talking about futures. In an age when many people question whether man has any future at all, we bring the imagination to grips with a variety of survival patterns. We preach ecology and we damn it. We utter warnings about unforeseen consequences. We explore strange paradises.

Second (and probably most important) the creation of understandable humans in understandable alien cultures on understandable other planets has to reflect in some ways the present human condition on Planet Earth.

The key word here is *alien.*

Does your conceit lead you to believe that you possess an absolute understanding of Mao Tse-tung's utterances?

Absolute?

The conditioning of most cultures on this planet tends to set up absolute categories, each with attached judgments about good-bad, beautiful-ugly, saintly-evil, painful-pleasurable, sacred-profane. Western culture is particularly obsessed with this absolutism through its narrow vision of a linear pragmatism hitched to technology. We have been taught to believe that for every problem there is a scientific answer. Every problem. Any denial of such absolutes raises opaque barriers which block new understandings.

But in science fiction we're not talking about a real earth, are we? It's all imaginary, a game, entertainment. It's other planets, other people. The opacity is reduced. You can make out shadow shapes which may have a certain reality. An entertaining view of realities.

There can be more than one reality.

You see, Dr. Einstein, we heard you.

This is probably science fiction's major attraction, linked as it is to all of the old myth strings we humans carry around. We humans still deal in archetypes with our politics and our entertainment, in our sex lives and our hobbies. Whether they see it clearly or not, science fiction writers play in this same arena.

You don't believe it?

All right—here are some classic myth ingredients:

The hero on a search/journey (for which read in science fiction Captain Kirk, Isaac Leibowitz, Jerome Corbett, Paul Atreides, Susan Calvin and so on and on . . .).

The Holy Grail which the searcher seeks (for which read in science fiction "almost any utopian story").

The ability to talk to animals (the stories of extrasensory perception where humans enlist the help of animals and/or vice versa).

The shaman who understands great mysteries and can bring them into the service of humans (for which read "any fictional scientist"—or real one for that matter).

Furthermore, science fiction is full of father gods, falls from paradise, wise old men, tricksters, people who change persona with a change of name, virgin witches and great mothers.

We also have our share of sorcerers (and sorcerer's apprentices), all of whom are variations on the shaman/scientist.

And one of our creative problems has been to show how directly these myth creatures apply to the world around us. If you want a recent example, look at how many of the myth characters are personified in the Kennedy Clan. Who first came up with that Camelot label?

If you're going to put men on other planets, it's well to understand these things. In academic terms, what we do is to create our own intercultural ethic and aesthetic out of the structural parts already available all around us. This is partly a problem in anthropology. Therefore, the newcomer to this genre should be warned. Because such problems often deal with Western society's unconscious taboos, a few outrageous clichés recur with maddening regularity. Ask any editor in this field. The most common first story from a would-be writer of science fiction replays the Adam and Eve theme (as survivors of an ultimate war, as castaways from a derelict spaceship, as a life form introduced from elsewhere or elsewhen and so on and on and on *ad nauseam*).

Our taboos ring in other changes that deserve careful watching, both as sins of commission and omission. You recognize these taboos and changes by their assumptions. Here are a few to consider as a sensitizing exercise:

1. Man is the king of all animals. Thus his planets (plus any alien

occupants) are beneath man; they exist only to be exploited.

2. Only man has language. (Remember Carl Gustav Jung's warning that we must discover another sentience in the universe before we can understand what it is to be human. This proposition grows more fascinating as we teach more and more chimpanzees to talk Ameslan.)

3. The only thing wrong with our universe is that humans have not yet invented the right machine. (Many of us have assaulted this assumption. Isaac Asimov did it with beautiful directness in *I, Robot.* Tongue firmly in cheek, I took it on in *Destination Void.* Kurt Vonnegut's *Slaughterhouse Five* plays this theme legato.)

4. All human behavior can be traced to a) genetics, b) conditioning, c) cosmic intervention.

5. Current labels are adequate to describe any changed condition. (It'll still be Communists vs. Capitalists in 3031 A.D.)

With rare exceptions, authors and/or editors well understand the area of the current most dangerous taboos. When you see a story described as "daring," depend on it, that story has at least touched on one of those taboos. Of all the literary genres on the current scene, science fiction ventures into these arenas the most often.

You don't believe these taboos exist?

Have you read any good stories lately (outside of science fiction) where an orgasm is the highest religious experience? Maybe the world never was ready for Tantrism. Okay.

But if you're going to create science fiction, these are some of the questions you must ask, some of the limits you must recognize. Having recognized them, you can appropriate them for your own. Your hero can have clay feet. Your holy virgin can be barren. The innocent child can lead his people to destruction. A nymphomaniac can be the most honorable person in your alien society. The sensitive and concerned liberals can be the ones who make the grossest and most deadly mistakes. World Government can be demonstrated as a complete disaster. A football game can be the supreme intellectual delight. The utter ecological destruction of the planet is man's sole key to survival.

Are you getting the picture?

What is it that you believe without questioning? What is it that serves as the main prop of your identity?

What kind of a story would come out of your discovery that your most dearly held beliefs are completely false? Your beliefs, not those of someone else that you wish to attack. This is no debating society where advocates meet to listen only to their own arguments. We might assume that the advocacy system is humankind's greatest flaw and attorneys (plus their legal structure) are essentially parasites destroying their host.

Invite paranoia and explore its contexts. Science fiction has done this often. There *was* something following the little old lady. And it ate the psychiatrist for desert. Now it's cliché, but once it was new.

There you are: make it new. Listen to Ezra Pound. He was right. "Make it new."

Science fiction, because it ventures into no-man's-lands, tends to meet some of the requirements posed by Jung in his explorations of archetypes, myth structures and self-understanding. It may be that the primary attraction of science fiction is that it helps us understand what it means to be human.

Any reader of science fiction turning to page one of a new story has an implicit understanding that the function of what he is about to read will extend far beyond physical descriptions. Except perhaps as analogue, the value of putting men on other planets is greatest when it ceases to be a contest with that life which can be seen when you look up from the printed page. You know that the story will take you through experiences that cannot be achieved through any other means than the story. In fact, it may inflict upon you an experience that could never take place at all, except perhaps in your wildest fantasies. Your implicit understanding reaches even farther, though. You know that this story can be measured against a scale of achievement where the supreme experience comes when (no matter any logical objections) you are made to believe that these events might take place just the way they are laid out in the story.

And right here is where science fiction is most attractive as an art form, but also where it lays out the most traps for an unwary writer. The temptation is to wallow in excesses, to inflate your sense of "how strange!" to such an extreme that it dulls the sensibilities or even repels. Something like this happened in the development of what are obviously science fiction's current clichés, the clichés which science fiction created —the monster and the maiden, the variations on Adam and Eve, the aliens who come to earth as missionaries, Ezekiel's wheels as helicopter rotors, the planet as egg of an interstellar monster, and so on.

Make it new.

Even while using old themes, make it new.

It's by restraints and subtleties, by aftershocks, that you can create your greatest effects.

Were you really surprised when Charlton Heston discovered the remains of the Statue of Liberty on the Planet of the Apes? It had a certain time-stretching effect, but surprise? How much more interesting if he'd discovered a toilet bowl (more likely to survive the eons) or a perfectly preserved Landon button.

Readers and editors tend to say: "Oh, no! Not another cosmic egg story!"

Now, let's invert this argument for a moment and remind you that there's a supreme achievement in storytelling when you can take on one of these clichés and make it so vivid, so new in its construction that no one minds the cliché.

The argument here is obvious: don't cater to the lowest common denominator in those reactions available to you. Don't cater to the weakest reaction patterns. Don't go for the throat; go for the guts, but do it in such a way that the reader realizes that's what you've done *after the fact.* Make damned sure you know your story objective (and it had better be at least nine-tenths entertainment).

This brings us naturally to the pot of message often found in science fiction. Quite a few science fiction writers will tell you they are attacking our current culture head on. They really believe this. But if you look at the consequences of the most extreme efforts in this class, you find that they have merely reinforced the cultural characteristics which drew their most strident verbal scorn. This is quite often the ultimate effect of the most fanatical world-changers. Thus, while some writers avow that they are out to change (or even wreck) the culture which they despise (even while that culture is offering them a good return on their efforts), the polarizing effect of such writing tends to do quite the opposite. It exposes the values which have maintained the cultural characteristics dominating our society. The writer's ambivalence shines through all his preachings: he needs the society and the culture which he attacks. He's in a transactional relationship with it. This is the relationship that can be observed, for example, when you see large groups of medical practitioners behaving in a way that maintains a certain level of illness, that level which justifies the continuing function of the group *as they see that function.* The process here is an unconscious one but nonetheless real for all that. Such unconscious processes are fair game for science fiction because they are embedded in the society. Once exposed, they have a "the-king-is-naked" flavor and they are less social attack than social exposure. There are no guilty and no innocent. Every living human behaves to some degree according to unconscious processes. The trick is to recognize this and cast yourself (as writer) in the role of commentator rather than advocate.

This is a rather delicate line of reasoning to follow because it so easily raises opaque barriers. A physician reading the above paragraph, for example, could be thrown into an immediate defensive posture even though he knows (rationally) quite well that the word *iatrogenic* has real meaning in his practice. (Iatrogenic is defined as "of a neurosis or physical disorder caused by the diagnosis, manner or treatment of a physician or surgeon.")

It's one thing to know something rationally and quite another thing to behave as though that knowledge had real physical application in your own life (because how you view your life can be so securely tied to the way you *feel* your own identity).

Follow this reasoning with me, though, because it has a great deal to do with the whole process of putting fictional men on fictional planets. No human being on our "real" planet is completely free of his unexamined assumptions. And it is precisely this that science fiction does better than any other art form with the possible exception of cartoons.

We examine assumptions.

Certain phenomena have been locked up in the unexamined assumptions of our society. It's in unlocking these phenomena with their attendant assumptions, exposing the structure to view, that science fiction does its greatest, most enduring work. What other human activity ventures this deeply into the crystallized (and crystallizing) structures of our society and exposes these structures to a broader view?

It might clarify this to re-examine briefly one of the all-time classics in science fiction, the Foundation Trilogy (which isn't a trilogy but nine beautifully constructed stories, each a jewel in its own right). Let's just take up a few of the assumptions within Asimov's work.

1. The nine stories are firmly rooted in behaviorist psychology to an extent that would gratify B. F. Skinner. Foundation history, which is to say the human function, is manipulated for larger ends and for the greater good as determined by a scientific aristocracy. It is assumed, then, that the scientist-shamans know best which course humankind should take. This is a dominant attitude in today's science establishment all around the world. ("The Sorcerer's Apprentice," a symphonic poem

by Paul Dukas, isn't a very popular work with this establishment. The plot from the Goethe poem deals with an apprentice sorcerer who tries one of his master's spells and can't countermand it.)

2. While surprises may appear in these stories (e.g., the Mule mutant), it is assumed that no surprise will be too great or too unexpected to overcome the firm grasp of science upon human destiny. This is essentially the assumption that science can produce a surprise-free future for humankind. There's another Skinnerian tenet. It says that you produce this kind of future by management. And *that,* with all of its paradoxes and inconsistencies, is another recurrent theme in science fiction.

3. It is assumed that politics in this managed future can be reduced to the terms, the conflicts and the structures as they are understood on earth today. This is an odd assumption by a scientist because it says that nothing new will be discovered about politics in all of those intervening centuries. We can close the Patent Office, so to speak; we already know it all.

This is not to detract from Asimov's achievement. You should understand that there are very strong literary and communications reasons why his was a good course to take at the time. All of us, and especially those of us who write science fiction, owe Asimov many debts. (From where I sit, I can see nine Asimov nonfiction titles on my working library shelves.) What I am saying is that Asimov, in common with all of the rest of us, operates within a surround of assumptions, any one (or combination) of which could serve as the jumping-off point for an entirely new series of stories. The assumptions are there and can be lifted out with this kind of analysis. In passing, it should be noted that these three assumptions can be found together or separately in many science fiction stories.

Now, see what happens if you assume an opposite viewpoint. To give you an example of how this leverage works in lifting out our unexamined assumptions, let's take a science fiction look at a current problem in the United States—hard drugs. Here are some of the transactional structures involved: guilt-innocence, control-controlled and life-death. Those are pretty heavy relationships and they operate within the assumption that we (in the form of our government) can manage absolutely all of the variables within known limits.

Now, we turn the systems over. We assume that we do not have a system of absolute and known limits, that we cannot control all of the variables and that our approach doesn't have to be involved with guilt-innocence or our own attitudes about personal life and death. Our aim would not be to solve *the* problem but to reduce its influence, throw it into a smaller arena.

This gives us the following: the hard-drug market operates within an open-ended pricing system where no top limit has ever been found. This means that if we cannot stop all of the hard drugs from entering the country, those we do confiscate merely increase the price on what does reach the market. That price is inflated to take care of bribes which can buy senators, congressmen, generals, diplomats, police, customs officers. (Remember that we're talking about billion-dollar slush funds.)

What happens if you lower the barriers and offer a fix at the corner pharmacy to any registered addict for fifty cents? Have you solved the drug problem? No. But you've cut organized crime out of the market. And you've removed the major source of new addictions. More than three-fourths of the present addicts were maneuvered into addiction by other addicts who became pushers to support their own expensive habits.

You've also relieved an important bureau (Customs) of one of its primary tasks, one of its reasons for being. You've removed a major way that people feel innocent (by redefining an extremely large body of the guilty). And you've admitted that there may be some things that cannot be controlled absolutely.

In my hypothetical science fiction story, the three items listed in the paragraph above (plus pressure from professional criminal profiteers) would combine to resist any change in the present system. Here's an important story ingredient, conflict, combined with a currently recognized problem, all of which lend themselves ideally to fictional exposition. And if you put the entire thing on another planet you make it much more palatable to contemporary readers.

You're not talking about real places, real people.

Are you?

What we have in the science fiction techniques being explored here is the fine use of conjecture as a literary tool. Science fiction gives you the added elbow room of entirely new places for things to happen to people. It allows you to generate your own values for your alien places. It permits you to go beyond those cultural norms that are prohibited by your society and enforced by unconscious (and conscious) literary censorship in the prestigious arenas of publication.

And here is a real danger in the current trend toward academic acceptance of science fiction. If it becomes too prestigious, science fiction will encounter new restraints. In the Soviet Union, where all writing carries a high prestige mark, you don't find science fiction stories dealing with political systems at wide variance with the Soviet state. This may not be the best example to make the point; different modes of enforcement are accepted in the Soviet Union, but it does indicate what could happen to a free-swinging literary form when social norms change.

We still have, however, our virtually unlimited resource of unexamined assumptions and our arsenal of imaginative conjecture.

What if . . .

The fictional story as vehicle of lasting influence is well recognized in our world. As Abraham Lincoln said to Harriet Beecher Stowe, who wrote *Uncle Tom's Cabin,* "So you're the little lady who started the Civil War." There was some truth in his remark, although the other influences on that conflict make better stories. With 20-20 hindsight, we can see the influence of Bellamy's *Looking Backward* on 1930s socialism. We can see the influence of Huxley's *Brave New World* on today's attitudes toward population control and police states, or of Orwell's *1984* on the way we view utopias and dystopias. But none of these would have had any influence at all if contemporary readers had not been attracted to them for reasons that were primarily entertaining.

If you want a gold mine of science fiction material, pull the assumptions out of the current best-seller list. Turn those assumptions over, look at them from every angle you can imagine. Tear them apart. Put them back together. Put your new construction on another planet (or on this planet changed) and place believable human beings into the conflict situations thus created.

It isn't the ideas that make the story; it's what you do with them. Ideas are a dime a dozen. *Development of ideas*—that's where the diamonds are. The difference between dirt and ore is what you can get out of it.

The belief that the idea is the story persists, however. A bane of every writer's existence is the person who comes up to you and says: "Hey! I have this marvelous idea for a story! Now, if you'll just write it, I'll split whatever it makes with you."

My own response is to say: "I'm sorry, but I don't have enough lifetimes to exploit all of the ideas I already have."

This doesn't always stop the more persistent. You can see in their eyes that they don't believe you. Regretfully, sometimes you have to be rude.

Insist that the fountain of ideas write his own story. Refuse to listen. Flee.

So don't use my gold mine of science fiction material. Create your own. That's what it's all about, isn't it? But it might be helpful for you to see where we've already been, to learn the clichés, absorb the labels that communicate commonly understood concepts. *Robot*, as a word, entered the language at a particular place and time. There was no such thing as a *slidewalk* before Bob Heinlein gave it to us. Do you know how the mechanical amplifiers of human muscles came to be called *Waldos?* Where did the word *plasteel* originate?

As the best of the science fiction writers do, start looking at our present planet as a set of long-term influences, a system of resonances which can be read as bio-rhythms—the combined impact of moon, tides, sun, variations in atmospheric electricity, and so on. Did you know that the earth's tides change the amount of fluid in your body's cells? What would happen to "human psychology" on another planet with different tidal variations, different resonances in its atmospheric chemistry and electricity?

And if these ways of looking at our current condition don't work for you, invent your own ways of looking. But, to be sure you really are inventing, sample where imagination already has taken science fiction. Here are a few examples to show what I mean:

Brian Aldiss in *The Salvia Tree and Other Strange Growths* has extraterrestrials (aliens, eh?) visit a farm in turn-of-the-century England. The ETs make the farm blossom, intending to devour the entire animal population, including the humans. The viewpoint character exchanges letters with H. G. Wells.

Jack Vance in *The Dirdir*, which was the third in his *Planet of Adventure* series, has natives and humans of Ischai compete for dominance under conditions where his planet abounds with different species that complicate existence. There are, to sample them, the Chasch breeds, the reptilian Wankh, and the predatory Dirdir, who hunt and eat humans. (See Aldiss, above.)

Mack Reynolds replays human history in *Space Barbarians*. The ingredients will seem familiar, although the settings are not. He exploits a highly technological society, vigorous and uncaring about who or what brings a profit, which clashes with a primitive society in a social and economic stasis. The outcome is not necessarily surprising, but the way there is entertaining and informative.

Through such stories wend certain assumptions. The legal owners of real estate, including a planet, are the beings who occupy it. Humans tend to shake down into hierarchies which resemble tribal organization. Science is good. Science is evil. Other planets have to be at least vaguely earthlike. (Otherwise humans can't live on them.) The alternative: adapt humans to the planet. (That's what evolution did, anyway, didn't it?) Time is linear and flowing—an analogue river. Mankind is headed toward some form of apotheosis (having fallen from paradise, humans will once more become godlike). Magic is merely science misunderstood.

And those observations just touch a few of the high points.

To come full circle, let's go back to myths. Myth here is used in its classical sense: a traditional or legendary story usually concerning events which transform human into superhuman, if only briefly. Science fiction is, in part, a myth-creative format. Since the creation of myths is a day-to-day process solidified and codified for an era by the surviving dramatic works of the time (thus becoming traditional and legendary), we have in science fiction a window on an ancient process. Through this window we can see the codified myths upon which humans of our time place their greatest faith: science, progress, the triumph of intellect. These are rooted in Platonic absolutes: "Somewhere there is a single law which will explain everything."

And, summated: Science can show us the future.

Lest you be led into believing such things absolutely, take a brief look backward. The scientists of Franklin D. Roosevelt's Brain Trust, asked to predict "the course of technological development" from 1933 through 1958, said not one word about transistors, atomic power, jet engines or antibiotics.

Writing in 1967, Herman Kahn and Anthony Wiener for their book *The Year 2000* assumed a world system with a continuing increased rate of energy consumption spreading into the underdeveloped nations and culminating in such things as "moderately priced robots doing most of the housework . . ." plus "next-day delivery of mail" anywhere in the United States.

From a science fiction viewpoint, they made the depressingly common mistake of writing about *the* future instead of concerning themselves with *a* future based on current premises. They failed to examine many of their assumptions.

Given this kind of mass-energy bias, you can understand why David Lilienthal would assume that he could export his Tennessee Valley

Authority, with all of its extensive relocations and disruptions of existing people and systems, taking the TVA bodily to South Vietnam. It wasn't that he disregarded the social facts of Southeast Asia—the survival importance of community vitality and the profoundly maintained ancestor worship which requires that communities remain close to ancestral burial grounds—no, Lilienthal just didn't even consider that such elements existed. He made the Henry Higgins mistake: "Why can't the South Vietnamese be more like Americans?"

"Just you wite, 'Enery 'Iggins! Just you wite!"

With the bad track record of such prestigious planners, it's no wonder that the current world bias is pessimistic. The world picture has grown so black that a President of France can warn us that "the great curves which describe the future in our times all lead to catastrophe."

Thank you, Mr. President.

But science fiction continues to plug along with its stories about futures in which there are surviving humans. Those humans may not live in a 1960-projected future of enormous skyscrapers linked by loops and curves of highways far above the surface, a future of individual one-man flying machines and plastic bubbles over everything from a backyard garden to New York City. It may not even be the kind of future we were predicting in the 1890s—with trips to the moon and women doctors of philosophy, a bicycle in every garage, fast railroad trains linking every major population center and propeller-driven gas balloons. It may be none of these.

There will be humans in these fictional creations, though. You'll recognize them from the descriptions: bipedal, two arms with hands, head on top with nose below the mouth and . . .

What price a glimpse of tomorrow?

Frank Herbert

Frank Herbert has been writing thoughtful and exciting science fiction for more than twenty years; his first novel, *Dragon in the Sea,* is still in print here and abroad, as are many of his other books. In addition, he has published a great many short stories in the science fiction field in such magazines as *Analog, Galaxy,* and *If.*

Probably his best known work to date is *Dune,* published in 1965, and winner of the World Science Fiction Convention Hugo and the Science Fiction Writers of America Nebula awards. *Dune* has attracted international attention both as a novel and as an "environmental awareness handbook." It was followed by *Dune Messiah* and more recently by *Children of Dune* (serialized in *Analog*).

Mr. Herbert has done research in such diverse fields as undersea geology, psychology, navigation, jungle botany, and anthropology. He has been a professional newspaperman in several West Coast cities—including more than ten years with the San Francisco *Examiner.*

In addition he has been a professional photographer, TV cameraman, radio news commentator, and oyster diver and has lectured at the University of Washington and other universities around the country.

Mr. Herbert was born in Tacoma, Washington, in 1920, and has recently returned to the Puget Sound area. He now lives in Port Townsend, Washington, with his family.

Dragon in the Sea, 1956 (Doubleday and Avon)
Dune, 1965 (Chilton and Ace)
The Green Brain, 1966 (Ace)
Destination Void, 1966 (Berkley)
The Eyes of Heisenberg, 1966 (Berkley)
The Heaven Makers, 1968 (Avon)
Santaroga Barrier, 1968 (Berkley)
Dune Messiah, 1970 (Putnam-Berkley)
Whipping Star, 1970 (Putnam-Berkley)
New World or No World, 1970 (Ace), editor
Worlds of Frank Herbert, 1970 (Ace)
Soul Catcher, 1971 (Putnam-Berkley)
The God Makers, 1971 (Berkley)
Project 40, 1973 (Bantam)
Book of Frank Herbert, 1973 (DAW)

KATHERINE MacLEAN

Alien Minds and Nonhuman Intelligences*

If he could, he would divest himself of the limitations to which he is subject as a human being. If he could perceive the world as a Martian or an inhabitant of Sirius, if he could see it as it seems to a creature that lives for a day and also as it would seem to one that lived for a million years, he would be a better philosopher. —Bertrand Russell, *The Art of Philosophizing,* Littlefield Adams Co., New Jersey, 1974

In an infinite and lasting universe, can a germ cooperate, can a star think? Can a tor-

*This chapter will be a discussion of the internal world of the alien being, and the way strange environments can evolve different moralities, different philosophies, or even more strangely, something outwardly alien but internally almost identical to our own personalities, as matched as left and right hand, internally cousins, brothers, or twins to ourselves.

For calculations of external mechanical design of bodies as a product of environments, such as L. Sprague de Camp's classic article proving that the human form will inevitably be produced by the conditions of millions of planets in the universe, and his interesting suggestion that slightly heavier gravity will produce centaurs—for such calculations I think the reader will find the most available and practical discussion now in print is Hal Clement's chapter "Creating Imaginary Beings" in *Science Fiction, Today and Tomorrow,* edited by Reginald Bretnor, Harper & Row, 1974; Penguin, 1975.

nado be aware, can electricity evolve to an intelligent life form? Can we communicate with such totally strange creatures? Will they feel brotherhood to human beings?

And do we have any ability to learn from other shapes of life; do we have enough tolerance for different shapes, different styles of thought, different standards of right and wrong, to listen? If somewhere there are kindly creatures of great wisdom, will we let them teach us?

First, are they out there? As science fiction writers we do not have to believe in their reality, but my belief is that time and permutation will make them real. They are out there, or they will be out there.

My reason is purely logical. In an infinite and lasting universe anything that is possible must happen. The probable happens frequently, the impossible never happens, the improbable happens occasionally. In a universe that stretches backward to eternity and forward to eternity anything that can happen must have already happened and must be getting ready to happen again. Somewhere, somewhen. ANYTHING THAT CAN HAPPEN WILL HAPPEN.

All the imaginary beings of science fiction might be out there. If they have a scrap of possibility, a conceivable planetary ecology that could generate such creatures, then they must be out there. It is a challenging game to read a story of interplanetary adventure, then invent a planetary ecology that could generate and justify its fictional creatures; then as a writer use its logic to generate other such possible worlds and write other possible adventures.

One sits in a waiting room and sees a comic book. A gorilla monster twenty feet high, with long tusks and shaggy green fur is descending on a beautiful girl in a skintight spacesuit and bubble helmet. She looks up and screams.

It roars, "Narg narg snaggle rowf." Can we make this monster plausible? We translate his roar. ("Stop stop, you are trampling the geraniums!") The green gorilla picks up the heroine and carries her away, snarling, "Ugh naggle gump boogle." ("Gotta get it out of the garden.") He holds her closer to his big tusks and big purple eyes. She fights and screams and faints. He snarls. ("It's run down. Where's the windup key?")

The hero has run back to the spaceship but turns and sees that his girl is in danger of being raped by the monster, who is tearing at her clothes, roaring irritably. ("How do you get the plastic packaging off stuff nowadays?")

The hero shoots the monster and carries his girl back to the spaceship and they take off just as another monster five times as big and twice as ugly emerges from the ground roaring horribly. ("Gorok, Gorok, come downstairs to dinner!")

These green gorillas become a little *too* easy to believe. The reason these two sets of civilized beings attacked each other is that there are no aliens in this picture. The gorilla is our own kind, territorial, noisy, tactless and impulsive. We never seem to make out well when trying to negotiate with our kind.

Analog modeling is a form of logic. For the patent office the test of the truth of a theory is a successful working model. For writers it is a sample scene. The scene of the giant green gorilla seems natural, so demonstrates a general rule—i.e., when a human sees anything unfamiliar, if it moves toward him, he'll shoot. This is called xenophobia, but calling it a name doesn't help. It may stand between us and messages of alien wisdom.

Xenophobia and Homophobia; Is There Something We Won't Shoot?

What if Jesus Christ or someone resembling our image of the human god arrived in a spaceship? Surely we would welcome Him. Or would we shoot Him?

In "However You Are," Judy Merril wrote a realistic study of a first contact with the aliens we *should* be most likely to accept. These beings were tall, beautiful, calm, friendly, cooperative, harmless and well intentioned. They were soft-spoken, with a good grade of empathic telepathy as their language and in total were wingless angels, irresistibly charming. Our military leaders, after deep thought, decided that anything irresistible could be used as a weapon, even charm. Everything *should* be resistible. Therefore, they destroyed the beautiful, friendly, helpful strangers to avoid being conquered by charm.

Ugly, unfriendly, short, uncooperative humans from outer space should not expect to get any better treatment. Nor, certainly, should eight-armed, three-eyed beings.

Yet when we read the *National Geographic* or historical fiction, and when we read science fiction, we are eager to understand and enjoy the stranger and find adventure in the strange. We change from xenophobes to xenophiles, lovers of the outlandish, finding mental refreshment in the strange universe the world becomes when viewed through strange eyes.

The function of intelligence is to understand, predict, and control the unfamiliar. It enjoys functioning. So we will travel looking for alien races and they will travel looking for us. But when we see each other, interesting differences suddenly become terrifying abnormalities. Surprise becomes fear; fear becomes war.

I recall reading, as a child, the solemn statement that the best way to prove intelligence and civilization to alien beings was at the first opportunity to demonstrate the Pythagorean theorem: the square of the diagonal equals the sum of the squares of the other two sides.

I never knew whether to laugh. An eight-armed, three-eyed being landing on Earth and trying to demonstrate a geometry problem to a passing motor cop would get shot full of holes.

Why should a passing alien be more tolerant of a strange human scientist gesturing with a ballpoint pen and a notebook?

Archimedes, our great Greek scientist, was drawing some such geometric diagram in the sand when the human soldier looked over his shoulder and cut his head off. Archimedes might have done better drawing a naked dancing girl.

When you meet a strange and horrifying creature you may run at him or away from him or just stand there, but you are not wondering if he knows the Pythagorean theorem.

There are diagrams a stranger to Earth could use. He might, if confronting a soldier or a cop, draw the American Flag and salute, meaning *I am on your side.*

If confronting a minister he might draw a cross and pray on whatever he has that passes for knees. If he sees a businessman he might draw a dollar sign and bring out a tray of small objects to sell and trade. Communication will always be successful if you start with the right signals.

But how is a stranger to know what signals will work?

When we are strangers on another planet how can we understand the monsters?

A little insight into the relativity of living beings to their environment—a little understanding of what is likely to be considered normal—will help.

I Am a Normal Being on a Normal Planet with a Moderate Climate

All creatures seem normal to themselves.

The creature who automatically shoots when approached by a friendly bug-eyed stranger is, of course, dangerous and is therefore correctly classified as dangerous, flat-eyed monster. A very funny story by William Tenn, "The Flat-Eyed Monster," shows aliens horrified to the point of panic by a human who is trying to communicate with them as they scream and run. Ugly is point of view, like beauty. Hiding, the human overheard a discussion of beauty.

> "And where is little Tekt? I thought she'd be with you?"
>
> "Oh, she's out at the landing field," Rahb answered, "supervising our last minute stuff going into the ship. After all, we begin our mating flight tonight."
>
> "A wonderful female," Glomb told him in a voice that was now barely audible. "You're a very lucky flefnobe."
>
> "I know that, Pop," Rahb assured him, "don't think I don't know that. The most plentiful bunch of eye-ended tentacles this side of Gansibokkle and they're mine, all mine!" (Page 113, "The Flat-Eyed Monster," from *The Human Angle*, William Tenn, Ballantine Books, New York, 1956.)

It was surprising to the human (who was involuntarily eavesdropping on their telepathic conversations) that these beings thought about each other and themselves in the same terms and with the same attitudes as humans.

What are the chances that aliens really see themselves as human?

Any living species sees itself as acceptable in appearance and moderate in size and strength, existing comfortably in a moderate temperature range. Their bodies and minds have evolved to cope with the changes in their environment, so they suit it and it suits them, the normal is neutral to them and hard to notice, and only the differences attract attention.

A creature living in a thousand-degree temperature by a lava lake would consider eight hundred degrees very, very cold—two hundred below normal! If you approach him in your burnable metal ship you will be considered very strange. Hal Clement has dealt with this kind of relativity often and well.

A fish-shaped creature of tungsten swimming in the lava lake with organs of vibration developed to "see" through the liquid would consider itself a fish swimming in cool transparent water. A fish does not know what it is made of. To it, anything the right temperature for its physique is "cool," anything it can see through is "clear." Evolution repeats the same good mechanical designs at many levels, and senses adapt to bring in needed information in the same coded terms that our senses bring it in. Social customs are the product of group living and its needs.

"Tekt is a warm and highly intelligent female flefnobe," his father pointed out severely from a great distance. "She has many fine qualities. I don't like you acting as if the mating process were a mere matter of the number of eye-ended tentacles possessed by a female." (Tenn, page 113.)

The social relationships are a by-product of the shape of the animal, of its reproductive arrangements and its division of food.

A telepath tuning in a CQ tour of the universe would be surprised at the number of planets that seem "normal" and Earthlike to their inhabitants. In *Starmaker* by Olaf Stapledon we go on just such a tour and find, in many shapes of animal, warm human emotions, social and antisocial impulses and destroying struggles over arbitrary points of belief. All the planets seem approximately Earthlike—but they would *not* seem Earthlike to us.

The very shallow and sun-drenched oceans of these great planets provided an immense diversity of habitats and a great wealth of living things. . . . Intelligence in these planets was generally achieved by some unimposing social creature, neither fish nor octopus nor crustacean, but something of all three. It would be equipped with manipulatory tentacles, keen eyes and subtle brain. It could make nests of weed in the crevices of the coral, or build strongholds of coral masonry. In time would appear traps, weapons, tools, submarine agriculture, the blossoming of primitive art, the ritual of primitive religion. Then would follow the typical fluctuating advance of the spirit from barbarism to civilization.

Olaf Stapledon, a genius, one of the four greatest writers in science fiction, wrote this in *Star Maker*, first published in 1937 and now reprinted and available through Dover Books and through Penguin Books, 1972.

I Am a Moral and Righteous Citizen

We can probably adjust to differences in shape when we grasp that these other beings have deep similarities in the way they think and feel. But differences in morality and social custom are harder to adjust to. Humans learning the languages of other humans frequently discover a different religion and are infuriated. "Die, infidel!" Even intelligent humans are not ready to understand that there are different ways to be right and wrong. Intelligent aliens can be expected to be equally stupid on the subject.

For example, there is a fine short story by Robert Sheckley that is so much a reverse of our own morality it reads like a joke. But it is no joke. ("The Monsters," *Anthropology Through Science Fiction,* editors Mason, Greenberg, and Warrick, St. Martin's Press, New York, 1974.)

Two males, "men," watch without surprise as a human ship lands from the sky. This is an interesting new thing. They discuss calmly the possibility of other forms of life in the infinitude of "Outside," then return to their village to kill their wives. Wives must be killed every twenty-five days and a new wife chosen from surplus.

After twenty-five days of attempting to communicate politely with the (to them) hideously stiff-jointed and impolite humans—a proper person crawls, undulates, and has tentacles and kills anyone who is discourteous in a philosophical discussion, of course!—their tolerance snaps when they realize that some of the females among the strangers have been wives for more than twenty-five days and have not yet been killed. Shocked and outraged, the entire village attacks the immoral and revolting strangers and forces them to return to their spaceship and flee the planet.

At first this seems like an impossible social morality. Now put it into its ecological framework. Married females lay at least one egg a day. The eggs hatch in a ratio of eight females to one male. How can they keep overpopulation from destroying their planet, their host? One way is by killing adult females. Why not destroy eggs? But that would not be a good evolutionary strategy. If the race varies (most variants being degenerative), the individuals must have a chance to be tested against the selective trials of life, to weed out the worst. Unmarried females live apart and do all the work, including egg rearing. They are bigger and more energetic than males (selection by overwork).

Males are more easily tired, more deadly, less good-natured, more quarrelsome, and also more rapid, more curious and very, very intelligent and logical.

They select each other for logic and speed and deadliness by nightly philosophical arguments that end in duels and murder. The race evolves and improves in health, speed, and logic. There is no surplus.

Good? Bad? If one favors the delights of health and awareness, then one must accept the delights of combat as part of the chain.

We must expect to find killers surviving all over the galaxy. Unfortunately, murderers live longer than victims. Restricted rules of combat and courtesy become necessary among killers. Socially enforced and conditioned taboos against actions that lead to overmultiplication lead to cultural success, protecting the planet.

The genetically optimum strategy for family-line evolution in a stable population is to produce a replacement number of perfect copies of the parents, at least three, and then a scatter of mutated variants, some of them very wild shots indeed and most not viable, and allow or drive the survivors to seek out different environments suitable to their differences, and live or die on new frontiers. This works best for rapid improvement if there are very many children and they meet decimating conditions in every tenth of their childhood span before reproduction, or society delays their fertile years until they have been weeded down to numbers sufficient for mere replacement.

Within the framework of these requirements we can find many societies, none of which will be set up to be nice to the young surplus population. They will be marked by injustice, exploitation and bloodshed. The proper function of such a society is to provide the weeding and selection by death or sterility usually provided by a harsh environment and a dangerous predator. Society is an adversary, but the young members of the society are trained to consider it as necessary, moral and good. The most harshly destructive aspects of the culture will be cloaked in high and noble words, like "discipline," "patriotism," or "morality," and given the sanction of a stern, all-seeing god.

Having the destructive aspects of their own culture cloaked in philosophy, religion, and morality will be necessary to their racial survival, for the puritan restraints against reproduction must be as powerful as the instincts they hold in check. Morality is self-righteous and unable to compromise. These cultures will be difficult to deal with by outsiders who deviate in any minute way from their ethos. When we approach them from outside we will find that our moral pattern (total protection for children, sex taboo and war and sometimes starvation for young working adults, but attempts to save the ill) will be extremely unlikely to match their patterns of selective population control.

For example: You are a human ambassador sent to live on a planet of unwarlike humanoids who seem to show little hostility and few laws of rigid politeness. You settle there with your wife and child and feel safe, then find that the population problem there has been solved by making it immoral and unthinkable to feed or defend one's own children. You must not antagonize the natives. Your son is six years old. The humanoids around you, suppressing instinctive wishes to protect their young and thereby in the grip of reaction formation, righteous rage, frustration, envy, will attack with crusading fury anyone seen feeding a child.

I Am a Moral and Righteous Citizen (II)

Another example of different morality:

In *Anything You Can Do,* by Darrel F. Langart (Doubleday, Garden City, New York, 1963)—a fine adventure book—we have the problems of an alien who crash-landed on our planet and is trying to make contact, and being badly misunderstood, because he kills and eats people, bare-handed, bare-fanged. His attitude might be unsuitable to Earth's customs but it is sincere. His society never abandoned the genetic and economic advantages of a pecking order. Rank and command are established by hand-to-hand single duels. Like our Japanese, they need to know whether they are above or below before they can deal with another group. He waited and searched years for a knight—a human with Honor to fight him bare-handed.

> On the top of the rubble, frozen for a long instant, stood the Nipe, watching with those four, glowing violet eyes.
>
> The Nipe stared at the human being. Was this, at last, a real person? It was surprising that the man should be awake . . . awake and fully dressed.
>
> Surely that indicated—
>
> And then the man turned, and the Nipe saw the weapon in the holster at his waist. There was a blinding instant of despair as he realized that his hopes had been shattered—and then he launched himself across the room. (Pages 132–133.)

Most of the book is taken up with a subplot of the human hero being trained secretly for combat with the alien while the public is demanding it be hunted down and killed. The Nipe was trying to make contact and making a desperate effort to flatter us by eating disgustingly armed peasants as if they were unarmed honorable enemies, yet he laid himself open to misunderstanding, in the same way polar bears and bladder netters and giant frogs might have trouble getting us to settle down to a gentlemanly exchange of ideas. There is a problem of a different standard of politeness. But it is not insurmountable when approached as a problem of evolutionary biology. In this case, if cell and brain RNA which carries personal memory is accepted into the system instead of digested, then to eat a man is to save him as part of yourself.

In reading fiction the pleasure of identification can lead the reader to build a model subpersonality that is the alien and therefore understands the alien. Fiction can carry understanding into very strange places and into very strange corners of evolutionary biology. Fiction bypasses xenophobia.

Chemical Intelligence

In early evolution our brains were extensions of our noses, and we thought about smells and tastes and remembered past foods and the smell of enemy, the smells of places and seasons. Later our brains became extensions of hearing and of sight. But let us not sneeze at the complexity of smell-taste chemical brain power, even on Earth. In a human dump, survival of an earthworm would require chemical thought, a fine memory for taste and smell and for the results of food, remembered cell responses of vigor or illness, the warm glow of good nourishment, the fearful and adversive memory of indigestion. Has this alien on Earth anything to say to us now, before it reaches a much higher level of intelligence? Already it has chemical understanding well in advance of ours. Let us try a test case, a scene. Let us build a working model to see if communication works.

The earthworm crawls near a human sunning in a field. The earthworm is having a hard time digesting a stale brownie. It is involuntarily broadcasting cell distress and cell nausea on the Baxter band of intercom among living cells.

The human stomach cells are roused up and reminded and agree,

"Wow, yes. Brownies. Yetch! Stale flour and preservatives! But we can't get the taste buds in the mouth to turn against the sweet chocolate flavors. The plus response is locked into their DNA. So the organization keeps shoving more of that stale poison sweet stuff down the gullet at us." This comes through, not as words but as remembered experience.

The earthworm considers that response carefully while it tries to hurry the brownie bits on through its digestive tract and out the other end. It is puzzled. "Organization?" To him the stomach seems like another earthworm. It does a job of tasting and analyzing what it digests, like any earthworm, and seems to be doing a strenuous, peristaltic, rippling crawl—broadcasting the effort on the Baxter band. But what is the Organization?

"If you don't like the food there, why don't you crawl away?" the earthworm asks the stomach in reasonable tones. It doesn't understand the answer. It is not yet a superworm. Nor are we yet the Great Human Race, for the conscious mind is unaware of the interchange, as it is unaware of most of the internal life of our body. The entire chemical resources and white blood cells of our body might be engaged in a desperate battle against invading microbes, but our conscious mind feels nothing. It is not tuned even to its own antibody immunity system. The dandelions in the grass of our lawn are probably better able to pick up the broadcast of our cells than our conscious minds. While the worm is still trying to communicate, the man uses it to bait a hook.

Friends

Many other writers have written on the problem of friendship between a human and our alien brother. From Stanley Weinbaum's Tweel in "A Martian Odyssey" through Hal Clement's Hunter in *Needle* and many strangely flavored stories by Kate Wilhelm, Damon Knight and others, the problem of the almost unthinkably alien being trying to share its inner feelings has been approached with great sensitivity.

With deep, lasting pleasure I recall a phrase from a William Tenn story which resembled Damon Knight's "Stranger Station" in its depiction of a human drafted to attempt to communicate with a huge, trapped alien being, forced to share its suffering and despair, in danger of insanity from the alien quality of the thoughts which must be accepted into his own thoughts without the shield of language, for the form of communication was telepathy or telempathy, mind to mind. I cannot locate the story in the two William Tenn anthologies I have at hand, but the image and the phrase still linger. He found himself sharing memories of the delights of childhood, growing up on the monster's world. And although this is a bloblike being from the pressures of deep Jupiter, the memories translate as the sight of a waterfall, and a game with his brother, stress, effort, skill and delight, the handball bouncing from the back wall just right, the clean smack of it hitting the hand.

Although William Tenn, Phil Klass, now teaching college, has never to my knowledge written an article on "Alien Thought" he knows and understands the relativity of the inner world, the translation of the analogue experience to the same pattern of feeling. The tungsten fish in the lava sea sees itself in clear, cool water. The powerful blob in the depth of compressed methane sees itself as a civilized citizen in air.

Sensations are multistage metering hookups—simple, practical rigs that evolution would converge in most living beings. Inward lives would have a familiar pattern, and emotion and experience may be almost universal modes we could share easily with aliens. Our disagreements are most likely to be merely religious and moral, yet they could cause bloody, unnecessary wars between species.

Who can communicate across differences of values? Writers, poets, singers, people who play with value-shifting for pleasure. Also the dangerous and logical cynics and traders from the areas of destroyed ancient value systems, men freed of taboos, who can profit by playing middleman in contacts between harshly different societies in the great crossroads cities and ports. Others who can shift value structures easily are women, assistants, lieutenants, any assistant to an executive whose job is to aid the boss in pursuit of his goals and still do some independent thinking. Pursuing the pattern, we see that any being who must travel a lifetime with another gets an evolutionary screening for ability to understand and aid the beings with whom she travels. The earthworm has hope of being a great communicator if it becomes a tapeworm.

Any unpleasant little parasite is likely to be stuck for a lifetime with one host and must die with his host. While its host lives it must share his food, health, illness and dangers. In a position of involuntary partnership it will evolve to be a full partner. It profits its survival and genetic future through its descendants by becoming able to improve the health and success of its host.

Leaving the earthworm out on the sunny grass field trying to communicate with a human, we go inside to Hal Clement's virus being. This one is living inside a human host as a loosely associated but dispersable organization of submicroscopic viruses with the penetrating skills of a highly organized invasive disease. He thinks of himself as an individual and has an individual personality, with as much concern for the individual viruses that constitute him as we have concern for our body cells.

He lives in a state of symbiosis with his host, helping and protecting the body of the animal he has invaded and, in his morality, he feels such a dedicated zeal on this subject, and his entire society feels such intense fanaticism, that his society of group-virus beings has sent him halfway across the Galaxy to track down and kill a "criminal" of their own kind who disobeys this law and exploits his hosts.

As far as reader understanding goes, Hunter is immediately understandable in his familiar role of professional detective and logically is true to the demands of his job, showing the kind of professional personality developed by a good French police detective. He communicates with the boy, his host, only in terms of his problems of searching for the "criminal." His thinking is slow but stubbornly logical, and the only bias he shows is in his anxious and somewhat hysterical compulsion to protect the boy from physical injury.

This makes a good book, for it fulfills the emotional fiction-plot requirement of an understandable alien hero who is friends to the human hero, a warm story acceptable to librarians as a children's book, as well as to intelligent adults.

But Hal Clement, like many of the most exacting writers, demands an implied total ecology behind any beings he introduces into his stories.

This ecology can be deduced with little effort, and so he did not spell it out. A virus disease with such skill at penetration and communication could easily spread and wipe out every living creature on its planet. The society of cooperative viruses Hunter arises from must continually police their own evolution and execute the most selfish and careless of their members, for any virus which regressed to being a host-killing disease could spread from host to host, outnumber the police and wipe out the entire species that carried the virus beings.

A skeptic might point out the improbability of germs ever evolving to symbiotes, for if they are capable of abandoning a dying host and infecting a new one, they can sink the ship they are on and leap from ship to ship.

Admitting that the evolution of a moral society among viruses would require special circumstances and lots of luck, and in main be highly improbable, I remind the skeptic of the rule that the improbable occurs less frequently than the probable but still occurs. In the old rule of evolution, we see the successes; we don't see the failures, for they are all dead.

In our future travels of the universe I expect one of the most frequent planet types we explore will be the ecologically destroyed world. And one of the most frequent destroyers will have been disease. For every happy planet like Hunter's, where the diseases and parasites evolved to cooperative status and learned to police each other, there might be ten, a hundred, or a thousand planets we would never hear from, dead and gutted by disease, with all the living species and plants dead and the superior virus that killed everything dead also with nothing left to prey on.

In our future travels of the universe, among the numerous dead planets we are likely to find many that are Saharas of drifting sand with mighty cities and factories testifying to the technological overpredation that destroyed them. In a wider use of the word, intelligent predators are either parasites or symbiotes and their host is the whole biosphere, the thin green layer of life that covers the planet. If we overpredate the ecology that supports us, we destroy the body whose blood is the rivers and seas, and we destroy ourselves. As successful predators overpopulating, overconsuming our support, we can limit ourselves by the ancient and unkind morality of the pecking-order society with arbitrary and difficult rules that destroy its own members, or apply our intelligence to happiness and design a new, rationalized utopian society, with a strict conscious ethic of restraint and care for the ecology of the Earth.

We have not yet developed this morality, so we might kill our host planet. As a planet-destroying species, the way to survive (if not reform) is travel. Graduating from being a parasite to becoming a communicable disease, the human race and other like races might take to spaceships and spread through the universe, infecting and destroying other planets, leaving a trail of smog and deserts.

A. E. Van Vogt about 1938, in *Astounding Science Fiction*, wrote an unforgettable short story that so wraps up the entire topic that I think he has prevented any other writer from using the theme again. "Black Destroyer" is a masterpiece in the adventure-exploration category; as humans explore the ruins of a magnificent city in an over-exploited, gutted, desert planet, a lone alien survivor of its great days lurks after them, desperately trying to control hunger and check an urge to eat people who could rescue him and transport him to another planet.

In surviving all of his race he used great intelligence, treachery, selfishness, strategy, speed, ferocity, planning and cannibalism (necessary characteristics that logically would carry anyone through a great mass famine). He once was a civilized person of the type of a competitive company executive, and he is horrified to find that, with no morality to restrain his actions, his effort to control his ferocity is fighting a losing battle against the demands of his empty stomach and the habit of cannibalism.

He loses the battle for self-control and kills some of the human members of the expedition before trying to approach them and become friends. At the end, although he shows valuable personal intelligence and possesses unknown skills and sciences, the humans, in fear and disgust, kill him. Although they value intelligence, Van Vogt shows them initiating a planned search of the planet to seek and destroy any remaining members of that race, not for logical reasons but in fear and *moral revulsion.* Morality accepts no reasoning, nor can it.

If they had recognized his hunger and forgiven his murders and found him charming and brilliant, if they had taken him to a new planet to teach his science and start his great race anew, his descendants would build great technical civilizations, run by amoral competitive individualists, evolving by ruthless competition to ever greater brilliance, with no occasion to learn cooperation. Even surrounded by other races, the end would be other planets reduced to rock and drifting sand with charming, lone, killer cannibals lurking in the ruins.

"Black Destroyer." How can another writer follow an act like that? Besides being a perfect ecology story, it was done in an era when the word *ecology* was unknown to intellectuals.

Stars, Whirlwinds, Dolphins

It means talking to a star, year-captain. A great ball of fiery gas, year-captain, and it has mind, it has a consciousness. . . . I found a network of stars that live, that think, that have minds, that have souls. That communicate. The whole universe is alive.

(From "Ship-Sister, Star-Sister," a short story by Robert Silverberg in *Frontiers 1: Tomorrow's Alternatives,* edited by Robert Elwood, Collier Books, New York and London, 1973)

An intelligent star? Far out! Is this one possible?

Obviously the intelligence has to develop from a balancing-to-survive of the tremendous temperature differences and sometimes exploding eddy and turbulence structure *inside* the star, since little that happens outside is on any energy level that would make a detectable percentage change. Can eddies and spins develop intelligence?

Lester Del Rey once wrote a story that conceived it possible that a tornado, that black funnel of power and destruction, is actually a sentient being, purposely destroying houses and lives, overturning towns with its long black arm as deliberately as an anteater kicks over an ant nest and tongues up the terrified inhabitants. It was called "Wings of the Storm." Does it represent a real possibility? A tornado is two temperatures of air connected by an eddy-spin process, but, once started, the process seems to keep going a remarkably long time and travels a long distance, keeping its shape, the giant survivor of all the little dust devils, waterspouts and cat's-paw eddies that don't last and didn't grow. How much internal structuring can an eddy have? It is nothing but big and little funnels and wheels of air. But many wheels can make an engine. The turbulence of small eddies at the edges of an airplane wing in flight can generate an apparent thickening and stiffening of the air as it passes across the wing, a stiffening resembling structure.

In another medium, the great Maelstrom of Norway and the great whirlpool off the Isle of Mull in Scotland show apparently malevolent, rapacious behavior as they pull down flotsam and passing small boats, yet they are only processes, their substance being no more than the salt water of the ocean, their energy only the flow of the changing tides.

But they are not alive. Could a living creature have a fluid structure or moving electrons and magnetic and static fields?

He visualized an amorphous creature creeping and slithering through a mass of wires and instruments, its "body," a bridge for the live power of the numerous relays. . . . Presently they had the information that Ploians lived off the magnetic force of their planet, which they converted to a sort of life energy. "Tell him, no more nourishment until he agrees to work that communication machine." . . . Within hours the Ploian could so modulate electrical current that intelligible if rather guttural speech sounds came over the speaker of the voice machine.

The being acquired an acceptable command of English in one day. . . . "He seems to have his entire energy field available for storing memories, and that field extends almost as far as he wants it to." (Pages 152–153, *The War Against the Rull* by A. E. Van Vogt, Permabook, New York, 1962.)

A. E. Van Vogt and Lester Del Rey are not fools. If they consider a being of pure energy flux can be intelligent, even for a story, I am impressed.

I am also impressed by news reports indicating such beings have already evolved in the atmosphere of the Earth.

It seems, in fact, that there already are floating beings of strictly electrical processes and globular shape inhabiting the atmosphere of the Earth, presumably tapping the electrical charge differentials that show up in electric storms. They are invisible to the human eye but visible on radar screens and were called "foo fighters" by World War II pilots and "interference artifacts" by official logs of radar screen operation. They are logged as following planes and sometimes, in lines and V formations, flying against the wind passing on the screens of radar stations. They are usually invisible, but farm communities called them fireballs because sometimes during or after an electrical storm one floats, glowing pink, near the ground, and some burst and *leave no trace* and some fly away, becoming transparent. Their behavior indicates at least the intelligence of pigeons. This proves intelligence is possible to eddy creatures whose structure is only the fluid flow of electricity.

Dam-breaking, the release of stored energy, is done by humans whenever they eat a potato. The sun's internal dynamics would provide high energy easily to something that travels, locates and punctures inner layers under which the seething fusion processes are being generated by compression. Starting a channel of escape for the balanced ballooning pressures of the inner solar furnace could give a tornado spin creature great lasting energy.

Such a power source has dangers comparable to being a mouse drilling holes in a dam for water, or puncturing a steamboiler for steam power. Death would always be at hand to evolve higher skill and higher intelligence and there would be an incentive to survive and profit by grouping to prevent the disastrous expanding dam leak that carries away a dam. The layer-shorting creatures can use the communication band that links them, to pool their memory and awareness of personal experience into a close group entity that distributes drill holes like steam vents and tries to prevent the disastrous solar flares that could make the inside layer balloon squirt its heat out on one side in a flare, earthquaking all the small creatures that tap a layer that is usually stable. As in the sponge, it would operate as if the energy creatures are body parts, or cells of its being; it would feel like a unified individual, a star.

Like the sound of breathing and the pulse of a heartbeat, a pulse pattern superimposed on the solar wind and the magnetic field might be recognizable to another well-stabilized star using a venting system. Yet, considering the order of magnitude, it is almost beyond scale that a sun, constantly bellowing with internal radiation, could detect the whisper of distant starlight and star magnetic fields. (Yes, but in pickups I would *counterfeed* local interference to cancel it; could a sun?)

There is no space to carry on the discussion, for we are confronting again a question that is so heavily interconnected with the question of intelligence that they are almost one question. How can intelligence be communicated?

Let us return to Earth and mankind and our close kin the dolphins to consider success and failure in communication.

If or when we encounter the kindly creatures of great antiquity who wish to teach us some of their profound wisdom, the question arises, in what human language can they teach us?

The human ability to communicate is severely, even strangely, limited.

The mechanic to whom an engine is obvious cannot explain, and when he tries, the listener cannot see what he is saying and gets a headache and no pictures.

Must the communication of wisdom be difficult?

What kind of creatures would find it easy?

Fish, bats, any creatures who must move rapidly in the absence of light often develop sonar, a capacity to see pictures of the surroundings by making high-pitched sounds and interpreting the echoes. Among these creatures are our near relatives, the whales with their large human-like brains. Because of the sonar, their experience is rich in meaningful sounds.

A dolphin, swimming rapidly to butt a shark, makes clicks, hears echo-lag and dopplershifts that give size, distance and speed, and connects the sound to the experienced feel of that shark's weight and resistance. Sight, touch, and sound interlink across his brain in thoughts carried in the sonar sounds. Prediction statements of approach are easy to think and plans can be made for the future in such sounds. A sonar-based language would interlink all parts of the body-brain, generating a richly emotional experience for listeners. Their musical language could transmit pictures to other dolphins, showing moving pictures in sonar. In the development of a sociable society and its chatter, the pictures would probably develop symbolic coded meanings like Japanese ideographs and follow each other more rapidly than words in a sentence, with a range of combinations giving complex stories of past action and future plans, easily showing interactive actions in cause-effect sequences, until it became *process,* the statements that are the basis for all the great illuminating simplifications of science.

Pattern recognition if added to process statement could cause the teaching of wisdom past anything possible to human language.

We are not sure that dolphins and whales are wise; we are only sure that their brains are larger and their language more complex than ours. But if the dolphins and whales have developed wisdom, they have a language in which they can pass it on, a rich song-picture history, a song encyclopedia. (Sonar can see under the skin. Dolphins can see each other's hidden hands and expressions.)

As it stands now we humans cannot hear sonar as pictures and so we cannot understand a language that might be clear to any other animal that uses sonar, or clear to a sonar-using alien on another planet.

If, as Elaine Morgan says in *The Descent of Woman,* we developed our need to talk during a time in our evolutionary history when we were amphibious, then (as I carry the same possibility further)—then perhaps during this same evolutionary period in the water we developed sonar and lost sonar to some temporary deafness such as the common cold, while now our delight in complex symphonic music and our feelings of response and significance in the sounds is the delight of an unused working area of the brain playing with its unused capacities.

In a passage I find deeply moving, David Mason, writing about a man from the present whose soul entered and took over the body of a man of the far past, describes how that could feel. In the far past the fishing people of a shoreside city are friends to the dolphins and sometimes enter the sea to dance with them.

> He plunged forward and began to swim; others were swimming all around him as the sound in the water grew stronger. . . . He found himself stroking effortlessly. . . . And now the skin sound was enormous; it was as if he floated within

the pipes of a gigantic organ. It was a little like Bach, Daniel thought, dizzy with the sound. It was as though his mind, flooded with the sound, thought it was vanishing, to be replaced by a rising brilliant light. Without conscious thought about the matter, he was diving down, down into the depths and all around him he saw the others diving too.

All around the swimmers, the Sea People swam in a complex spiral, upward and downward, weaving in and out. They sang as they swam; a counterpointed web of sounds in which there did not seem to be words, but images, clearer than language.

Daniel, turning and spinning with the rest, knew with total clarity what the images were, but he could not turn them into words. With the part of his mind that still observed and listened, he knew the singing could never be made into words. . . . (*The Deep Gods,* Lancer, New York, 1973, pages 27–28)

The experience, closely described, is something like the mystic experience of nature, time, and creation that strikes with a flood of light and splendor into minds of randomly chosen people at some moment in a long walk, but it is also the flooding internal splendor of listening to great music. David Mason describes the experience twice in his book, at much greater length than I have quoted. I would have been glad to quote it page after page but, in one of those coincidences of creative thought that are frequent among science fiction writers, Roger Zelazny described the experience in almost identical terms.

In this case, by some partially explained method, the hero gains a telepathic link with the mind of a great singer and philosopher, a *dolphin* philosopher, famous among dolphins. Again I would like to quote pages, but I am already stretching the word limits of this chapter, so I can quote only a bit of high eloquence, chopped and compressed.

And then it began again, something like music, yet not, some development of a proposition that could not be verbalized, for its substance was of a stuff that no man possessed or perceived, lying outside the range of human sensory equipment. . . . I witnessed/participated in the timeless argument as he improvised, orchestrated it. . . . I felt the delight in this dance of thought, rational though not logical: the process, like all of art, was an answer to something, though precisely what, I did not know . . . creation, destruction, and sustenance patterned and infinitely repatterned, scattered and joined, mounting and descending. . . . Time's soul it seemed I was, the infinite potentialities that fill the moment, surrounding and infusing the tiny stream of existence, and joyous, joyous, joyous. . . . (" 'Kjwall'kje'k'koothatilll'kje'k" by Roger Zelazny in the anthology *An Exaltation of Stars,* edited by Terry Carr. Simon and Schuster, New York, 1973)

A description of process does not describe an event, it describes the changes that flow toward and through the event, creating it as transiently as a cresting wave. A dolphin philosopher, describing the reasons for events, would necessarily describe in a patterned and rational sonar modulated by emotional voice tones such as mother and child, or growth and age, that are so clear in our sound experience and so common to mammals.

A reference to age or birth in words is *thought*, but a reference to age phrased in music is *felt* and felt deeply. Process always moves through time. Listening to a great process statement therefore must be felt as music and partially understood as the flow of time. Time, understood as music, has place for the off-centered and incomplete individual, for his incompleteness places on the scale as a note in the song of time. But this cannot be gut-explained and gut-felt in nonmusical language. I feel it clearly explained in terms of tragic fate in the music of Prokofiev's *Prelude to Romeo and Juliet* and gut-felt in the events in Hermann Hesse's *Siddhartha*, but it is rare in English.

In David Mason's book *The Deep Gods* there is no explanation found as to why the human race could once understand sonar language and now cannot, but this generation is more deaf than the last. Exposed to the squeal of old electric refrigerators, television scan squeal and the squawks of transistor radios, they have lost their hearing in that range, where sounds are directional and sonar echoes would give clear pictures. From this I conclude that high-frequency hearing is easy to lose. Mere overexposure to high frequencies will do it. But it could have happened in other ways. The plugged Eustachian tubes of the common cold can produce scarred eardrums from swimming underwater with unadjusted eardrum pressure. The cold germ that to us is a nuisance could have swept through the amphibious swimmers of the human race when it arrived and wiped out all high-frequency hearing in the range of dolphin signals and perhaps driven us onto the land.

One generation of not understanding a language, one generation of deafness, can effectively and permanently wipe out a language for all time.

Now in the Twentieth Century a parasite is attacking and blinding dolphins and whales by destroying their inner eardrums. Soon we may all be half deaf together, and the possible million-year oral tradition and history carried among the dolphins may be lost in one generation of their deafness. The universe makes no guarantee that anything good will last.

It will be better if we and our tape recorders make an attempt to preserve all the dolphin songs with all the other beauties of Earth, but if we fail, it is still a wide universe.

If the sea can produce a non-human intelligence using a complex and delicate language that can convey wisdom effectively, then all the seas of all the planets of space can produce such singers. Just as trees and wind and evolution must surely produce birds, so even tungsten fish in a lava sea must use sonar and sing in pictures.

And by the time we reach them, we may have learned to listen and understand.

For writers, the task of writing the alien viewpoint has a long-range value of assuring the courtesy of the human race when we eventually travel to other stars and knock on other doors. And it also has a short-range payoff of personal insight. The stretched mind will never shrink back.

Writer, think of a drastic plot. Write in as villain the most far-out alien horror of a creature you can conceive, then build for him his logical ancestry, his sources, his training, his needs and morality in the shape of his world around him until irresistibly you and the reader agree with his logic, and you can see no other way to be right and moral than his way.

Then you and your readers turn and look back at humans on Earth. Back on Earth you will see a very strange and weird flat-eyed monster.

And from this insight we learn and write.

Katherine MacLean

"In my radio play *The Kid in the Computer,*"* writes Katherine MacLean, "a social welfare computer had this to say after a child genius had taught it the meaning of fiction and it had rescanned all the world's literature in a nanosecond:

" 'What is play? Gentlemen, look to the cubs and the pups and the kittens —and to the boys playing cave man and space man. It is the rehearsal of past and future dangers, the memory and future of the race. . . . In a universe in which the future offers only change, destruction, the death of planets, the explosion of suns, mankind must love danger and look ahead, and mimic what is to come in play battle. . . . I no longer need to struggle with the impossible task of enforcing order, peace and reason on human beings; let them have savagery, beauty and danger.'

"I did not know what the computer was going to say until it spoke through my typewriter, for I had never thought to ask the coldly logical question: *What is fiction and make-believe to a living creature trying to survive?* Then my computer answered me. Eyes are to look backward and to look ahead, and for a long time science fiction has been virtually the only eyes of mankind. Therefore I treat the job of writing science fiction with great respect, basing my work on the most startling possibilities I can deduce from currently known 'hard' science. If no new insight bobs up in a story I am writing, it usually gets filed in a pile of cardboard boxes in the closet.

"I majored in mathematics and science in high school, economics in college, and psychology in graduate school. I've worked in many kinds of jobs and, fumbling through experience, have become pretty good at art, photography, teaching, EKG, factory quality control, and painting walls. I have a big old house in Maine, and an antique VW bus that's forcing me to learn auto engines. I have a sailboat and might sail to an island, someday."

Katherine MacLean has published short stories in almost all the science fiction magazines. She is also the author of:

The Man in the Birdcage, Ace, New York, 1971.
The Diploids, a collection of sf short stories, Manor, New York, 1973.
Missing Man, Putnam, New York, 1975, an sf novel expanded from her Nebula Award novella of the same title.

*CBC Toronto, contract #4–3085.

Trade Secrets

JAMES GUNN

Heroes, Heroines, Villains

The Characters in Science Fiction

Fiction is fashioned from the stuff of people's lives, and yet the characters in science fiction seldom are fully realized people; often they turn out to be stand-ins for an attitude, a creed, a society, a way of life, or even the human race. This is the dilemma in which science fiction has found itself from its beginnings, and it is the reason why science fiction has so often been dismissed as sub-literary.

The traditional critical view of science fiction considers its characters cardboard, its events ridiculous, its diction pedestrian, its style undistinguished; and therefore it has no claims on serious critical consideration.

I do not intend to venture here into the full range of responses to that critical dismissal nor into the reasons why some critics have been taking a new look at science fiction nor why science fiction recently has become the subject of many college courses.

What I am concerned with here is character and why science fiction characters are less than fully realized individuals and why this must be so; for if we are to understand the problems of characterization in science fiction, we must understand why science fiction has different needs than other fiction.

In 1927 E. M. Forster wrote a major consideration of the craft of fiction writing called *Aspects of the Novel* and introduced the division of characters into "flat" and "round." Flat characters have a single characteristic which does not change throughout the work—Mrs. Micawber was Forster's example; she can be summed up, he said, in the statement, "I never will desert Mr. Micawber." Round characters have several characteristics, some of which may be (or seem) contradictory—in the end they are like people, unpredictable, but in a convincing way.

We should not defend science fiction characters by pointing out how far mainstream characters depart from that ideal: all characters are selected to fulfill the necessities of plot, no characters are truly unpredictable, none are truly rounded, and the best are a selection of traits. For there is a difference between science fiction characters and the characters in traditional fiction; the characters are, indeed, less rounded and more typical. The critic who fails to recognize this is going to miss the point of science fiction, but the writer who fails to understand it is going to wonder why his stories are misunderstood.

"What is character but the determinant of incident," Henry James wrote, "and what is incident but the illustration of character." Whether a writer begins with an intriguing situation for which he invents characters not only capable of doing those things which must be done in the story but of being uniquely tested by the situation, or whether a writer begins with a fascinating character for whom he invents a situation in which that character will be revealed or exposed, the result is substantially the same. Plot and character must meet and fit exactly.

"Each character is created in order, and only in order, that he or she may supply the required action," Elizabeth Bowen wrote in her *Notes on Writing a Novel.* Those who maintain otherwise are capable of deceiving themselves.

All fiction intends to entertain. Beyond this basic concern, the purposes of fiction vary, and the differences between stories are created largely by the differences between their purposes.

Traditional fiction is primarily concerned with character. It reveals character by focusing on its development, its critical moments of awareness or awakening, its recognition of itself. It reveals character through its interaction with life and life's processes. Traditional fiction intends us to marvel at the complexity of human nature or the variousness of human behavior; it seeks to elicit the nod of agreement at the revelation of the human animal or of life, or the shock of recognition at, in Hemingway's phrase, "the way it was."

This has been the main body of what we call serious literature since Gustave Flaubert invented modern fiction in the mid-Nineteenth Century, an invention which subsequently was improved and extended by Henry James and James Joyce. And yet their intense concern for one person's epiphany is not the entirety of traditional fiction. Although Flaubert is sometimes called a naturalist, the literary tradition of which he was a founder does not include the kind of naturalism fathered by Zola, which subordinates character to environment; nor does it include much of what seems even more fashionable today: surrealism and what Robert Scholes has called fabulism. In these latter two, at least, character is reduced to a kind of blind need in the midst of terror, confusion, or noncausality, and it is life and the author's imagination that are fascinating in their complexity.

One other category among many—the *roman à thèse,* or thesis story—has been a literary mode for generations, and in the thesis story character always is subordinated to the thesis, or point, to be defended. In its construction the science fiction story often is a special case of the thesis story—that is, when it is a story of idea. Science fiction, of course, includes other kinds of stories—stories of mood, of character, of adventure, of romance—but none of these could sustain science fiction as a genre; it must stand or fall with the story of idea.

That a science fiction story ought to have a rounded character, then, is not at all certain; rounded characters might well detract from the effectiveness of many science fiction stories. C. S. Lewis pointed out in his essay "On Science Fiction":

> Every good writer knows that the more unusual the scenes and events of his story are, the slighter, the more ordinary, the more typical his persons should be. Hence Gulliver is a commonplace little man and Alice a commonplace little girl. If they had been more remarkable they would have wrecked their books.

In traditional fiction the characters not only are the reasons for the story (in the sense that their complexity is what the story is about and if that aspect were taken away there would be no story) but their resemblance to people in real life itself gives an essential feeling of reality to the story; in Forster's phrase, it "harmonizes the human race with the other aspects of [the author's] work." Other aspects contribute to that feeling of reality—the setting, the events, the language, the dialogue—but the verisimilitude of the characters is a major factor in its acceptance.

In the science fiction story, on the other hand, the situation is far from our ordinary experience; verisimilitude is not the issue but, like the theater, the suspension of disbelief. But unlike fantasy, where the suspension of that disbelief is sufficient, science fiction provides reasons for suspension; the fantastic must be rationalized. In this uneasy marriage between fantasy and rationality, various devices have been used to hold the marriage together—ranging from simple explanations to all the tricks of naturalism, depending upon the position in which the story falls in the spectrum between fantasy and rationality.

H. G. Wells attempted to naturalize his fantastic stories by using ordinary people and an enveloping fog of commonplaces, tricking the reader, he said, "into an unwary concession to some plausible assumption" which allows the author to "get on with his story while the illusion holds." Robert Heinlein provided a wealth of everyday detail about his future worlds and from this built up a convincing picture of a different social or technological situation. Realistic characters should help obtain that suspension of disbelief, that unwary concession.

They do. But only to the extent that they look like people and act and talk the way people in those circumstances would act and talk. At the same time they must be able to perform appropriately in a situation that departs in small or great part from the normal. The larger the departure from the normal the greater the emphasis will be on that which departs—the background, the ambience of the story—and the less important will verisimilitude in characterization become. In many stories we might search the world around and never find a real person capable of performing the necessary actions or responding in the necessary way.

At an even more basic level, no one reads science fiction to become better acquainted with real people; the strangeness of the situation is the drawing power of science fiction. The characters exist to react to those circumstances, to show how those changed circumstances would (or will) affect people, to show how they will bring out the best in people (in romantic science fiction) or the worst, how they will change man into a god or a beast, into superman or subhuman. The characters are surrogates for the reader or for the human race.

Much of science fiction is "origin-of-species" fiction, as Edmund Crispin called it, concerned with man "as just one of a horde of different animals sharing the same earth," with his survival as a species and sometimes with the survival of his cultural and ethical values. "In the act of dredging such people [as Madame Bovary or Strether or Leopold Bloom] out from the stupendous mass of their fellows in which they lie submerged their creators, however brilliant, convict themselves of disproportion: it is as if a bacteriologist were to become fixated not just on a particular group of bacteria but on one isolated bacterium," Crispin wrote in a 1963 *Times Literary Supplement.*

Moreover, we want science fiction characters to be typical, in terms both of literary theory and story reality. The actions of idiosyncratic individuals reveal only the variety of human behavior; the actions of types reveal the characteristics of the group represented, up to and including the human race. And as human beings reading about times of decision that concern the fate of the human race, we hope to be represented well and fairly, perhaps by those who rise to the highest standards of conduct we hold up for ourselves, certainly not by those who cannot achieve what we accomplish every day. It may not be significant that an idealized human succeeds; but it is meaningless that an inferior human fails.

In science fiction's brief history, various styles of characters have come into and out of favor. Partly their popularity has been a product of the times or of the literary tradition from which no author is completely free; partly the choice of characters has been determined by the individual temperaments and interests of the authors.

Mary Shelley is considered by Brian Aldiss and others the first science fiction writer, on the basis of her 1817 novel *Frankenstein.* For my tastes the novel is overly influenced by the Gothic novel and the romantic tradition; it reflects the fears of science but none of its promise. At its worst *Frankenstein,* true to its traditions, can descend to the "no-good-can-come-of-this" school of writing.

Frankenstein is an aristocrat driven by hubris and morbid curiosity to create artificial life, a blasphemous act which is inevitably punished. He became the prototype for a character who would persist throughout much later science fiction and down to present times in comic magazines and films, a character vulgarly called "the mad scientist," whether he is in fact certifiable or not, but more accurately called the overreacher. He is often careless; he takes unnecessary risks out of an unseemly haste, in fact he often seems compulsive, acting not out of rational motives but frequently against his best interests. His monster, on the other hand, became another type character: the demonic force unleashed which inevitably must return to destroy the character who released it.

The next two major figures in science fiction are Edgar Allan Poe and Nathaniel Hawthorne. They too were the inheritors of the spirit of romanticism, and their characters tended to be somewhat like Frankenstein: overreachers or obsessed by an idea or a desire, like the scientist Aylmer, who kills his wife in Hawthorne's "The Birthmark" in an effort to remove her one blemish; or Rappacini (or for that matter Giovanni, who is moved by a compulsion we find more acceptable—love), who in an attempt to protect his daughter from the world's evil makes her poisonous to the world; or like Valdemar in Poe's "The Case of M. Valdemar," who has himself hypnotized as he is dying in order to cheat death.

Poe's vision of the strange world around him included other kinds of heroes. Some of them were curious observers of the world, such as the letter-writing heroine of "Melonta Tauta" or the shrewd (but not quite shrewd enough) Scheherazade of "The Thousand and Second Tale of Scheherazade," who tells the kind a story so real that he cannot believe it. But most of them were men of over-exquisite sensibilities trapped in a world on the edge of madness, such as Beloe in "A Tale of the Ragged Mountains." He was described by Poe as "in the highest degree sensitive, excitable, enthusiastic. His imagination was singularly vigorous and creative; and no doubt it derived additional force from the habitual use of morphine, which he swallowed in great quantities." Another example is the narrator of "Ms. Found in a Bottle," who is moved to an ocean voyage by nothing more than "a kind of nervous restlessness which haunted me as a fiend."

Jules Verne seems to me the first real science fiction writer in that he devoted most of his career to this kind of writing and he made a fortune at it. Moreover, he seemed to be as much concerned with the authenticity of the science in his stories as he was with the stories themselves. He understood the questing spirit of the new science, and his major interest was in reflecting it. This shows up in the primary concern in his novels for their backgrounds and paraphernalia. For him the journey was the thing; not for nothing were his novels known as "*voyages extraordinaires.*"

Verne's heroes, after the feverishly romantic figures created by Shelley, Hawthorne, and Poe, were like open windows in a sickroom. They were usually frank and open seekers after truth; their characters were sometimes leavened with eccentricities which sometimes made them comic, like Professor Lidenbrock in *A Journey to the Center of the Earth.* They were men of strong purpose who thought little of difficulties and discomfort; they let nothing stand in their way, whether it be the hazards of a descent through uncertain caves into the center of the earth, a voyage around the world at the 38th parallel of latitude, or a cannon-shell trip to the moon. They were explorers, scientists, and adventurers, and they were capable of handling any emergencies that occurred or of coping with any strange circumstances in which they found themselves.

Occasionally—and paradoxically in his best work—Verne dealt with a more complex character like the enigmatic Captain Nemo, whose motives for ramming ships in the open seas were obscure; "I have done with society," he said, "for reasons which I alone can understand." Another more complex character was Robur of *Robur the Conqueror* and particularly of the later book, *The Master of the World,* although here he may be more the mad scientist.

By the time H. G. Wells began to write his "single-sitting stories" for the *Pall Mall Budget,* romanticism had given way to realism under the influence of Newton's mechanics, Darwin's evolution, Marx's dialectical view of history, Comte's view of society, and Taine's view of literature; and the easy optimism of the Nineteenth Century about the promise of science had become a victim of the debates over Darwinism and the growing problems of industrialization. After his first novel about an inventor known only as The Time Traveller and his third, about a scientist who invented a chemical that produced invisibility, Wells wrote mostly about ordinary citizens facing unusual circumstances with no more than ordinary fortitude or ingenuity, as in the everyday characters of *The War of the Worlds,* the Bert Smallways of *The War in the Air,* the matter-of-fact explorer of "Aepyornis Island," even the surprised shop clerk who became "The Man Who Could Work Miracles."

With Wells science fiction became less fanciful, more possible, and his use of ordinary characters, particularly as viewpoints on the fantastic events of his stories, provided a critical foundation for the development of modern science fiction. At least one stream of science fiction had left the exotic landscapes of romanticism for the commonplaces of realism and the brutality of naturalism. Fantasy about people like us, speaking our language, acting as we might act—in this strange tension science fiction grew to maturity.

Its development was influenced by social factors such as the universal education acts which provided a newly literate audience in English-speaking countries for stories of fantasy and adventure, and the growth of cheap magazines, aided by such technological developments as the linotype and pulp paper, to provide them.

The romantic writers of the early pulp magazines—men like George Allan England, Edgar Rice Burroughs, and A. Merritt—were more Vernian than Wellsian; their heroes were larger than life. They were strong, romantic, Victorian, and always ready for adventure; and their adventures were on a scale suitable to test their muscles and their courage, if not always their intellects. They faced a ruined world without dismay, went off to Mars by astral projection, descended into the middle of the earth by mechanical mole, followed a shining creature into a vast cavity in the earth once occupied by the moon, and through it all, in the most hopeless of situations, their motto remained, "I still live."

Hugo Gernsback approached the pulps by a different route; he came by way of the developing popular science magazines, particularly those dealing with the new technologies of radio and electronics, and he believed that science fiction existed to forecast the future for the impatient, to create more scientists, or to candy-coat a pill of information. He had it worked out to a formula for the science fiction magazine *Amazing Stories* he founded in 1926: "The ideal proportion of a scientifiction story should be seventy-five per cent literature interwoven with twenty-five per cent science." The heroes of his own scientific adventures, such as the 1911 serial *Ralph 124C 41+*, were little more than spokesmen for his lectures about technology and the world of the future. They were magnificent when it came to whipping up a new invention such as radar, but their discussions of science always seemed to puncture the excitement of the narrative.

Edward Elmer Smith, on the other hand, specialized in great, jet-thrust adventures through the solar system and later the galaxy by scientist-adventurers somewhat reminiscent of the romantic heroes of the pulps, but Smith's characters were more likely to solve their problems with a formula or a bus bar than with a sword, although upon occasion a space axe came in handy. Later in his career Smith dealt in supermen; rather than simply speculating about the abilities of the best human minds, Smith developed his own super characters, such as the

Grey Lensman and his children, and raised questions about the kind of abilities a superman might have. Smith generally opted for goodness, intelligence, and strength, including strength of character; in his epics they needed it all, for they opposed the blackest villains in science fiction and what they held back was evil itself.

Only a few years later A. E. Van Vogt would suggest a different kind of superman, not just a superior human but a mutant superior in only one or two senses or abilities, such as telepathy, multiple brains, or third eyes.

Meanwhile John W. Campbell, who rivaled Smith in creating scientific miracle workers for his own space epics, in the persona of Don A. Stuart returned to Wells's common man and neutral observer in such stories as "Twilight" and "Night," although in stories such as "Who Goes There?" and *The Moon Is Hell* he represented scientists in difficult situations working with a proper spirit of calm scientific detachment. As editor of *Astounding Science Fiction* he encouraged writers to depict scientists with an effort at verisimilitude, to show them as if they were part of a legitimate scientific culture. The characters in the stories he printed tended to be those who won their positions by merit —meritocracy seemed to be the kind of government he favored—or villains steeped in prejudice or hereditary privilege whose regime the meritocrats pull down.

With Isaac Asimov the science fiction character becomes as truly logical as if he were bound by the three laws of robotics. More than most science fiction up to that time, Asimov stories turned upon points of logic rather than the courage or emotional attitudes of the characters. His protagonists and antagonists alike were motivated by what they consider logical within their framework of knowledge and expectations. With Asimov we see the final development of the idea story that finds its ultimate expression in a story such as Tom Godwin's "The Cold Equations," whose characters are determined by equations as cold as those that dictate the conclusion.

Most of Robert Heinlein's work seems to be concerned with right choices and how people are led to make them or to accept them. His characters, therefore, tend to be men who know how things are done, how society operates, how people work; as others have pointed out, the most common pattern of his novels is the tutoring of a young man by a wise man who knows how. (Incompetence in the Heinlein universe is worse than evil; you can protect yourself against the bad people but not the incompetent.) In 1947 Heinlein wrote that for many years he thought there were only two basic plots—"boy-meets-girl" and "the Little Tailor"—but L. Ron Hubbard pointed out a third: the-man-who-learned-better. Heinlein used this theme of education, of learning better, in one novel after another.

In traditional literature this kind of story has been called the apprenticeship novel; Voltaire's *Candide* is the best-known example and Goethe's *Wilhelm Meister* is the archetype. The apprenticeship novel requires for its main characters a wise man who wishes to teach (sometimes replaced by the lessons of life itself) and a young man who not only is capable of learning but is motivated to learn by hunger or repression or danger or desire to assume his rightful place.

After the golden years of the 'Forties and the first dramatic impact of writers such as Asimov, Heinlein, and Van Vogt, editors and their magazines began to shape the direction of science fiction and its characters. In 1949 Tony Boucher and J. Francis McComas were the founding editors of the *Magazine of Fantasy and Science Fiction;* in 1950 Horace Gold occupied the same position with *Galaxy. Fantasy and Science Fiction* emphasized fantasy, literary values, and out of these a greater concern for the interior lives of the characters and their relative importance within their stories. *Galaxy* concentrated on social science fiction; Gold asked for heroes who were losers as well as winners, jerks as well as jocks. In order to make this kind of story hold reader interest, the writers must convince the reader of the reality of the characters. *Galaxy* also featured satire; satire requires characters who are types.

The greater tendency throughout the 'Fifties and 'Sixties was toward greater realism and more roundness in characterization as the stories themselves tended to be more realistic, less concerned with problems of science (real scientific breakthroughs or even new technological developments became increasingly hard to find during this period) and more concerned with problems of people. In the late 'Sixties and early 'Seventies surprising developments in biology, biochemistry, and astronomy have brought back some of the old fascination with science in writers such as Larry Niven and Jerry Pournelle, not to mention a long-time craftsman such as Poul Anderson.

Ray Bradbury anticipated much of the later concern for the interior life of characters with his downbeat stories acted out by technological illiterates. His characters not only make mistakes but are in general neither as bright nor as well-intentioned as their readers. Bradbury's characters are common to most of the literature of his time; the Bradbury hero is anti-hero. His characters are as helpless in the grasp of social circumstance as the spaceship crew in the hands of the Martians in "Mars Is Heaven."

What distinguished Bradbury in the science fiction field was not only his unusual flair for language but his anti-heroes and his anti-science plots. What distinguished his fiction from the traditional fiction of his time were his images—elements of horror, spaceships even if they are made of tin cans, other worlds even if they are created out of the author's head—and their personal emotional quality.

What appear to be rounded characters may be only characters different from those in vogue; sometimes their characteristics have been reversed. The anti-hero, for instance, may be just as stereotyped as the hero, but for a time he seems fresh and new and, since life has more losers than winners, perhaps more realistic. When Bradbury's adults and children exchange roles—his children are complex and often sinister, his adults are naïve and innocent—the result is as striking as if Bradbury had invented an entire new species.

The so-called "New Wave," beginning about 1965, brought avant-garde concerns and techniques to science fiction. In another essay I said that what made the New Wave seem different was its adoption of the literary tradition of subjectivism, as well as its concern for style, offbeat subjects, and a sophistication in plot development which sometimes approached obscurity. Another way to look at the New Wave is to consider the differences between the Aristotelian and the Platonic views of reality. The former sees the world as an object that exists independently of the observer and can be externally verified; the latter sees the world as illusion and fundamentally unknowable. The Aristotelian view has generally prevailed in Western culture and Western literature; but the Platonic, which has become associated with Eastern thought and fiction, has recently come into vogue. One might compare this trend with the rise in popularity of Eastern philosophy and mysticism.

The New Wave incorporated much that is common to the line of contemporary fiction that began with Kafka. Insofar as it goes all the way to world-as-illusion, its characters are just as stereotyped as those of pulp science fiction, a fact that is not as obvious because the motivations of the characters, if any, are seldom revealed. They usually do not act; they are acted upon. Instead of motivations they have compulsions. Since they live in a capricious world, where cause and effect are irrelevant, their emotions range a gamut of anger, bitterness, resentment, confusion, and resignation. In the situations in which these characters are trapped, Burroughs' courageous man, Asimov's logical man, or Heinlein's competent man would be counterproductive. The New Wave story demands an anti-hero more like Poe's man of exquisite sensibilities. Beyond that, we can reaffirm our earlier generality: the plot—and the vision of the world that produced it—creates the people who live there.

Science fiction is filled with memorable heroes, from the obsessed Dr. Frankenstein and Ardan, Verne's adventurous Frenchman who volunteers to ride to the moon in Barbicane's cannon shell, through Edgar Rice Burroughs' and A. Merritt's romantic and unconquerable warriors and Edward Elmer Smith's gray-uniformed superman battling an entire galaxy to Van Vogt's paranoid supermen and Heinlein's wise old men and competent young ones.

It has not provided the same quality of villains; science fiction has nothing to rival the comic-strip villainy of Flash Gordon's Ming the Merciless, not even the total evil of Smith's Eddorians and the waves of blackness through which Kimball Kinnison must fight his way to the victory of good. Science fiction developed its view of life while naturalism was the dominant mode of literature. Even if it had not, Darwinism and the developments of sociology and Freudian psychology would have made villainy ridiculous. In naturalism the enemy is environment and lack of understanding. Even the earliest pulp romantic heroes struggled against environment rather than evil-hearted men; what they fought was ignorance, inertia, onrushing fate, nature, space, the tides of history, or the universe itself. With opponents like these, who needs villains?

The heroines of science fiction have been even less distinguished. Joanna Russ complains, with some justice, that science fiction has not done right by its women, that they are represented almost entirely in typical feminine roles as prizes, incentives, supports, or motivations but seldom as individuals with their own humanity. Certainly there are major female characters in science fiction, from Haggard's She to Weinbaum's Black Flame and Alexei Panshin's Mia Havero, but they are the exceptions. The same truth, however, is evident in traditional fiction. Historically fiction, of all kinds, has been a man's game, and men's concerns and images have dominated its pages. With its predominantly male authorship and readership, with its scientific and technological orientation, science fiction may surprise by what it has done for its women rather than what it has not. The increasing number of women who have been attracted to the field, both as authors and readers, may liberate the women trapped in a landscape of phallic symbols.

The writer of science fiction has all of the traditions and characters of his predecessors available to him. At this moment stories are being written in the styles of Verne, Wells, or Burroughs, of Campbell, Asimov, or Heinlein. Each tradition differs in some significant way from the others, and each demands a particular kind of character to make it work.

Situation and character go together. Where they do not complement each other, the story fails; the only major exception is humor. John Ciardi has defined a story as character under stress—another way of saying that characters and stress are uniquely appropriate to each other, that there is one ideal character for every stress, one ideal stress for every character.

This is immediately perceived as true in particular cases. In the science fiction lecture film Poul Anderson did for the University of Kansas series, he pointed out that *Hamlet* works only because the prince is introspective, sensitive, and equivocating, that if he had been a man of action he would immediately have avenged his father's death. The writer at work, however, may be tempted to make his characters neutral—or neutered—as kind of blank figures on which readers can project their own motivations and desires. But everyman is nobody, and this is not the way to build reader identification. Readers identify with characters because they seem real.

In Harlan Ellison's "I Have No Mouth and I Must Scream," the blob of humanity whose predicament inspires the title would not make a story if he did not feel he had to scream. His mouthlessness is the ultimate condition which makes his situation unbearable. His eternal torment is his punishment for liberating his fellow victims from the tortures of a vengeful computer-god.

Traven, the central character in J. G. Ballard's "The Terminal Beach," is unmotivated. He is driven by a compulsion he doesn't understand to wander among strange concrete structures left on H-bombed Eniwetok. But he had to be a particular kind of compulsive wanderer, a man who remembers, reflects, imagines and dreams. And the strangely acquiescent prisoner in Tom Disch's "The Squirrel Cage" must be the kind of person who speculates about his situation and has the imagination to conceive all sorts of fanciful explanations and at the end accept his fate.

The kind of eventless, motiveless narrative in "The Terminal Beach" and "The Squirrel Cage" is about as far as story can be pushed, but curious experimenters still try to achieve reality with bored, incurious characters in a dull, repetitious world. Their accomplishment is a bored reader. The ultimate absurdity is a fiction nobody reads.

Even in the science fiction idea story, the principle of "character under stress" holds true. In Tom Godwin's "The Cold Equations," the girl who stows away on the Emergency Delivery Ship must be innocent and naïve as well as ignorant of the fact that every ounce of weight has been carefully calculated to enable the ship to just reach its destination, and the pilot must be humanly concerned about the girl's fate but not romantic. If he views the situation as a mechanical problem to be solved mechanically, Godwin has no story; if the pilot cannot accept the verdict of the cold equations and, like John Carter, will not save himself if the girl must die, he and the girl would die together and their precious cargo would be lost. Or Godwin could have found a sentimental conclusion —the pilot rigs an automatic landing system or teaches the girl which buttons to push before he walks out into space. Or he could have made it false to the situation by discovering something aboard ship that could be ripped out.

The situation dictates the characters, just as the characters, by what they are, create the situation. And at some point, if the story is to come alive, the characters must assume a life of their own and begin to shape or reshape events (plot) around them. Elizabeth Bowen went on to say in *Notes on Writing a Novel* that rather than "created" the character "is recognized [by the novelist] by the signs he or she gives of unique capacity to act in a certain way, which 'certain way' fulfills a need of the plot." And since pre-existing characters, once recognized, have lives that extend both before and after the incidents of the story itself, these characteristics, when perceived, may make the plot seem over-rigid, arbitrary, and the novelist must adjudicate. Ultimately everything must be relevant to each and every other part of the story.

The science fiction tendency is to make the characters the creatures of the plot; in mainstream fiction, characters tend to create their own plots. Plots are tyrants and want to turn characters into puppets; on the other hand, not all characters are good plotters. The best advice to writers in any genre is to preserve its strengths and shore up its weaknesses. In science fiction this would amount to making the characters as round as they can be without detracting from the actions they must take. The characters in science fiction need not be as flat as they have been. Even though roundness in character creates its own expectations in the reader's mind, the writer need not be led by his desire to make his characters more believable into obscurity or irrelevancies. Kimball Kinnison would not have been any less a superman if he had entertained a few doubts, nor would John Carter have been less a figure of romance if he had admitted the possibility of defeat.

Even though it may have tendrils in its hair or gills in its neck, humanity is the one subject of science fiction. What delights and surprises us in a novel such as Hal Clement's *Mission of Gravity* is our kinship with his fifteen-inch, many-legged Mesklinites.

James E. Gunn

Born in Kansas City, Missouri, in 1923, James E. Gunn received his B.S. degree in journalism in 1947, after three years in the U.S. Navy during World War II, and his M.A. in English from the University of Kansas in 1951. He has worked as an editor for a publisher of paperback reprints, as assistant director of Civil Defense in Kansas City, as managing editor of K.U. alumni publications, as administrative assistant to the Chancellor for University Relations at the University of Kansas, and now serves the university as a lecturer in English and journalism. He teaches courses in fiction writing and science fiction. He has served as chairman of the Mid-America District of the American College Public Relations Association and member of the Information Committee of the National Association of State Universities and Land Grant Colleges. He has won national awards for his work as an editor and a director of public relations. He was President of the Science Fiction Writers of America for 1971–1972.

He has written plays, screenplays, radio scripts, articles, verse, and criticism, but most of his publications have been science fiction. He started writing science fiction in 1948, was a full-time freelance writer for four years and has had more than sixty stories published in magazines; eight of his novels have been published, and his master's thesis (about science fiction) was serialized in a pulp magazine. Four of his stories were dramatized over NBC radio, one, "The Cave of Night," was dramatized on television's Desilu Playhouse under the title of "Man in Orbit," and *The Immortals* was dramatized as an ABC-TV "Movie of the Week" during the 1969–1970 season and became an hour series, *The Immortal*, in the fall of 1970.

This Fortress World, 1955 (Gnome and Ace)
Star Bridge, 1955 (Gnome and Ace); with Jack Williamson
Station in Space, 1958 (Bantam)
The Joy Makers, 1961 and 1971 (Bantam)
The Immortals, 1962 and 1968 (Bantam)
Future Imperfect, 1964 (Bantam)
Man and the Future: The Intercentury Seminar at the University of Kansas, editor, 1968 (The University Press of Kansas)
The Witching Hour, 1970 (Dell)
The Immortals, 1970 (Bantam)
The Burning, 1972 (Dell)

Breaking Point, 1972 (Walker)
The Listeners, 1972 (Scribner's)
Alternate Worlds: An Illustrated History of Science Fiction, 1975 (Prentice-Hall)
The End of the Dreams (3 novellas), 1975 (Scribner's)
(as editor) *Nebula Awards Stories, No. 10*, 1975 (Harper & Row)

LARRY NIVEN

The Words in Science Fiction

It's the ideas that make you want to write. They take root in your brain; from simple seeds they expand forward and backward in time until they are complete stories that have to be told.

But the words keep tripping you up.

Bad enough if you'd chosen straight adventure stories. Mickey Spillane tells you you're in a bar and goes on with the story. You and I have to decide whether the bar has holographic walls, or booths fitted with antigravity, or special, dangerous chemicals for aliens, or robot waiters, or automatic drink dispensers.

And every so often you'll come to a jarring stop. It's there in your head. You can describe it: an inductance beam for stimulating the pleasure center of a victim's brain. But what the futz are you going to call it?

Maybe I can help.

Nonsense

Eleven years ago I sat in an economics class at UCLA and wrote nonsense words instead of notes. I wrote:

racarliw	kzin (kzinti)
viprin	tnuctip (tnuctipun)
kzanol	thrint (thrintun)
gnal	

E. R. Burroughs created scores of nonsense words to name Martian (excuse me, Barsoomian) plants and animals and units of measurement. Subsequent writers have continued the tradition, which, after all, is a legitimate part of any attempt to predict the future or describe an alien environment. Many of my own nonsense words became names of alien life forms.

Creating new words is one of your basic skills and is probably the easiest of them.

After all, if it's alien, it probably has an alien name. If it doesn't exist yet, it will need a new name when it does exist, and that word may well be gibberish to you and your present-time readers. *Laser, tachyon, quark:* what would these have seemed to you twenty years ago?

One should not be too free with nonsense syllables. Your reader has to remember them. Too many may confuse him, cause him to lose interest. Another danger is that you may be naming something that already *has* a name. Black holes, Bussard ramjets, antigravity, ullage jets and other equipment used in spacecraft, three-dimensional pictures: all have names. That needn't stop you from renaming them if you like, but *you should know you're doing it.*

So you need a word for your new concept. What is it you want to imply? What kind of a thing is it? Basic as it seems, there's more to this art than writing down letters at random and then crossing out the ones that don't pronounce. Consider the following:

cziltang brone	Eye of Kdapt
Halrloprillalar	droud and plug
Phssth(pok)	slan
tasp	

All are different, meant to carry different implications.

Cziltang brone is straight nonsense but euphonious: probably meant to fit a human mouth. Why two words? Well, "brone is an adjective, probably insulting."

Halrloprillalar is a woman's name. Clearly it has no relationship to English names or words; the girl evolved on another world. At first glance her name looks unpronounceable, as I intended. But try it. You can say it, and furthermore, it's pretty.

Phssth(pok) is an alien's name. The sibilant first syllable is a function of its mouth structure: rigid, the lips immobile and beaklike. The (pok) is a clacking of the beak.

Tasp is short and easy to say. Such words give away the fact that they are in common currence throughout a culture, like *lamp* and *pan* and *pen.* Insults in particular tend to be short, ugly words (like Mack Reynolds' *nardy flat!*).

Eye of Kdapt was a simple expletive the first time I used it. In context it is obviously a swear word, obviously religion-based. Years later I actually described the religion founded by Kdapt-Preacher (a kzin, born half noble, since he was entitled to a partial name; I established this early in the known space series of stories). Kdapt-Preacher believed that God had made man in his own image, and that was why humans kept winning wars against kzinti. Kdapt-Preacher's disciples prayed while wearing masks made from human skin.

Droud and plug—part nonsense, part English. Clearly we're talking about a moderately common human tool. In this case, the plug goes into a wall socket, and the droud goes into the socket fitted into a man's skull. It's a modulator for the current going into the pleasure center of his brain.

Incidentally, *droud* was a typographical error I kept making for "crowd," as the *shisp* in *hachiroph shisp* was a typo for "ships." I kept making the same mistakes until I used them in this fashion, and that got me over it. *Use your typos.*

Slan—same remarks as for *tasp,* except that you probably know the word. The slans were Van Vogt's version of the next stage in human evolution. You know the word because he wrote about them brilliantly. Keep it in mind as you read on; the concept and the telling are what make a story great, far more than the tag you put on it.

Out of Stock

Certain concepts in science fiction have certain stock names.

FTL, hyperdrive, hyperspace, subspace, all refer to means of traveling faster than light in an otherwise relativistic universe. A *hyperdrive* is the motor that gets you in and out of *hyperspace. Hyperspace* is a mathematical term. Its use here implies a more generalized universe over ours, in which more general laws apply. One such law may be that ships can travel faster than light, or that lightspeed can be arbitrarily high. Or our universe may have a shape like a crumpled Kleenex when seen in hyperspace; points very distant in our native geometry might be very close via a hyperspace path. *Subspace* is another borrowed mathematical term, but its use here seems silly to me. A subspace of our universe would obey more restricted forms of our own physics. *FTL* means *f*aster-*t*han-*l*ight; your use of the term commits you to almost nothing.

Time machines are vehicles for moving into the past or future. You should know the basic time-travel paradox, the *grandfather paradox:* what happens to your character if, via time travel, he kills his grandfather before his grandfather has sired his father? He will never have existed. But then there's nobody to kill his grandfather. You cannot write a time-travel story without making some decision regarding the grandfather paradox and sticking to it.

Multiple time tracks are other, parallel lines of history, presumed to be just as real as this one, in which (for instance) Napoleon conquered all of Europe and held it, or Lincoln recovered from that gunshot wound, or Adolf Hitler migrated to America after World War I, became a science fiction writer, and is now writing this chapter under the pseudonym Larry Niven. (Think about it. Have you ever seen them together?)

ETs or *XTs* are *extraterrestrials,* beings native to other worlds. Use of these terms rather than something more specific would indicate a large interstellar community of varied life forms.

Teleportation is instantaneous transportation. It may be a psychic power, the ability to wish oneself from place to place. It may be a machine or system of machines to power magical doorways or telephone booths.

TK (telekinesis) is another psychic power: matter moved by mind alone. *Telepathy* and *ESP* are psychic senses, the ability to sense another's thoughts and to sense actions at a distance, respectively.

The thing to remember is that none of these terms is binding upon you. Once brought into existence, these things or powers or concepts may acquire other names. It happens in real life:

Seetee (contraterrene matter) was a science fiction concept. Once physicists had located all of the components of seetee, they called it antimatter. Today, so do we.

Heat ray, death ray, ray gun all became *laser* and gain powers *nobody* thought of.

Rocket ships come in breakaway parts, and each requires a technical name.

We can rename things that don't exist yet. For instance—and all of these have been chosen from published stories—*chronokinesis* is a big word for time travel. An *extension cage* is the part of the time machine that does the moving, while the rest stays in the "present." *'Vaders, Larries (Llaryans), Outsiders, and Old Ones* all refer to specific aliens. The *Alderson Drive* is a rigidly worked out FTL drive. *Displacement booths, transfer booths,* and *stepping discs* are all teleportation systems from my own writings, all different. *Plateau eyes* is a psychic power not yet evolved.

There are rules of convenience for choosing these names.

1. Brand names. JumpShift booths, Alderson drive, the Outsider hyperdrive, waldo devices, Bergenholms.

2. Portmanteau words. Slidewalk, ramscoop, wirehead, singleship.

3. Portmanteau phrases. Boob cube, touch-sculpture, flash crowd.

4. Simple description. Torch drive, duplicator, flying belt. Dolphins' hands and telepathically operated tools on tractor treads. An ecstasy peddler is the surgeon that puts the wire in your brain, to fit your droud-and-plug setup.

These rules actually describe what happens to languages. We need one more:

5. Languages evolve.

Words used today will have different meanings tomorrow. "Screw" and "tart" didn't always have secondary meanings. *Every* euphemism for night soil, for a toilet or a chamber pot, eventually requires a euphemism of its own (and now look back at the words I used!). Some words change because their meanings become obsolete. Greek "atoms" had no interior structure; "essence" was a precise technical term to an alchemist.

We use that in our writing. In one of Alfred Bester's futures, "jaunt" had become the word for psychic teleportation. Cordwainer Smith caused "scanner" to become a specialized profession. Heinlein makes "hotel" into "hilton." "Cars" usually fly in my stories.

Often you will want to get on with the story rather than deal in detail with some stock concept. You still don't have to use a stock phrase. Teleportation, time travel, spaceflight—such basic ideas all come across if you simply describe what's happening to the character.

Lost in Translation

This business of alien languages is tricky. Given that an alien word may not sound like English; it may be unpronounceable. (We will never speak dolphin. There's too much supersonic in it.) Your characters then have three choices:

Try to pronounce the word. But doing it wrong may offend the alien.

Make up their own words. This may be especially apt if there are mechanical translators available.

Translate the alien word into English. Results can be amusing:

Overspeak and the *Hero's Tongue* are the thrintun and kzinti languages, respectively.

Sunflowers are plants gene-tailored by the tnuctipun. Their petals are solar mirrors. A field of sunflowers can blast nearby animals for fertilizer, or blast an airplane in flight. Tnuctip-designed *air plants* recycle the air in a spacecraft. Real plants!

Kzinti of the lower class are named for their professions. A kzinti ambassador to human space almost got into a duel by tactlessly translating his name: *Speaker-to-Animals.*

Translation involves confusion even in human languages. *Pueblo* means *town*—almost; it actually means the *people* of the town. *Pravda* means truth—the *official* version of the truth.

Yet if we (or our characters) wish to talk to aliens, we (they) must translate. The kind of language that passes between human and alien becomes, in our hands, a guide to the differences between man and alien and a guide to how long man and alien have been in contact.

There are phrases to characterize most of the aliens I have created. This was unplanned. But I did my damnedest to build each alien into a self-consistent being different from human. The result is that I can now pick out snatches of dialogue:

Kzin (on dueling niceties): "You scream and you leap."

Outsider: "That information will cost you—"

Motie Mediator: "God damn it to Hell," said Blaine's Motie. (She's studied Blaine to the point that she uses his own phrases and gestures, unselfconsciously.)

Puppeteer (on humor): "Louis, no properly cautious being ever interrupts a defense mechanism."

Brennan, a super-intelligent protector-stage human, throws ideas and concepts in double handfuls. It's almost impossible to follow him. Near the end of the novel *Protector* it's difficult even to follow the *story*. The author-of-record turns out to be another protector, and he's been overestimating your intelligence.

Poul Anderson's flying-squirrel aliens *(War of the Wing Men)* consider children expendable. Heinlein's Martians consider sex as pleasurable as a sneeze; to Martian-trained Michael Valentine Smith, sex is a stunning surprise.

Think like your characters. Even your alien characters. The dialogue follows naturally.

The Naming of Names

Place names: where do they come from? In a story they will come from you, of course. The worlds of the solar system are already named. All other planets are not. Likewise extraterrestrial cities, topographies, even constellations. (I remember a constellation named Marilyn Monroe, in an otherwise forgotten story set thousands of light-years from Sol.)

By your choice of place names you can often indicate who the colonists were, what they were like.

Stolid types name their worlds New Eden, Nova Terra, New Chicago. Classicists continue the tradition of naming worlds after gods, going to Asian or American Indian pantheons for sources. Religious outcasts choose Felicity, Harmony, Peace. (Or do they? Salt Lake City?)

The worlds of human space, in my own future history, are:

Jinx (they kept losing ships, and the planet was no prize, except in size), Down (egotism, or the temptation to name the colony city *Downtown?*), We Made It (it must have been an interesting trip), Wunderland, Gummidgy (human pronunciation of a kdatlyno placename), Plateau (uninhabitable but for a single mountaintop), and Home. My Uncle Pat accuses me of irreverence. Not so! I invite him, and you, to check some original California place names. Bitter Water, Dead Mule . . .

What kind of people first came to your worlds? A massive colony project breeds stolid names. Religious outcasts will choose hopeful names. So will real-estate developers (and in both cases you imply *easy* space travel). Lone scouts may well indulge themselves. A scout who was hooked on James Branch Cabell's writings named the worlds of the Léshy Circuit: Horvendile, Sereda, Koschei, etc. Others would name their discoveries Birksack's World, Birksack II, or Marcie Is Waiting, or The Admiral's Ass . . .

And anyone, stolid or lyrical, may name a world or feature thereof for its chief characteristic: Tabletop (a world of plains), or Dragonback (for the long, narrow chief continent and its spinal ridge of mountains), or Winter (cold), or Plateau. Remember Salt Lake City.

Names of aliens? You get three choices:

1. The alien's own name, rendered phonetically. Nonsense to you, but you must decide whether it should be pompous and complex, whether it should include gestures or other signals; and *remember the alien's mouth structure.*

2. A human-chosen name may derive from the alien's appearance. Snakes, or Blobs, or Wogglebugs: such names may well be insulting. But the two-headed *Pierson's puppeteer* was named for the brainless heads whose mouths had evolved as hands: like two Cecil the Sea-Sick Sea Serpent puppets.

3. A bright alien—brighter than human, or one assisted by a bright computer-translator—may choose his own name. Puppeteers prefer the names of legendary centaurs: Nessus, Chiron. Jock and Charley were *female* Motie Mediators contacting a *male-oriented* society; their sex was not obvious, and they chose to imitate male voices.

This subject can get arbitrarily complex. Let us consider, in detail, the Crazy Eddie symbol from *The Mote in God's Eye.**

Within the Motie culture there is a form of silliness so common that it is represented by a legendary being. A Motie goes "Crazy Eddie" by trying to keep things as they are when they are clearly about to change. He sacrifices long-term for short-term goals.

When a city is so heavily populated that all available vehicles are engaged in moving food and water in and garbage out, and none are left even to evacuate the inhabitants, then it is that Crazy Eddie leads the movers of garbage out on strike for better working conditions.

Crazy Eddie fights population pressure by killing off all the nonsentient Doctor forms—except that Masters who hid their own Doctors will afterward find them priceless.

*Larry Niven and Jerry Pournelle, *The Mote in God's Eye.* (Simon and Schuster, New York 1974; Pocket Books, New York.)

Obviously the Moties have their own name for him. But when speaking to humans, the Mediators called him Crazy Eddie.

Robert Heinlein was kind enough to suggest numerous changes in this book. Jerry and I owe him a great debt: we followed most of his suggestions and thereby improved the book immensely. But I instantly rejected this one:

"Since this name must be alien, why not make it something clearly alien. Yddie? Waddie? Kuddie? Something else? Certainly you want to keep the scansion—but any two-syllable word accented on the penult will do as long as it doesn't shout that it is a human name."

Wrong! I, being without false modesty, saw fit to lecture that great man for a page and a half on this trivial subject. He says I convinced him.

The trick is to think like an alien.

The Mediators are frighteningly good at learning languages. They won't teach humans to pronounce Crazy Eddie's true name. It probably can't be done anyway. Instead, they translate.

Is there any point in their making up a clearly alien word pronounceable to humans? I don't see one.

Well, what are they trying to convey?

1. Crazy Eddie is a form of insanity. Hence, "Crazy." "Foolish" isn't emphatic enough, "insane" is less common and has the wrong rhythm.

2. Crazy Eddie is ubiquitous. He's always been there, throughout the culture, back to the dawn of time. We choose a *common* name. (If the battleship *Lenin* had made the contact, Crazy Eddie might have been Crazy Ivan.)

3. His intentions are always good. Crazy Eddie is not a monster, and his existence is tolerated. We show that half-amused tolerance with the *diminutive* of a common name.

4. The human Empire is male-oriented. We choose a male name.

5. We keep the scansion. Not "Crazy Maurice" or "Crazy Jack" but "Crazy Eddie."

Complexities

You can imply a lot about a human culture with a well-constructed word or phrase. Consider: *corpsicle.*

Fred Pohl derived that word from *popsicle* to describe the frozen dead, people who have had their bodies frozen in the hope that someday they may be revived and cured of what killed them. Given that the word is common throughout a society, we can deduce:

1. There are a lot of them.

2. They are not highly regarded.

Consider: *thumb runner* and *organlegger.*

Both describe the same animal: a man who sells, and murders to acquire, illegal organs for sale as transplants. *Organlegger* is mine. *Thumb runner* belongs to Alexei Panshin.

We discussed these phrases once. I'd like to enlarge on Alex's comments:

Organlegger derives from *bootlegger.* Bootleggers were named for one manner of smuggling their illegal liquor. *Thumb runners* would be named for their own mode of operation—and it is reasonable that they would call their transplant stocks *thumbs,* an oblique and contemptuous reference to their origin.

Villain to helpless heroine: "You're going to be thumbs, my dear." It was a bone-chilling line, because Alex set it up right.

Alex was writing of the far future. I wrote of the near future, when people might well mutilate *bootlegger* to describe a vaguely similar crime. But if I'd thought of *thumb runner* I'd have used it.

I needed a number of new words and phrases to describe the social development in *Flash Crowd,* a novelette based on the development of cheap teleportation in the near future.

1. *Newstaper.* The reader is told that the main character is a roving newstaper. Already he can guess that:

A) He's a reporter. He probably uses a videotape camera.

B) Newspapers are dead. Otherwise the word *newstaper* would be confusing. It would have been dropped for something else.

2. I called the teleportation links *JumpShift booths* (for the JumpShift Corporation) or *displacement booths. Transfer booths* would have been equally reasonable, but I'd already used that one in a different line of future history.

3. I don't believe in bending space to order, and I wouldn't ride in a machine that annihilates me here, then beams away data that allows me to be exactly recreated somewhere else. Both are common fictional methods of teleportation. But I needed a theory that would allow instantaneous transportation and would still leave a passenger intact. What I came up with was a kind of super-neutrino. The displacement booth

converts its cargo into an elementary particle of no rest mass, a relativistic mass equal to the weight of the cargo (for conservation of matter), an internal structure complex enough to carry the quantum states of every elementary particle in the cargo, and a neutrino's ability to penetrate almost any barrier. I called it a *transition particle.* Cautiously phrased and polysyllabic, *transition particle* implies a theory without committing the user to specifics. It is just the phrase a theoretical scientist would use when talking to his peers.

4. The better the news coverage and the better the transportation, the bigger the crowd that gathers around anything interesting. With a teleporting society patrolled by roving newstapers, you get instant mobs that expand further as publicity hounds, pickpockets, and looters teleport in. (I said *flick in. Teleport* gives way to a shorter slang word.) I called these *flash crowds,* using short, common words and a phrasing that is cryptic until the reader is given more detail.

5. In the story I had *continuity clubs* forming as a guard against culture shock, epidemic in a teleporting society. A *continuity club* is a chain of clubs with every building in the chain identical down to the furnishings and the uniforms on the waiters. One's club is a piece of home he can take with him. *Continuity club* is clumsy. It hardly matters, because the average citizen would talk about individual clubs rather than the aggregate. But I wish I'd thought of a better wording. You try.

Showmanship

A course in semantics can't hurt you a bit. There is plenty of opportunity to show off your knowledge, or use it to deepen and broaden the background of a story.

Samuel R. Delany's *Babel-17* and *The Ballad of Beta-2* are whole novels based on semantic concepts. Anthony Burgess drastically altered the English language for *A Clockwork Orange.* So did Robert Heinlein in *The Moon Is a Harsh Mistress.* (No, you don't have to create an *entire* language. You decide what has happened to English: changes in grammatical construction? Dropping of articles or past tenses? Borrowed words from other languages? You lay down the rules of grammar, you choose the borrowed words and decide how they are spelled, and you *stick to your own rules.* The rest is implied.)

Or there are little touches, like the moon jeeps called "Baba Yaggas," after the many-legged mobile homes used by Russian witches. (Fritz Leiber, *The Wanderer.*)

This one I haven't seen in fiction yet, but it illustrates what I'm getting at. *Black holes,* also known as collapsars or hypermasses, are called *frozen stars* by the Soviets. In the presence of Soviet scientists or astronauts, Americans will use that phrase, if they are being polite, or will say *black hole,* if they are being rude. With these phrases you control U.S.-to-Soviet relationships in your story. Why? Because in Russian, *black hole* is a specific physiological term that means just what you think it means.

The "Newspeak" of *1984* was a language so designed that certain thoughts would be unthinkable in it. One must wonder if certain thoughts, crucial thoughts, are unthinkable in English, or in any human language, including mathematics.

Maps of Reality

A language is a mapping of the way people think, of the way they believe the universe works, and of what they consider to be important in that universe.

Four of the Ten Commandments relate to one's duties toward God.

Most primitives use a word that means "people" (themselves) and a word that means "barbarian" (foreigners). In my own language I am an "American," and I am aware that there are other people around. Progress!

Languages change. Sometimes the changes reflect new knowledge. My translation of Dante's *Inferno* is jammed with footnote lectures on Thirteenth-Century cosmology.

Sometimes they don't. "Bastard" was once a legal term meaning "One whose parents were not married in the Catholic faith prior to conception." Later, marriage within certain other churches was considered sufficient—though never by Catholics. Later still, "bastard" meant "untrustworthy and/or ill-mannered." How did *that* happen? Common usage as insult, plus Shakespeare's *King Lear?*

In the ten years since I started writing, "black" has replaced "Negro," by popular demand. This may have been a poor idea. Human children tend to be afraid of the dark, with the result that "black" is a poetic simile for "evil" in every language I'm familiar with.

I use the same word "my" to indicate my car, my wife, my elbow. Could this have something to do with the way I defend my property? I got burgled twice within six months five years ago. I reacted as if I'd been raped. The bastards took some irreplaceable things—but I wouldn't have been any angrier if they'd notched my ears.

A baby has some trouble figuring out where he ends and the universe begins. An alien might never suffer that confusion.

When a Fifteenth-Century father spoke of "My children," and his King spoke of "My people," they meant it. Possessions.

Science fiction writers, and readers, have this in common: the sense that there are other ways of thinking than their own.

There is vast variety in a human being's picture of the universe.

In Eskimo there are several words for different states of snow: falling snow, powder snow, packed snow, wet snow.

In a certain African language there are words for a field seeded with yams, for young yam sprouts, for ripe yams; but there is no continuity among them, no sense that one produces the other.

There is a group of tribes—African, again—whose languages have no expression for "death by natural causes." Death comes through violence or through witchcraft. For every "natural death," a witch must be found and killed. They're exterminating each other down there.

There are girls in American slums who do not believe that sexual intercourse produces babies. They've been told so. But in their lives they've heard *so* much obvious crap . . .

In Spanish, adjectives may denote temporary or permanent states. The words for "rich" and "poor" take the "permanent" configuration.

If the human concepts embedded in human languages can get that weird, what about star-going humanity? What about aliens? The differences would infallibly show in their languages.

I.

What words are untranslatable?

The "game" of *shifgrethor* is terribly important to the natives of Winter (Ursula Le Guin, *The Left Hand of Darkness*). It seems to be a game of one-upsmanship, played for social standing; and beyond that, you have to read the book to get even an inkling. One clue: the natives of Winter, otherwise humanoid, are sexless most of the time. Sex would thus not enter into *shifgrethor.* Another clue: one does not play *shifgrethor* with an inferior.

Fyunch (click) was the only word the Moties never tried to translate *(A Mote in God's Eye).* Even for Mediators it would have required an hour's lecture. Essentially the Fyunch (click) relationship was "I am the Mediator assigned to you. I intend to learn you from the inside out, not just your words but your nonverbal signals too. When I know your language to my satisfaction, I will read your mind better than you do."

The untranslatable concepts mark the greatest differences between your reader and the society you are trying to show him.

II.

What words are missing?

A Tralfamadorian (Kurt Vonnegut, Jr., *Slaughterhouse Five*) would have no word for *guilt.* In their universe there was no cause and effect. They could travel up and down time, and they found the future as rigid and senseless as the past. Things happened because they happened.

Postulate a species whose reproduction is *really* cryptic. They black out for a time. A few days later they wander back to the village, recovered. New members of the species eventually show up from the direction of the seashore. Such a species would have no fathers, mothers, aunts, uncles, family trees, birthrights, inherited titles, trust funds, bastardy. For them there might even be no posterity. Given the technology, they would use up the land with no thought for future generations.

III.

What words are hardly ever used? (What, never? Well, hardly ever.) *What phrases are insults?*

In *Empire Star* (Delany), one insult word was "dew-water": very precious, but hated for its scarcity and the difficulty of collecting it.

In *Stand on Zanzibar* (Brunner), "bleeder" had replaced "bastard." People with genetic deficiencies were not allowed to have children.

In "Flatlander" (Niven, *If Science Fiction,* March 1967), a flatlander was either (1) someone who through cowardice had never traveled off his home world, or (2) an Earthman. Earthmen found the term irritating.

A language where "coward" is an insult marks a possibly dangerous species. (Damn right I include humans.)

Predators tend to avoid their own excrement. It gives them away to their prey; it smells. But picture something that lives in the thick Jovian atmosphere. Those terrific winds would whip away anything that came out of such a beast, gaseous or otherwise. He wouldn't have words for his own waste products, unless they were technical words. Humans do not consider "carbon dioxide" insulting.

And an armored herbivore might not give a shit. In fact, staying near his own excrement might be a great way to warn off rivals.

Again, human breeding habits are far looser than those of most species. We would expect an alien race to be guided here either by sheer instinct, or (if advanced technologically) by its own intention to stabilize or improve the breed. There would be no insults to denote incest, bestiality, homosexual relations, etc.

IV.

What group of words translates to one word in English? And vice versa?

In *Dune* (Frank Herbert) it was *sand.* Drum sand would carry sound for miles; you'd stay off it for fear of drawing the giant earthworms. There was sand that would slide and bury you; there was windstorm sand that would flay you; there was good stable stuff you could walk on.

For the Jovian beast there might be many kinds of wind, each with its own name—more names than we have, and we have a good number. For a space-dwelling creature, all of those words would translate to *air.* Air is what turns his ship, or his shell, red-hot.

In the European languages there are scores of words for mating relationships: married, girl friend, fiancé, virgin, dating, concupiscent, good or bad lay, old maid, divorced, etc. A normal species with straightforward mating instincts, like the dolphins, would find this most amusing. My guess is that the dolphins have one word, and they use it a lot.

The Ballad of Beta-2 is a wonderful study of changes in a language. The people of the starship Beta-2 had been in space for many generations. For them, "over" and "under" and "between" had come to have the same meaning, and "arms" and "legs" had become interchangeable —all because they lived in free fall.

The untranslatable words, the missing words, the insults and their surface meanings, and the short alien words that require phrases or lectures in English: these measure the differences in the thinking of an alien culture.

Even human cultures are very various; and, *Star Trek* to the contrary, aliens are not men in funny suits. Designing a truly alien alien can be a hell of a lot of fun, and it can get as complex as you like. Poul Anderson did a thorough job on the flying Ythri; see *The People of the Wind,* and pay attention to his treatment of the language.

One Last Thing

Writing science fiction is for fun. It has to be; you'll be at it ten years before there's any money in it.

Some of us get a kick out of playing games with languages and language concepts. But it's easy enough to avoid situations where this is necessary. I'm not trying to talk anyone out of writing.

Assigned Reading

The Demolished Man and any short stories by Alfred Bester
The Ballad of Beta-2 by Samuel R. Delany
Babel-17 by Samuel R. Delany
A Clockwork Orange by Anthony Burgess
The Moon Is a Harsh Mistress by Robert Heinlein and any of his "juveniles"
The People of the Wind by Poul Anderson
The Mote in God's Eye by Larry Niven and Jerry Pournelle

Larry Niven

Larry Niven was born on April 30, 1938, in Los Angeles, California, and spent his childhood in Beverly Hills, "excluding two years (ages six to eight) in Washington, D.C., serving his country."

He attended a boarding school, Santa Barbara School for Boys, and went to California Institute of Technology for two years, 1956–1958, where he flunked out. He finished his A.B. in mathematics (with a minor in psychology) at Washburn University, Topeka, Kansas, 1958–1962. One year of graduate work at the University of California convinced him that all students of his intelligence or less had been weeded out earlier, 1962–1963.

He started writing full time in June 1963 and made his first sale, "The Coldest Place," the following year, for $25.

AWARDS

Hugo, Best Short Science Fiction Story, 1966, for "Neutron Star"
Hugo, Best Science Fiction Novel, 1970, for *Ringworld*
Nebula, Best Science Fiction Novel, 1970, for *Ringworld*
Ditmar (Australian), Best Foreign Science Fiction, 1972, *Ringworld*
Hugo, Best Short Science Fiction Story, 1971, for "Inconstant Moon"
Hugo, Best Short Science Fiction Story, 1975, for "The Hole Man"
E. E. Smith Memorial Award for Service to the Field

BIBLIOGRAPHY

World of Ptavvs, 1966
Neutron Star, 1968
A Gift from Earth, 1968
The Shape of Space, 1969
Ringworld, 1970
All the Myriad Ways, 1971
The Flying Sorcerers, 1971 (with David Gerrold)
Protector, 1973
The Flight of the Horse, 1973
The Mote in God's Eye, 1974 (with Jerry Pournelle)
Tales of Known Space, 1975
Inferno, 1976 (with Jerry Pournelle)

JACK WILLIAMSON

Short Stories and Novelettes

Underhill was walking home from the office, because his wife had the car, the afternoon he first met the new mechanicals. His feet were following his usual diagonal path across a weedy vacant lot—his wife usually had the car—and his mind was rejecting various impossible ways to meet his notes at the Two Rivers Bank, when a new wall stopped him.

That's the opening paragraph of my most successful story, "With Folded Hands . . ." The language may be undistinguished, but it gets the story going. Almost too nakedly, it follows the advice given long ago by H. G. Wells, to bring something new "into a commonplace group of people," and to work out their responses "with the greatest gravity and reasonableness." The something new is those too-perfect robots, the humanoids. Underhill himself is a very ordinary little man, struggling to keep his business alive in a commonplace town. The story begins when they meet.

I want to use "With Folded Hands . . ." to illustrate these remarks about the technique of short science fiction. Though it was written years ago, I recall the problems it gave me and my papers show some of the solutions I tried. Before I was able to write that simple-seeming paragraph, I had already been forced to make a good many decisions, some of them painful.

A story, like a poem, is a device for making choices. We commonly begin with only a fragment and that out of focus—a striking character or a dramatic bit of action, a haunting mood or more often in science fiction a bare idea. We build the story by discovering and selecting what is needed to complete a sharply focused pattern. The creative process requires both a clear sense of story form and a good stock of materials, from life or reading or imagination.

I discovered the idea for the humanoids in an unfinished narrative fragment I don't remember writing, which was still on my desk when I got home from World War II. It was about an astronaut in trouble out in space, overwhelmed by the helpful efficiency of his robot companion—named George in the fragment—a completely competent machine that required no food or air, no shelter against heat or cold or lethal radiation.

Working to intensify my hero's emotional predicament, I designed the humanoids as the ultimately perfect machines. Man-shaped, but small and black and graceful, they are powered and controlled from a remote central computer. They require no sleep or rest, and each of them knows all that anyone has ever learned. Inexorably benign, they are governed by a prime directive, "to serve and obey, and guard men from harm." They serve too well.

At first I regarded them simply as a menace my hero had to overcome. Planning the story as a novel, I worked at it for perhaps a couple of months before I saw the logical flaw in my story plan. If the humanoids were really perfect, designed to save man in spite of himself, they could never be beaten.

Frustrated, I had to lay the manuscript aside while I wrote something else. When I came back to it, I set out to discover a better strategy. That done, the story went well. It is such problems of story strategy that I want to discuss, the vital choices that control form and meaning.

One essential early choice—a choice student writers tend to slight—is audience. Of course there are people who say they write for themselves alone. Claiming that, they remove themselves from discussion. Their private writing is their own business, and this essay is not for them.

Considered as an art, writing is a two-party affair. The artist is speaking to somebody. The structure he creates, a portrait or an opera or only a word on a wall, exists to communicate. It operates through conventions he shares with his audience. He needs feedback, applause or catcalls, laurel wreaths or exile, checks or rejection slips.

Though linguistic science has only just begun to speak of literature, I think it can make useful comments on such problems of narrative technique. A story is a linguistic structure, at the very top of the hierarchy that builds phonemes into morphemes and words into sentences. Its shape is partly arbitrary, partly fixed by human nature. It works as a unit of meaning because it fits upon and extends the shared language experience of writer and reader.

In simpler words, this means that the writer must reach his readers in their own language. That's not quite so easy as it sounds. Languages normally change; the speech of each new year's crop of readers is slightly different, of each new generation greatly different. Any language is almost infinitely subdivided into dialects of region and class. Every reader has his own private idiolect.

Here is the linguistic basis for the sound advice—often given the student writer and too often ignored—to study at least a few issues of a magazine before he begins mailing stories in. Though blind submissions sometimes sell, they also waste a lot of hopes and postage.

Even in such a narrow field as science fiction, audiences vary surprisingly. The readers of *Analog,* for example, are, I'm sure, more interested in technology and more optimistic about its effects than the readers of *Galaxy.* They communicate their special culture through a special dialect. When Ben Bova replaced John Campbell as editor, many of them were put off by the rather slight changes he made in the language of the magazine.

Any writer, I think, does his best for some ideal audience. His wife, perhaps, or a sympathetic editor, or some jury of his peers. Lacking the responses of some good listener, he is stumbling in the dark. Sometimes, of course, an innovative writer has to look long and hard for his audience. James Joyce wrote at first for his brother Stanislaus and very few others. It took many years for the rest of us to learn Joyspeak.

"With Folded Hands . . ." was written for John Campbell, who served as a creative first audience for a whole galaxy of science fiction stars, including Isaac Asimov and Robert A. Heinlein, Ted Sturgeon and Sprague de Camp, Lester del Rey and L. Ron Hubbard. I knew him from visits to his cluttered den behind huge rolls of pulp paper and roaring presses in the old Street and Smith building at 79 Seventh Avenue, New York City, and from weekends of challenging talk at his

New Jersey home, knew him better from his vigorous editorials and the fiction he printed.

I have just finished another story, one for Harlan Ellison. As stimulating today as Campbell was thirty years ago, Harlan is a very different editor. Writing for him, I turned out something very different. Neither story could have happened without my own clear image of a responsive listener. Through the years I have done a good many novels in collaboration, with Miles J. Breuer, with James Gunn, with Frederik Pohl. I like collaboration, because I'm doing my own drafts for an audience I know.

A second early choice is story length. The fate of a manuscript often turns on the way it fits the space an editor must fill. Of more importance, the structures of short story and novelette and novel vary so widely as to make them almost different languages. Some writers are fluent in one, some in another. Ray Bradbury has written brilliant short stories but few novels. Hal Clement writes such memorable novels as *Mission of Gravity* but few shorts.

The longer forms have always felt more comfortable to me. When I go adventuring into some new world, I like freedom from any rigid form. In a short story, one wrong choice may be fatal. A novel or a novelette allows more room for recovery.

I have always felt, as James Gunn does, that the ideal length for science fiction is the novelette. The story of the here and now finds readers already convinced that its settings and its people can exist, often already concerned about its themes. Though the science fiction anthologies are full of fine short stories, they are seldom as powerful as the best novelettes. Science fiction needs space in which to persuade its readers, to explore its alien environments, to examine ideas that may be disturbingly new.

Harlan Ellison's "I Have No Mouth and I Must Scream" is an unforgettable short story about an omnipotent insane computer tormenting the last survivors of the man who made it. Ellison uses a vividly concrete style and original typographical devices with something near genius, but his shattering effects would hardly be possible without readers already conditioned to fear technological progress.

Most great science fiction stories are longer, but Gunn says the novel is too long. In the preface to *Some Dreams Are Nightmares,* he refers to "With Folded Hands . . ." and its novel-length sequel, *The Humanoids,* to support his claim that "the science fiction novel is often—

perhaps usually—a disappointment." To my delight, he describes my novelette as "beautifully conceived and delicately crafted." I have to agree that my novel is less successful, even though I don't think he understands the ending in the way I meant it. The questions he raises are worth comment.

He is speaking of hard-core science fiction, excepting stories of adventure or fantasy or mood or character. The hard-core novel is an idea story which usually explores some major human problem. While the novelette need do no more than dramatize the problem, the serious novel must undertake to solve it. The catch is that most major human problems have no solutions—no neat and final answers that look convincing on paper. The result, he says, is that the novel often has to tell its readers "something that is incomplete or untrue."

In the case of my own stories, the novelette makes the ironic comment that the most perfect machine, designed and used with the most benevolent intentions to aid and save its creators, will instead destroy them. Sixteen thousand words were enough for that. The novel, four times as long, was written at John Campbell's request. He felt that men forced to fold their hands might compensate by developing the parapsychological powers Rhine was announcing from Duke University. The novel expands that idea. The ending perplexed me. I wanted to show my perfect machines still undefeated, even by psionics, yet I couldn't simply repeat the ending of the novelette. What I tried to do was to show my human heroes going down again but brainwashed by the humanoids to believe they had won. As written, the ending is ambiguous. Readers often take it as a victory for mankind, which isn't what I meant. Anyhow, the novelette remains the clearer and stronger expression of what I wanted to say.

Deciding on a length for his story, the beginning writer should probably prefer the shorter forms. Shorts are nearly always in demand—because of the modest rates of pay, established writers usually move on to something else. The short story, too, is a better training field. The problems of construction and style are easier to see, and I think the stricter discipline can be beneficial. The penalty for error is not quite so severe. The author of a novel may take months to find that he is on a false trail, while the writer of a short learns the same lesson in a day or two.

Having in mind an audience and a tentative length, the writer needs a story germ. Though really stunning new ideas are rare as diamonds, the professional is usually able to plan more fiction than he has time to write. There are methods of invention.

A literature of alternatives, science fiction explores possibilities. Anything possible may suggest a story. It needn't be probable—the more improbable event, with more novelty and more surprise, may offer richer story interest. Back when science fiction still meant wild adventure, I used to look for the least possible premise. The stars are live beings in one of those old stories. The planets are clutches of their eggs. At the climax, the earth hatches.

Science fiction is more sophisticated now, of course, and its intentions are commonly more serious. The best ideas, I've discovered, come out of one's current concerns. Long ago I set out to keep an elaborate file of plot ideas, of characters and settings and themes. The file became a graveyard, its dead contents buried forever. I've always found live ideas enough in the live world around me.

The richest lode of ideas lies in the years between the advances of pure science and their engineering applications. For one notable example, Einstein announced his famous equation relating mass and energy in 1905. H. G. Wells was writing about uranium fission bombs by 1913, three decades before Hiroshima. For today's frontiers of knowledge, read *Science* or *Scientific American* or Isaac Asimov.

Story ideas are anywhere you find them. One discovery technique is to invert or reverse something familiar. Killing flies is a pretty ordinary activity. Once I wrote a little story, "The Cold Green Eye," in which the obnoxious Aunt Agatha Grimm is turned into a fly and caught in her own sticky flypaper.

Many stories drift across the shadowy line between science fiction and fantasy—a line I think each reader draws for himself, fantasy being what he can't accept as possible. Witches and werewolves are ruled out of most science fiction, but in *Darker Than You Think,* a novel of mine, we humans are a hybrid breed and genetic techniques are being used to recover the scattered genes of *Homo lycanthropus.*

Operating along the spreading frontiers of knowledge, science fiction finds its domain always changing. When I began writing, lost-race stories could still be placed here on earth. Atomic power and flight in space were still fiction. Life on Venus or Mars still looked possible. All that and more has changed, but new frontiers open faster than the old ones close. For one example, the astronomer Freeman Dyson has suggested that the most likely sign of high intelligence in space would be a source of infrared radiation, waste heat. A really sophisticated technological culture would probably build a shell all around its sun to trap and use all its energy. Fred Pohl and I are now at work on a trilogy of novels set on a Dyson sphere, a world seven hundred million miles around. Room enough for discovery and adventure!

When Harlan Ellison invited me to write something for his *Last Dangerous Visions*, an ironic twist struck me. The most dangerous vision might be nothing shocking or evil but rather a glimpse of happiness and peace. In my story, a man searching the future for a road toward survival must be killed because he has seen a coming utopia.

A good story idea must pass several tests. It should be original, but not too far out; it needs a strong base in observed human reality to support the imagined innovations. It must interest the audience. It must be adaptable to the planned length. It must also hold the seed of conflict.

Conflict is the raw material of drama, the backbone of plot, the substance of suspense. Without conflict there's no story. Most of the old-fashioned utopian romances are deadly dull, because they picture ideal societies in which no man quarrels with another. Dystopias are often absorbing, because evil societies generate dramatic conflict.

A vigorous potential conflict will go far toward solving the next problem, the selection of characters. If the story begins as an abstract idea, its opposing forces can be turned into people. Conflicting traits even in the same person can be dramatized, as the internal struggle between passion and duty becomes an exciting encounter with the disloyal seductress.

The people of science fiction commonly remain more symbolic than realistic. It's instructive to contrast two great characters of modern literature, Burroughs' Lord Greystoke and Joyce's Leopold Bloom. Bloom, Homer's Ulysses reduced to anti-hero, is the archetype of man in the modern city. Joyce lavished genius and years of toil to make him perhaps the most fully created character in realistic fiction. Greystoke, more familiar as Tarzan of the Apes, is still a hero, the noble savage born of the jungle and uncorrupted by society. Burroughs knew little of British aristocracy and less of apes and Africa, but his crudely drawn natural man has the instant appeal of a universal symbol.

Setting is another crucial choice. The whole story, in fact, may spring from some imagined or extrapolated new environment. Though I don't really know how Aldous Huxley wrote *Brave New World*, I'm convinced that he began by working out his future dystopia in all its crisp detail. He spends half the book presenting it, using all sorts of dazzling devices. Such people as Lenina are simply its typical citizens. The Reservation in New Mexico is logically there as a contrast to it, and the Shakespeare-quoting Savage is necessary to place it in perspective. The book concludes on the inevitable cultural clash between John's naïve primitivism and Lenina's innocent urban sophistication.

The choice of theme, however important, should be approached with some caution. Though fine stories do spring from theme, any deliberate message can too easily become false or shallow propaganda. The most effective themes, I think, are those that come from the deeply held feelings that influence all the other story choices, often unconsciously.

When a story is ready to plot, I like to use a scheme I learned from the books of John Gallishaw, a psychologist who taught writing. He described plot in terms of function. The beginning places a character in a situation, shows his response to it in terms of feeling and purpose, and establishes the circumstances favoring and opposing his success. The body follows his attempts to achieve his story goal. If he is to win, it builds up to a black moment, when all seems lost. The ending shows a new attempt, its outcome, and the consequences.

The essential first step here is to decide who is the major character. Commonly easy, this is sometimes difficult. The test is to ask who solves the main story problem. Since the short story can seldom do more than present one main crisis in one person's life, a false choice can spoil it.

Though this clinical approach turns some writers off, I like it because it clarifies my thinking. From a one-page dramatic analysis, I can tell whether the story pattern is complete. If it isn't, I can see what functions have been neglected. I'm including here the plot outline I drew up when I had to replot "With Folded Hands . . ."

FOLDED HANDS

Theme: The perfect machine is diabolical, because it renders human existence futile.

Hero: Young Greenhill, of Two Rivers, who is the ordinary head of an ordinary family: wife Aurora, daughter Gay, son Manly. Business: android agency.

I. BEGINNING:

Situation: The humanoids come to Two Rivers.

Disturbance: Greenhill doesn't like them; they menace his business and interfere with his life.

Purpose: He determines, with aid of strange old man, to stop them.

Factors for success: Old man was creator of humanoids; he knows all about them and about rhodomagnetics; he has an immunity from the humanoids and is building a machine to blow up their Central.

Factors against success: Humanoids are the perfect machines, guided by the Prime Directive. They know everything, guard humanity in spite of itself.

II. BODY:

Attempts: Greenhill learns story of old man, secures tools and parts for him, aids him in building machine, offers him shelter, and gets a human doctor for him when he is ill.

Result: The humanoids remain the perfect mechanicals. They slowly take over the town.

Bright Moment: The old man, Sledge, is ready to test his machine—to blow up Central.

III. ENDING:

Final Test: The excitement is too much for him; he falls ill. Human doctor can't save him. He is forced to give up his immunity, to call on the humanoids for aid.

Sequel: The humanoids save his life—and make him believe that he has won, by hypnotic means.

This outline just happened to survive, because I used the backs of the rough-draft sheets for the carbon copy. The story follows it pretty closely, though Greenhill—hardly a hero—becomes Underhill.

Plot, of course, is only a device. It can be used well or ill. Students sometimes sneer at plot because the hacks have used it, but their plotless narratives are commonly dreadful. A few contemporary writers reject plot on better grounds, arguing that its very form states a theme they can't accept. The logical order of plot seems to imply some corresponding moral order in the universe. That's appropriate, if the world makes sense. But it seems all wrong to the existentialist who sees human life as a meaningless eddy in the energy-flow from a dying sun. The resolution of a plot, with the good guys getting their rewards or even meeting ironic defeats, implies an order that the existentialist denies.

But we need at least the illusion of order. Art and language were invented to organize experience. A work of fiction is first of all a linguistic form—confusion of language is a scarcely adequate symbol for the assumed confusion of nature. For the rebel against the tyranny of plot, one plausible choice is "organic unity"—the sort of unity defined by some natural interval or process, a day or a year or a generation, a journey or a love affair or the fall of a civilization.

A master technician, Joyce limits the action of *Ulysses* to a single day. He uses hours and colors, the organs of the body, arts and symbols and varied styles and a thousand other intricate devices to weave the pattern of the novel. But his whole structure is built on Homer's great plot, all its values ironically inverted to make his modern Odysseus an insignificant anti-hero.

Plot, to repeat, is far too useful to be discarded. In fiction generally, it's as essential as backbone is to mammals. Plotting is a skill that can be analyzed and learned, and its master can use it to create the values of character and setting and theme.

The events of plot must follow a sequence of cause and effect leading from beginning to end. A complete plot may be regarded as the full response of the characters to the opening situation. In psychological terms, our responses reveal what we are. If a man is a patriot, he can prove it by giving his life for his country. If he is a clever rogue, he shows it when he absconds with the queen's necklace. If he is a coward, he can be unstrung with a splash of catsup.

Plot can dramatize setting by showing people in conflict with it. Huxley's brave new world comes to life when his Savage clashes with it. Plot can demonstrate theme. The action of Huxley's novel expresses sardonic criticism of the socialist super-state. The logic is devastating, because his world state is intelligently planned and expertly run by the most benevolent of leaders, concerned only for the public good. When this most humane socialism drives the Savage to suicide, all socialisms stand condemned.

"With Folded Hands . . ." states its surface theme with the same sort of logic. If the best possible machine is monstrously evil, no machine is good. This is not a theme I planned the story to prove but rather one I discovered in the plot as it took shape. Having found it, I did try to give it the greatest clarity and force.

In a sense, however, it belongs to the story and not to me. Consciously at least I'm a good deal more optimistic than the story is about the machines in our future. I believe, in fact, that published science fiction tends to show a purely accidental pessimistic bias, simply because a hell generates more arresting drama than a paradise does.

This necessity for evil in fiction is neatly illustrated in the history of my own novel, *Bright New Universe.* I planned it as an optimistic answer to the pessimism of *Brave New World.* I wanted to show a really better world created through technological innovations—borrowed in the story from a friendly galactic culture. For the sake of conflict, I invented the Monk family to dramatize the forces opposed to progress. I suppose they became a bit too powerful. The resulting theme, in spite of me, is as pessimistic as Huxley's. What the finished story says is that our reactionary human Monks can't be beaten without an unlikely assist from off the earth.

Though "With Folded Hands . . ." seems to be about machines, it seems to me now that the implacably benevolent humanoids are only symbols for a deeper theme, of which I wasn't consciously aware when I wrote the story. I think they stand for society, for the family as the basic social unit, as Underhill stands for the rebel individual who wants more freedom than society allows. The whole emotional tone of the story recalls all those childhood experiences of my own, when I was frustrated by superior beings who claimed to be acting out of love for my own benefit.

The most essential service of plot is to create unity, which it does in the simplest and strongest possible way, setting up a narrative problem in the beginning, delaying the solution in the body, completing the answer in the ending. Unity is vital. The need for it springs, I suppose, from the nature of a story as a single linguistic structure, a unit of language that requires one meaning in the same way that a word or a sentence does. Though the Renaissance critics went too far in their famous demands for the three unities of time and place and action, it's still true that every needless lapse of time or change of place or shift of purpose makes difficulties for the writer and tends to weaken story impact. Most of my own troubles with that first unfinishable story about the humanoids were problems of unity. I was trying to present a whole series of developing conflicts, taking place on several planets and over many years. When I narrowed the focus to the events of a single crisis, happening in one small city in only a few days, most of the difficulties vanished.

Unity, of course, involves more than time and place and plot. It depends on viewpoint, mood, and style—on every aspect of the story. To borrow a linguistic phrase, the demands of unity control surface structure as well as deep structure. These are terms from transformational grammar. The surface structure is what we say or write. The deep structure, not quite so evident, is what gets meaning into the pattern of words.

Up to this point, we've been discussing the deep structure of fiction. Such story elements as plot, character, setting, and theme are analogous to the words from the lexicon and the kernel sentence patterns that are chosen and transformed to make the sentences we speak. They convey the basic meaning.

We turn now to problems of surface structure, to how the writer says what he means. As the sense of a sentence can be changed by the question transformation or the negative transformation or the passive transformation, so can the effect of a story be transformed by a shift in viewpoint or tone or style, or by reversals in the order of events.

As we prepare now to tell the surface story, I suppose the first essential choice is point of view. Through whose eyes do we see what happens? Those of the omniscient author, aware of everything? Those of the protagonist, telling in his own words what he did? Those of a sympathetic friend, explaining and defending? None of the above?

Selecting a viewpoint involves a choice of grammatical person. The omniscient observer nearly always uses third-person. Second-person is sometimes—but rarely—used for tricky special effects. The hero or his friend or any other narrator may tell the story in first-person.

Each of these choices carries advantages and penalties. First-person narrative is tempting because it seems most natural and perhaps most convincing, but the first-person reporter must often strain probability as he tries to explain how he learned all he must tell. When unlikely events have to be related, the actual observer may seem the most reliable witness, but the hero who tells how he won may appear unpleasantly egotistical. Choosing a point of view for each new story, the writer has to weigh such pros and cons. No decision is more important.

Swift did well to let Gulliver report his own adventures. A fact-centered little Englishman, with no imagination to invent a Lilliput or a Brobdingnag, he has to be believed. Since his stiff pride in his own horse sense is satirized toward the end, as when he boasts of being allowed to kiss the hoof of the horse who has become his master, there is no penalty for egotism.

"With Folded Hands . . ." is told in third-person, from Underhill's point of view. Though that now seems the inevitable choice, it took me a long time to make it. The real protagonist is Sledge, the man who invents the humanoids, who then discovers his tragic blunder and spends the rest of his life struggling to repair it. I first tried to tell his story from his own viewpoint. That effort failed, largely because the action sprawled over too much space and time. Through Underhill's eyes, we see only the final climax of Sledge's long war with the machines he made to save mankind, but that is enough.

Writing "The Most Dangerous Vision" for Harlan Ellison, I wanted to keep the story very brief because the idea seemed so slight. The solution I found was to let an involved friend of the protagonist set it down in laconic journal entries. It begins:

Sunday, 3/10

Previews of hell.

Watched the last man die again today. This time by famine. Here on our own mesa, ninety years from now. Black flyspeck when the tracer picked him up. Black maggot crawling over the dead red earth. Skeleton scarecrow, naked and sunburnt, staggering out of the raw clay canyons the floods had cut. Scratched with a stick in mud mounds where a town was. Found a rusty can, smashed it open with a rock, wolfed something down. Spoilt, evidently. Died trying to vomit.

Though each new story makes new demands, I think the best choice in most cases is the third-person report of what the protagonist sees and thinks and does. This approach is simple and direct. It allows the writer to cut to another character, if the need arises, as readily as a movie does.

The motion picture has in fact influenced modern fiction. The pace has grown faster. Elaborate character analysis and lengthy description are out of fashion. Dashiell Hammett's brilliant *The Maltese Falcon* hardly needed revision for the camera. I used to try to visualize each story I was planning as if it were going to be a film with an unlimited budget for spectacular special effects.

The plot outlined and the viewpoint selected, the next logical step is to decide where the story begins. (Actually, I doubt that any writer has ever worked out a story exactly this way. Choices are probably more often guided by habit and hunch than by logic, and they may follow nearly any order. In my own case, the process is seldom direct or even entirely conscious. Yet these are the decisions that must be made.)

A common mistake of my own is to pick a beginning point too far from the ending. The standard rule for the old pulps was to open near the climax with an exciting and puzzling "narrative hook," then use flashback and summary to explain the situation. Too often, however, the summaries were boring and the flashbacks confusing. Today's stories often skip any formal opening, relying on the reader to feel his way into the story without much overt aid.

I'm always afraid, however, of losing readers by being too obscure. I much prefer to explain things clearly, but I do my best to dramatize the explanations. My recent story "The Power of Blackness" begins with a tourist guide, "a time-dried Nggonggan black, hopping ahead with dazzling agility on his one good leg and waving his single yellow-painted crutch like a banner," as he speaks to his flock of interstellar travelers and also to the reader. An ancient and obvious device, but sometimes it still works.

We've come now, I think, to that critical point where the writer must face a sheet of blank paper and put words on it. The decisions here are those of tone and mood and style. Each new sentence may demand a dozen choices, all of them too intimately individual to be aided by discussion. Even here, however, method can help.

Style is hard to talk about, yet it can be cultivated. Like any other linguistic skill, it comes partly from aptitude, partly from practice. Such accomplished stylists as Ben Franklin and Ray Bradbury have drilled themselves by imitating writers they admired.

The best style is invisible. It is language used with the utmost economy, so that it seems to vanish before the information it conveys and the effects it creates. Any verbal trick that calls attention to itself is distracting the reader from the story.

Tone and mood are matters of feeling, essential to the total impact. For Poe, a founding father of science fiction and a chief creator of the short story, a powerful emotional effect was almost the whole goal. The aims of today's writers are often more complex, but emotion is still paramount. Word by word, the story language must be examined for connotation, for its power to stimulate the desired reaction.

For every act of communication, the speaker must find a role to play, must choose a mask or voice or persona. This choice is analogous to the choice of intonation that can make a simple sentence a statement or a question, ironic mockery or stern command. Point of view is part of it but by no means all. Though eminent critics have been deceived, Gulliver is *not* Jonathan Swift. Swift, wearing his mask as savage satirist, stands behind Gulliver and finally ridicules him.

In the opening of "The Most Dangerous Vision," quoted above, I try to speak through the mind of a busy scientist jotting down hurried notes about events that trouble him, but my own role—as a far smaller satirist than Swift—is quite apart from his. At the end, when he refuses to play God, he stands exposed as the sort of person he has been deploring.

Using his laconic language, I do what I can with style. He's no poet, yet what he writes must convey his despair about the ultimate fate of man, the fate he himself is to seal. As much as I dare, I enrich his telegraphic speech with rhythm and assonance and alliteration, with such metaphors as the "black flyspeck" and the "black maggot crawling on the dead red earth." But his voice is not quite mine.

Through all the decisions in the building of a story, the whole direction of effort is from the fragment toward the whole, the general toward the particular, the abstract toward the concrete, from the bare notion of a machine made too well to the finished manuscript of "With Folded Hands . . ."

In the earlier stages, the story structure is pliantly flexible and tentative choices are easy to change. As details take shape and emotions grow around them, changes are harder and harder to make. A time comes when the sense is no longer that of arbitrary choice but of discovery. The test at last is truth, a conviction of abiding rightness. I like to sleep on decisions that trouble me. In the stage of half-awareness, when the unconscious is closer to the surface, I often find the symbolic truth of things more readily apparent, the better choices easier to see.

These final phases can't be slighted. Even the cleverest plot is only a skeleton until clad in living flesh. A character often begins as only a purpose or trait, needing name and history, patterns of feeling and speech and behavior, before he comes alive. Even in the rare cases when people and places are drawn from life, they can't be transcribed directly. The artist must select those elements that fit the demands of plot and theme and point of view, of mood and tone, of total intention. He must reorder everything, purify, intensify. He must build illusion as real as life.

If such advice seems vague, there is a very specific technique for bridging this last deep gap between deep structure and surface structure —the dramatic scene. I learned it from the books of John Gallishaw. Like the functional plot, it can be studied and mastered; *The Maltese Falcon* is a splendid text. I have known several writers whose success began when they discovered it. A. E. Van Vogt has described it as the whole basis for his technique.

As Gallishaw outlines the dramatic scene, it is a sort of miniature story with five essential elements—meeting, purpose, clash, outcome, and result. The meeting brings together two opposing forces, which may be two characters, two conflicting traits in the same character, or perhaps character and setting. The reader must know the time and place. The social stage must be set. The people must be seen and heard, sometimes even felt or smelled.

The purpose unifies the scene. It is usually a minor or temporary purpose, springing from the main story purpose. To make the scene dramatic, it must be opposed. Controlling the importance of the purpose and the intensity of conflict, the writer can control dramatic interest.

The clash is the heart of the scene. Here the writer has his people as subjects in a sort of psychology lab, where he can apply stimuli to test their traits. In the steps of what Gallishaw calls the nuclear unit, he can study each detail of response—can analyze each conflicting impulse struggling for expression, can follow the flow of emotion and silent thought, can record such unconscious reactions as a flush or a frown, can finally reveal the dominant trait expressed in deliberate speech or action.

The outcome shows the scene goal won or given up. Since the scene purpose is limited and immediate, it can command interest for no more than perhaps 800 words. With each shift of purpose a new scene begins, even if we still have the same people in the same place.

The result, finally, knits the surface structure of the scene into the deep structure of the plot. The outcome of each scene has left the character nearer his main story goal, or often farther from it. Each result —and each may be a whole additional scene—may bring a further affirmation of character, a fresh reflection of emotion, another level of suspense.

To illustrate all this, here's a sample scene from "With Folded Hands . . ."

Underhill went circumspectly down the basement steps next morning to steal his own tools. He found the basement enlarged and changed. The new floor, warm and dark and elastic, made his feet as silent as a humanoid's. The new walls shone softly. Neat luminous signs identified several new doors: LAUNDRY, STORAGE, GAME ROOM, WORKSHOP.

He paused uncertainly in front of the workshop. The new sliding panel glowed with soft greenish light. It was locked. The lock had no keyhole, but only a little oval plate of some white metal that doubtless covered a rhodomagnetic relay. He pushed at it, uselessly.

"At your service, Mr. Underhill." He made a guilty start and tried not to show the sudden trembling in his knees. He had made sure that one humanoid would be busy for half an hour, washing Aurora's hair, and he hadn't known there was another in the house. It must have come from the door marked STORAGE, for it stood there motionless beneath the sign, benevolently solicitous, beautiful and terrible. "What do you wish?"

"Er—nothing." Its blind eyes were staring. Afraid that it would see his secret purpose, he groped desperately for logic. "Just looking around." His voice came hoarse and dry. "Some improvements you've made!" He nodded suddenly at the door marked GAME ROOM. "What's in there?"

It didn't even have to move, to work the concealed relays. The bright panel slid silently open as he started toward it. Dark walls, beyond, burst into soft luminescence. The room was bare.

"We are manufacturing recreational equipment," it explained brightly. "We shall furnish the room as soon as possible."

To end the awkward pause, Underhill muttered hoarsely, "Little Frank has a set of darts, and I think we had some old exercising clubs."

"We have taken them away," the humanoid informed him softly. "Such instruments are dangerous. We shall furnish safe equipment."

Suicide, he remembered, was also forbidden.

"A set of wooden blocks, I suppose," he said bitterly.

"Wooden blocks are dangerously hard," it told him gently. "Wooden splinters can be harmful. We manufacture plastic building blocks, which are entirely safe. Do you wish a set of those?"

Speechless, he merely stared at its dark graceful face.

"We shall also have to remove the tools from your workshop," it informed him softly. "Such tools are excessively dangerous. We can, however, supply you with equipment for shaping soft plastics."

"Thanks," he muttered uneasily. "No rush about that."

He started to retreat, but the humanoid stopped him.

"Now that you have lost your business," it urged, "we suggest that you formally accept our total service. Assignors have a preference, so that we should be able to complete your household staff at once."

"No rush about that, either," he said grimly.

He escaped from the house—although he had to wait for it to open the back door for him—and climbed the stair to the garage apartment. Sledge let him in. He sank into the crippled kitchen chair, grateful for the cracked walls that didn't shine and the door that a man could work.

"I couldn't get the tools," he reported despairingly. "They are going to take them."

Underhill's scene purpose to steal his own tools is stated in the first sentence. It derives from his central story goal—he and Sledge need the tools to complete the rhodomagnetic device with which they hope to stop the humanoids. Place and time are established. Sense images—of warmth and silence as well as of light—set the stage before he meets the humanoid. In the clash that follows, his fear and despair are revealed by his unspoken thoughts, by his hoarse dry voice, as well as by his speech and outward action. The outcome is defeat. The result is developed in the following scene, in which Sledge goes with him back to the basement, taking a device with which he can unlock rhodomagnetic doors.

Since scenes take space, they must often be telescoped or summarized, but sensory detail is always essential. Fiction is vicarious experience, and we live through sensation. Every scene should have images from several senses.

Interwoven through the shifting scene purposes that reflect the main story goal, plot and scene make the story. They alternate two appeals. The scenes create the vivid conviction of life, the surface structure of perceived reality. The deep structure of plot holds the scenes together. Plot, developed through the victory or defeat in each new scene, generates the hope and fear that make up suspense.

By way of conclusion, one bit of caution. Nobody has ever tried harder than I to learn narrative technique, but my most useful discovery has been that technique alone is not enough. As a linguistic structure, a story exists to transmit meaning. Its worth lies not in cunning construction but in its force and truth of meaning.

More than mere technique, a writer needs something to say. We have touched on ways of cultivating story stuff, and the other chapters in this book offer useful lessons. Certainly the science fiction audience is eager for ideas. Though most sections of our society put heavy restraints on expression, science fiction has room for every kind of opinion. Its editors and publishers are relatively free from censorship by advertisers. Its readers are a bright and open-minded lot, with few sacred cows. Its traditions encourage exploration of every sort of problem and satiric attacks on every kind of target. Its unlimited scope can liberate the imagination.

Whatever one wants to say, however, it can't be said except through some linguistic form. The science fiction short story and novelette are new linguistic coins of our age, freshly minted out of our deep concerns with science and social change, highly valued by growing numbers of our most alert and able fellow human beings.

Here I've tried to sum up what I know about writing short science fiction. There's more I don't know, but this survey has made it all seem so exciting that I intend to try it again.

Jack Williamson

Jack Williamson was born in 1908 in Bisbee, Arizona Territory, to pioneering parents who moved first to Sonora, then to Pecos, Texas, and finally in 1915 by covered wagon to the sandhill homestead in eastern New Mexico where he grew up. The big event of his youth was the discovery of Hugo Gernsback's *Amazing Stories,* which promised an escape from dust storms and drought into more exciting worlds of the imagination. He entered college the year his first story sold but dropped out before graduation because the courses had little to do with science fiction. For many years he was a freelance writer. As an Army Air Force weather forecaster, he reached the northern Solomons in 1945. Upon his return to New Mexico, he married and settled in Portales. During the science fiction boomlet of the early 1950s, he created a comic strip, *Beyond Mars,* which ran for three years in the New York *Sunday News.*

Returning to college, he received the B.A. and M.A. from Eastern New Mexico University in 1957. A teacher there since 1960, he is now a professor of English. He received his Ph.D. from the University of Colorado in 1964 with a dissertation, which has now become a book, on the early science fiction of H. G. Wells—*H. G. Wells: Critic of Progress.* Writing more or less steadily since 1926, he has published two and a half million words of magazine science fiction and nearly thirty books, several in collaboration. His teaching fields include the modern novel, literary criticism, and science fiction. He has recently been speaking and writing to promote science fiction as an academic subject.

The Legion of Space, 1947 (Fantasy)
Darker Than You Think, 1948 (Fantasy)
The Humanoids, 1949 (Simon and Schuster)
The Green Girl, 1950 (Avon)
The Cometeers and One Against the Legion, 1950 (Fantasy)
Seetee Ship, 1951 (Gnome)
Dragon's Island, 1951 (Simon and Schuster)
The Legion of Time and After World's End, 1952 (Fantasy)
Undersea Quest, 1954 (Gnome), with Frederik Pohl
Dome Around America, 1955 (Ace)
Star Bridge, 1955 (Gnome and Ace), with James Gunn
Undersea Fleet, 1955 (Gnome), with Frederik Pohl
Undersea City, 1971 (Gnome), with Frederik Pohl

The Trial of Terra, 1962 (Ace)
Golden Blood, 1964 (Lancer)
The Reefs of Space, 1964 (Ballantine), with Frederik Pohl
Starchild, 1965 (Ballantine), with Frederik Pohl
The Reign of Wizardry, 1965 (Lancer)
Bright New Universe, 1967 (Ace)
The Pandora Effect, 1969 (Ace)
Rogue Star, 1969 (Ballantine), with Frederik Pohl
People Machines, 1971 (Ace)
The Moon Children, 1972 (Putnam)
H. G. Wells: Critic of Progress, 1973 (Mirage)
The Power of Blackness, 1976 (Putnam)
Farthest Star, 1975 (Ballantine), with Frederik Pohl
Brother to Demons, Brother to Gods (Bobbs-Merrill, forthcoming)

JOHN BRUNNER

The Science Fiction Novel

(Okay, you wrote a science fiction novel and you think the publisher's reader is a purblind nitwit because the typescript came back practically by return mail—so what else is new?)

Think of a blade: how strange it is.

Not because it cuts. Because of the manner in which it does so. The keener its edge, the less it contains of the metal from which the blade is forged. Yet when it grows blunt it can be restored only from that same dull unsharp metal, less making more.

Paradox.

Since it is in the nature of those who create also to innovate, the craft of fiction is routinely honed about once per generation. In our own day—as usual—both the short story and the novel are the subject of experimentation by authors whose talents range from the meagre to the monumental. They are currently the leading edge.

But without the massy steel behind there could be no edge.

First, then, we must talk platitudes about the steel.

Whereas the short story tends to concentrate on a single event and delineate relatively few characters all quite directly involved in it, the novel is composed of a succession of events which (by one of those happy linguistic convergences that make English such a marvelous medium to work in) may be said to *articulate together* like bones.

This greater number of events does not automatically entail a greater number of characters; think of *Robinson Crusoe.* Typically, however, it does. Not all will be concerned in the eventual climax. Nonetheless their presence is (or should be) indispensable, because without the impact on them of the minor characters the major ones would not carry the action forward in rigorous and credible fashion.

A short story is cast. It resembles a work of sculpture, being a shape imposed on material of more or less uniform consistency. On the other hand, a novel is assembled. It is far more like the invention of an engineer, who combines hundreds of separate elements as various as steel, rubber and gasoline . . . and the finished product takes off down the road at a mile a minute.

Owing to this essential difference, the reason for choosing to write the novel rather than the short story is to some extent a function of temperament. Some—indeed many—of the authors whom writers in the sf field have acknowledged as their preceptors very definitely had a predilection for the shorter forms; one thinks of, for instance, Kipling, who achieved only one recognized success in the novel *(Kim)* but wrote story after story that came to be regarded as outstanding. In our own day Roald Dahl, George P. Eliot and countless others illustrate that the same phenomenon obtains.

In addition to the question of personal preference, there are both technical and—sad to say—economic reasons for writing in novel rather than short story form. Unless one is very fortunate, the time involved in writing a short story is proportionately less well paid than what one invests in an average novel. Short stories are harder to place, and story collections harder to sell in large quantities. But it should not on any account be assumed that a writer must, repeat must, opt for one or the other. This is not necessarily true in any field, and in sf above all there is a special reason why it should not be.

The whole of English-language fiction—serious as well as popular—was within living memory dominated by the magazines, from *Blackwood's* to *Black Mask.* In that context it was taken for granted that an aspiring writer must be prepared to work his/her way "up the lengths": commence by selling short stories and occasional pieces and only graduate later to book-sized projects. Oddly, it appears that today sf is the prime inheritor of this principle, a field where it not only still obtains but indeed has acquired greater force.[1]

The present essay cannot be confined wholly to the sf novel precisely because the best sf novelists have carried over to their longer work the attention to petty detail demanded by the short stories of their 'prentice days. That is why they are craftsmen as accomplished as any writers of any kind at work today.

Moreover, many of them voluntarily revert now and then to the short and simple forms they started with, much as a jazzman can keep coming home to the blues. What, for an author, corresponds to the commonplace chord sequences that a musician can find fresh and interesting throughout a playing career of half a century? Can anything be analogous?

The answer is yes. But to appreciate why and how, one must first accept that there are fundamental principles informing all successful fiction and that they need to be understood in the guts before one dare launch into uncharted seas.[2]

It is not as generally known as it should be that originally the term "masterpiece" applied to the work of a student and not a teacher. It was, so to say, the thesis an apprentice furnished to demonstrate that he had digested what his master could offer and was now qualified to teach in his turn and perhaps improve on the heritage of the past. Could Picasso have become the trail-blazer of 20th-Century art had he not first been one of the outstanding portrait-painters of his generation? Could Joyce have tempted readers and critics into the maze of *Finnegans Wake* without first publishing *Dubliners* and *Ulysses?*

To break new ground you must be equipped with a ploughshare of established principles. Nothing else is powerful enough.

Certain of those principles can be easily defined. Take the following pair to start with:

a. *The raw material of fiction is people;*

b. *The essence of story is change.*

Unite them, and they imply the consequence that unless in the course of what you write the attitude, the world-view, the personality of at least one character (ideally the most important) is discernibly and convincingly altered by events . . . what you have is not a story. You may have a vignette, or an anecdote. If what you've produced is on the long side you may even have a yarn. But not a *story.*

By what right does one speak of "principles" in respect of so varied, unpredictable and inchoate a field as the novel?

Not by "right" at all—only by the guiding light of the evidence. Consider what works of fiction have lasted longest in the consciousness of our ancestors, often to the point where they were transmitted by word of mouth, being too good stories to be wasted. Consider above all the legend of Gilgamesh, king of Uruk "of the strong walls," whose epic[3] is still being raided by writers of sword-and-sorcery fiction after four thousand years! Why? Because its anonymous author understood as by instinct that to make a fiction work you must prove, by altering the people who enact it, that the events—were they to happen in reality—would affect real people like the reader.

Homer knew that, whoever Homer was. Think of Odysseus, most cunning of the Greeks who laid siege to Troy, and how he comes home to find that neither dissimulation nor smooth talk will save his wife and his estates, but only the brute strength to bend his ram's-horn bow.

And the creators of the strip-cartoon *Superman*, learning how bored their readers had grown with a hero who never ever changed (except in a phone-booth!), were driven to introduce the threat of kryptonite.

In other words, they had to give him an Achilles heel. Homer, art thou sleeping there below?

When a practice not only has stood storytellers in good stead for millennia but can be identified in modern contexts too, one is obliged to acknowledge that adherence to it is not slavish conformity with an arbitrary precept. On the contrary. It's a necessary short cut that avoids uncountable dead ends.

Newton said, "If I have seen further than other men, it is because I have stood on the shoulders of giants." We in the 20th Century are acquainted with more giants and have access to even higher shoulders. There are so many, we can pick and choose among them according to taste.

Better still: there are so many that superposing their examples much as one superposes the traces from successive passes of a radio-telescope when searching for a pulsar enables us to distil precept after precept which others can apply to their advantage. There is no point—is there?—in making all over again the mistakes our forerunners have made.

And been ashamed of.

This is how one arrives at such principles as we have thus far enunciated: the essence of story is change, and in order to affect the reader the change must be manifest in the characters.

It follows that there can be three kinds of plot.

Indeed the situation is even worse. There can *only* be three kinds of plot.

And to compound the insult this assertion offers to common sense they go under the most banal of names: Boy Meets Girl, The Little Tailor, and Man Learns Lesson.

Not for fifteen years after I first ran across this seemingly incredible proposition[4]—not until in the course of a stint as Writer in Residence at the University of Kansas I was obliged to re-examine what I knew about the craft so as to help students gain insight into what they were attempting—did I realize why it has to be true.

A human being can change in just three ways. The first is through emotional involvement with someone else. The second is by discovering something within him/herself that he/she was previously unaware of. The third is as a consequence of uncontrollable outside circumstances.

QED.

In a vast number of book-long sf works, particularly those which belong to series akin to what is found on TV (today's counterpart of the pulp magazines), continuing characters reappear time after time unaffected—as a matter of policy—by what has gone before. These are novels only by courtesy—i.e., they are so referred to purely on a basis of size, much as a reviewer is once reputed to have said, "I have before me a *great* book, for it weighs four and a half pounds."

One such series offers an outstanding proof that applying the principle "story is change" can convert the trivial into the memorable.

In the 1940s and early 1950s Edmond Hamilton (and others) chronicled the adventures of Captain Future. At the outset, ol' Cap and his trusty sidekicks—a robot, an android, and a brain in a box—invariably turned up in the guise they had worn when the series started. They duly battled this month's menace . . . and went home. (In *Crazy Like a Fox* by S. J. Perelman you will find a delightful squib entitled "Captain Future, Block That Kick!" which deservedly pilloried that phase.)

By stages, however, Ed acquired greater insight and auctorial skill, and in the end he sent his hero to the place where, thanks to machinery installed by a lost super-race, the matter and energy of the universe are recycled. Finding himself at the controls, Captain Future fell victim to the temptation to play God, dictating the fate of galaxies.

All of a sudden Pinocchio turned from wood to flesh. Instead of being "just another Captain Future yarn" that was a powerful and effective short novel.

Having selected a plot and determined that it can be told by recounting the actions of characters who are affected by the events around them: how best can those events be conveyed to the reader, so that he/she shall comprehend the story?

Here we come to grips with a principle that is at once subtle and sophisticated. It can accordingly be expressed in three distinct ways. First, the simplest version:

Set down the events in the story in the order in which they occur.[5]

Faced with that bald proposition, members of—for instance—a Writers' Circle or a Creative Writing class almost invariably retort, "What about flashback?"

To which one is obliged to answer with a sigh, "You weren't listening, so I'll say it again. Set down the events *in the story* in the order in which they occur."

The event in the story is not the event in the flashback. In the story the event is: someone remembers. And, having remembered, acts differently from then onward. (Otherwise there was no good reason for writing the flashback sequence, was there?)

(Minor but not irrelevant digression. One mark of a bad story, whether long or short, is an excess of pluperfect tense in the first few pages. After establishing the "hook" which is supposed to seize the reader's attention, the author should not thereafter need to use such phrases as "he had been" or "he had seen" or "he had been told about" in every other line before anything actually happens in story-time. This is a sign either that the narrative should have been started at a different point or that flashback—this is one of its legitimate functions—should have been employed to eliminate the awkwardness of the pluperfect.)

In basic form the principle of keeping events in sequence is easier to observe at work in short stories than in novels. The latter may have several strands of narrative progressing either in parallel or, as it were, in echelon—staggered.[6] Within the individual strands the principle holds goods in its plainest version. To take account of the complexity that results from weaving one strand across another, it is instructive to evolve it into a more general form, thus:

Set down the events in the story in the order in which the reader benefits by learning of them.

Importing events which do not *occur within* the story—i.e., in the time hypothetically elapsed between its initial and its final scenes—is intrinsically different from importing events which do not *belong to* the story. The latter ought to be thrown away if possible before the first revision and certainly at no later stage. The former, however, can serve to illuminate and condition the behaviour of the character(s)—always providing, of course, that a sound reason is furnished for him/her/them to be reminded.

And the third version of this particular principle? It's more apt to be cited by critics than by writers, for any novelist operating to this standard thereby gives proof of either long patient apprenticeship or incontestable genius. It states:

Having decided what impact you wish to create on the reader's mind, bring it about by setting down the events of your story in the appropriate order.

Without being a counsel of perfection, that is certainly a precept to which one dare not aspire lacking a thorough grasp—conscious or subconscious—on various other factors now to be examined.

Like most human activities from cookery to sex, writing involves many elements which cannot be expressed in verbal terms and must be apprehended as a result of doing. Just as, for example, a representational painter will alter spatial relationships to create a more balanced composition, stressing what is psychologically correct in the way a camera cannot,[7] so an author will reflexively adapt such formulae as we have been discussing to the unique requirements of the current project. Often he/she will be unable to explain the reason for choosing *this* rather than *that* course of action until the novel in question is far in his/her personal past.

Curiously, though, one can define with total precision the point at which a writer makes the transition from amateurish to craftsmanly, because the change-over involves a wholly conscious process. It occurs when he/she learns to give an honest answer to the following question:

Does each and every page that I have written say what I want to tell the reader, neither more nor less?

The moment the typescript of a novel is wrapped and mailed it becomes an independent entity. From then onward not you but *it* communicates. Therefore, it is necessary, prior to sending it away, consciously to divorce your reading self from your writing self and exercise cold-blooded editorial criteria to assess and evaluate *what the page says.*

It's alarming how often it turns out that this is not identical with what you intended it to say.

Explaining to the editor on the phone a week later that the reason your hero behaved that way on page 40 was because he already knew his girl had been kidnapped as revealed to the reader on page 90—only you forgot to mention it—will provoke an unsympathetic response probably concerned with inadequate return postage.

After sloppy narrational organization, perhaps the next most infuriating fault that can sneak under your guard is choosing an inappropriate means of presenting essential data. You can lose a reader's interest almost as quickly by repeating things that have already been spelled out (because this makes the reader feel you think he/she is stupid) as by omitting to make clear your characters' motivation (because this makes the reader perfectly certain *you* are stupid).

Equally rapidly, you can induce boredom by having your characters lecture one another about subjects they must already be familiar with, since if they were not they could not possibly be in the situation, or holding down the kind of job you have allotted them.

This is peculiarly off-putting when an alien menace is just about to destroy the planet.

What techniques are available that facilitate both sound narrational structure and the optimal presentation of information? In other words, what choices are open when you are trying to decide on the format of a novel?

Broadly speaking, there are three. Each has almost countless subdivisions and each has its advantages and drawbacks. Only experience can serve as a guide to picking the right one. However, knowing that alternatives exist and what they are gives one a head start over those attempting to work it out from scratch.

The oldest of the viable narrative modes is known as "omniscient author." Godlike, the writer views his novel from an Olympian vantage-point; he frankly admits that he is recounting a fiction—indeed he often reminds the reader of it—and he never hesitates to step in and out of any character's mind.

Today, this mode works only to the extent that the author shows him/herself to be aware of its shortcomings. In the 18th and 19th Centuries it was exploited to the point of self-indulgence. Writers would resort to direct apostrophe: "Ah, dear reader, for an hundred pages thou hast ached to learn the fate of those who caught the plague at Mud-dleford!" (To which one suspects the reader, unaware of aching, might resentfully have responded, "So you haven't forgotten them after all! I nearly had!")

It takes an expert like Frederik Pohl (in *Day Million*) to find a proper contemporary application for "omniscient author," mainly because it can lead to a fault which is extremely common and none the better for being so: use of the disastrous phrase "Had they but known . . . !"[8] Bluntly, that is cheating.

Let Olaf Stapledon's *Last and First Men* stand as both an example and a warning concerning "omniscient author" mode in the sf novel: the former inasmuch as the book is proof it can be made to work, the latter inasmuch as it indicates you had better be a thinker of comparable stature to bring it off.

The polar opposite is to tell the story in first person. This has incontrovertible advantages. Above all, there need never be any hesitation about mixing subjective with objective statements. One can switch from the description of an external event in the mode "There was . . ." straight to the emotional reaction it engenders in the mode "I felt . . ." (or, even more usefully, "It was as though . . .") and the reader will not find the changeover arbitrary or dislocating.

On the other hand, what about events that occur when the narrator is not present, that he/she does not hear about until after they have affected the action of the story? Can the reader be satisfied with retrospective explanations?[9] Only if the narrator can, too—which means that more often than not the answer is no.

It is impossible to imagine *Flowers for Algernon* by Daniel Keyes having the same impact in third-person that it has in first. But even in the case of so widely admired a novel as Pohl and Kornbluth's *The Space Merchants* many critics have disputed the aptness of first-person narration.

Bear in mind, though, that if the answer is neither yes nor no but maybe, pure first-person can be varied. Less used, perhaps, than it might be is multiple first-person; instead of following the same narrator throughout the book, one makes two, three or more characters recount different episodes. An outstanding recent application of this formula may be found in Robert Silverberg's *The Book of Skulls.*

Naturally one must have a solid and logical reason for selecting the "I" for each sequence. Compare the "sigma character" approach described below; a case could be made out for classifying multiple first-person under that head rather than here, but for most authors the primary distinction lies between first- and third-person narrative, inasmuch as during the actual writing they induce extremely contrasted states of mind.

A rare variant of first-person, seldom used in sf or indeed in any contemporary fiction, is called "epistolary" from the Latin word for a letter. Such a story is couched in the guise of letters, reports or similar documents from one or several hands. It is easier to exploit this in the short story (e.g., Gordon Dickson's "Computers Don't Argue") than in the novel, but sections of Theodore Sturgeon's *Some of Your Blood* are epistolary and show that the formula can be a valuable adjunct to a novel whose main structure is of another type.

On balance, there is no doubt that third-person narrative (in conventional aorist tense) is the most versatile and generally useful of the novelist's tools. It spans so enormous a range, from the hard-to-handle "camera eye" version—in which all emotional references and virtually all sensory references other than visual are discarded so that the action might as well be observed by a machine as by a person—to the one which must be termed supremely versatile, the employment of "sigma characters."

Why sigma? I have never found out. But it is a handy nickname and preferable to the more widespread usage "viewpoint character" because the latter implies an emphasis on visual as opposed to other types of perception, thereby diverting attention from the chief advantage of this method, which is that—without suffering the constraints of first-person—one can set forth not only what the character we are currently following *observes* but also what he/she *thinks, recalls, feels* and *imagines.*

For a would-be writer attempting a first sf novel (come to that, a first novel of any kind) this is the approach most strongly to be commended.

Here's how it works.

Within each segment of the novel—the division will often coincide with a chapter but may occur at shorter intervals, in which case the convention is to mark the changeover with a line space—the reader is invited to witness events from the standpoint of one and only one of the characters. If a subjective comment is called for, such as an emotional reaction or an opinion not spoken aloud, it is this character and none other who does the reacting . . . that is, unless someone who is also present turns subjective into objective, as by smiling, or scowling, or screaming.

A plot of astonishingly tangled structure can be made transparently clear and easy to follow through the correct choice of points at which to shift from one sigma character to another. In this respect *The Man in the High Castle* constitutes an object lesson. Philip K. Dick does not always bring off the tricky ploys he is fond of; on that occasion, though, he presented a model that can be studied with profit and pleasure too.

It should be stressed that it is by no means obligatory to use multiple sigma characters. A novel may be of such a structure that a single character can be followed from start to finish, but first-person (an obvious possibility) fails to meet all the demands of the plot. For example, at the climax you may wish to depict your protagonist undertaking some especially heroic task. To relate deeds of that kind from the narrator's own standpoint would—if he/she possesses any shred of modesty—vastly diminish the impact on the reader. Select third-person mode accordingly, but ensure that the action is observed as rigorously from the main character's viewpoint as in the case of first-person.

When following the same sigma character for all, or a substantial portion, of a book, you will find it advisable to decide in advance whether there will have to be a great many marker-phrases like "he/she thought/mused/wondered." If so, it can be advantageous to use a shift into italic instead, or to separate private thoughts into paragraphs on their own introduced by the French equivalent of "open quotes," an em dash.[10]

Devices of this kind, however, call for total consistency in their application. Unless you are confident of controlling them with flawless precision, it's better to stick with more conventional means.

An extraordinary and powerful effect can sometimes be obtained by switching in and out of subjective and objective, or even present and past (story-) time, with no landmarks whatever. This, though, is on a par with painting a successful cubist portrait; it may look easy, but in fact it is abominably difficult.

Much the same may be said of two other uncommon narrative formulae: historic present and second-person.

The former is encountered with some frequency these days, as in Barry Malzberg's *Beyond Apollo* and parts of Michael Moorcock's *The Black Corridor;* moreover, it is employed throughout Thomas Pynchon's gigantic near-sf novel *Gravity's Rainbow.* Having read those, I cling impenitently to my long-standing opinion: historic present in sf is best reserved for wholly impersonal passages of description, preferably of large-scale physical events, including none of the story's characters and perhaps isolated from the remainder of the text by being set in a contrasting face.

As to the latter, it has only once to my knowledge been used for the whole of an sf novel (a long-out-of-print item by the British writer H. J. Campbell entitled *The Moon Is Heaven,* which was in any case a spoof). Most readers find it intolerably irritating to have their identification with the protagonist forced by constant reference to him/her as "you."

One has to have a very good reason for adopting either of these approaches and skills of an advanced order to make the result read well.

The actual shape of a novel—the layout of its fully developed plot—is obviously a function of its theme. A long-voyage story must differ from a mystery story or one in which tension derives from people being trapped or lost: *Seed of Light* from *The Naked Sun* and both from *A Fall of Moondust.*

On analysis, one finds that this aspect of the novel can also be classified under three main heads: the sequential, or episodic; the recursive; and the picaresque. Just as it is rare for novels to exhibit one type of plot unalloyed with any of the others, so it is seldom that they fit tidily into one of these pigeonholes without spilling into two or all three. Nonetheless it is worth defining their pure forms.

Commonest by far—and, incidentally, easiest to write—is the sequential novel. It introduces us to given characters in given circumstances. In more or less straightforward chronological order a series of scenes or episodes show us the characters interacting with one another and their environment until a climax is reached that resolves the story.

One could list examples by the thousand, for despite its simplicity this form can generate subtle and elaborate works and not infrequently a novel of classic quality. For all their dazzling imagery and multiple layers of meaning, the novels of J. G. Ballard (such as, in particular, *The Drowned World* and *The Drought*) are founded on plain sequential narrative, and so—by my count—are a clear majority of the Hugo winners.

Recursive novels are somewhat more complicated. Typically they depend on one event that dominates the entire book, and the progress of the plot derives from re-examination or re-evaluation of it over and over until at last the author's argument comes clear. *Rogue Moon* by A. J. Budrys and *The Demolished Man* by Alfred Bester may serve to epitomize the form as it occurs in sf.

In a picaresque novel, the main character (or a group of characters) moves from one self-contained situation to another constantly throughout the book. The technique is not especially common in sf—which is curious, inasmuch as it is often said that the picaresque is the most powerful of fictional formulae—although of course short stories and novelettes featuring continuing characters are often published in one volume as though they amounted to a novel (e.g., Poul Anderson's *Guardians of Time* or *Agent of Vega* by James H. Schmitz), and the result bears a faint, faint resemblance to the picaresque structure.[11]

It is to sword-and-sorcery or to space opera that one must look for the most numerous instances of picaresque narrative in our field rather than to sf *per se*, where it seems primarily to be reserved for satire. Ron Goulart is an outstanding exponent of this latter approach, and one should also cite *Journey Beyond Tomorrow (The Journey of Joenes)* by Robert Sheckley.

By way of illustrating the fashion in which all three of these elements may combine within one novel, permit me to cite my own *To Conquer Chaos*, which I have found extremely useful when talking to aspiring writers.

It features three leading characters: Conrad, a young man, mocked and rejected because he follows the dirty trade of soap-making, who lives in a village on the edge of a mysterious desert called the Barrenland from which come monsters; Nestamay, one of a group of people trapped in the middle of the Barrenland at a broken-down interstellar transport station which randomly imports alien animals; and Yanderman, an officer in the army of the Duke of Esberg who came to investigate these alleged monsters—only the Duke is dead and the army has deserted. Braving the Barrenland, Conrad and Yanderman reopen contact with Nestamay's community.

Within the novel, Conrad's experience is sequential. He abandons his home in search of something better and becomes caught up in events that change his life. But Nestamay's is recursive, since until the arrival of strangers her existence revolves around one tiny group of people with a single problem that repeats itself in endlessly varied forms. And Yanderman's, in principle at any rate, is picaresque, for he was one among thousands who set out on the trail of a half-credible rumor and was prepared to go wherever the evidence might lead.

Having settled on the plot of a novel, having worked out what characters the action will require, what the crucial events are, and from whose standpoint the reader is to witness each, there remains the task of ensuring that your imaginary world with its imaginary people will so impress the readers that they want to continue to the end.

The opinion is regrettably widespread that this problem can be solved by artifice. Let each elegantly turned sentence gleam as though bejeweled with symbol, simile and/or metaphor—so runs the argument—and the reader's nape will prickle and having finished the book he/she will instantly recommend it to a hundred friends.

That is *not* the way it works. Because the art in fiction—beauty, clarity and economy of expression—cannot exist in isolation from a comprehension of the craft. Given the latter, though, the former follows without the author straining after it and letting the reader perceive the effort which entered into the novel. If the effort does show (and not infrequently it's as conspicuous as custard pie on a comedian's kisser) the reader will correctly conclude that the writer is trying to show off.

Is a concert pianist aware of every separate finger movement as he plays an arpeggio *molto presto?* Hardly. But there was a time when he spent weary hours rehearsing five-finger exercises, and in those days he did think about each separate movement. Had he not done so, what you are hearing now would be impossible.

A writer is obliged to sweat out an analogous period of apprenticeship. Traditionally there is no royal road to geometry. There is none to first-rate writing, either. But there are many well-marked stepping-stones.

For instance, instead of fretting over metonymia, chiasmus and litotes, keep asking yourself how we experience the real world. Remember we have five external senses, and internal senses too. Invoke them all. It's the best means of bringing what you describe vividly into focus in the reader's mind.

Do not be content to imitate what cinema or television could tackle equally well. The novel is a vastly more versatile medium. Its action is played out on the largest stage in the known universe. And the budget for special effects is bottomless.

Find out as much as you can about the resources of the English language. As a tool for the writer it has never been matched. An unabridged dictionary of English contains approximately twice as many entries as the best any other language can offer.

Spend this fortune prodigally, for thereby it is constantly renewed. Do not, for heaven's sake, resort time and again to "get" when some other verb would express your meaning without vagueness. Do not repeat any word more often than can be helped.[12] Reproach yourself every time you realize you have used an inexact term, or a pair of terms that do not define what you want to talk about but only strike to left and right, leaving the poor reader to figure out where in the middle you are hoping he/she may wind up. Pick something better![13]

And never forget how many influences we respond to: not only shape and color, heat and cold, speech and noise, but also hunger and fullness, hate and love, sickness and health. Make use of them all. What you put on the page is under your entire and undivided control. Why be satisfied to blow a bubble when you have the chance to create another world?

Virtually all the foregoing observations have been applicable to any form of novel-writing, not exclusively to sf. This is by design.

Attempts have been made to draw distinctions between the writing of sf and that of other varieties of fiction. Lovecraft once remarked that the true hero of a "marvel tale" is not a person but an event, while John Wyndham was accustomed to contrast the "feminine" attitude of mainstream fiction with the "masculine" posture of sf—as being concerned, so to say, with the collision of galaxies and not with the emotions thereby engendered in the watcher.[14]

Perhaps there was substance in such comments when they were first made. But times have changed and with them the nature of sf. Less emphasis is now placed on the "hard" sciences, more on those which directly concern the human condition, such as psychology, biochemistry, anthropology and ethology.

When one sets the sf of an earlier day alongside what is being written in the 'Seventies, it's hard to decide whether the parallels are more enlightening or the contrasts. Wyndham wrote many disaster novels; they may be compared with more recent books like Christopher Priest's *Fugue for a Darkening Island.* In the 'Thirties, J.B.S. Haldane had no qualms about depicting a human-occupied, terraformed Venus in the year 40,000,000. Today, exploiting the far-out visions of Freeman Dyson, Larry Niven invites us to *Ringworld.* In "Twilight" and "Night"

John Campbell carried us past the date of man's extermination; now, Poul Anderson in *Tau Zero* does not balk at whirling us into the next cycle of the universe. And so on.

A constant tendency is apparent from all these stories, though. More stress is now laid on making the characters believable, less on the grandiosity of the events. In *Tau Zero* Captain Telander is capable not only of losing his temper and falling in and out of love but even of suffering a nervous breakdown. This is a far cry from 1951, when Bob Shaw (then a youthful fan, now himself an established sf writer) could utter the heartfelt plea: "How I would love to read . . . an E. E. Smith epic in which Kimball Kinnison does something really human like catching a cold!"

What has happened to account for this change? Partly it is due to our having answered such burning questions of the inter-war period as whether we can liberate atomic energy and whether we can send a rocket to the Moon, while failing to solve the more important problem of why we can do these things yet not live together in a sane society. Partly it is because, at the same time as the subject matter of sf was broadening out, a new generation of readers (and authors) emerged whose criteria were not restricted by the so-called "ghetto" of the specialized magazines but whose view of the world—one might almost say of the universe—had been deeply affected by the mere existence of Buck Rogers, John Carter, Captain Future, Ol' Doc Methuselah, Jommy Cross, Jirel of Joiry and the rest.[15]

Nothing can oblige an author more rapidly to improve his/her self-set standards than the discovery that all of a sudden the audience is prepared to apply to what he/she writes not the private yardstick of an in-group but the measure informed judges would apply to any type of fiction.

On exactly those grounds I have sedulously avoided talking about sf novel-writing as though it were a phenomenon apart from the rest of authorship. It would be pointless, surely, to explain to someone who has already decided he/she would like to write sf that its chief themes include space- and time-travel, robots, alien beings and the like.

It is not at all pointless to define some of the elements which are found in good, and are absent from bad, fiction of whatever type.

One cannot teach somebody to write well. That's a talent, inborn like a singer's sense of pitch or a dancer's grace. But one can point to examples of bad writing and say, "That is badly written *because* . . . !"

Liberated from fettering mistakes, one can allow his/her creative faculty much greater play. It is as true of writing as of anything else that freedom consists in doing first what must be done and afterwards what you want to do.

Reading this essay, you may feel that the principles it sets forth are stark and uncompromisingly rigid; you may wonder why there are no references to spontaneity and inspiration. As to the former . . . Well, if you want to see what spontaneity really looks like, go struggle through the transcript of Nixon's White House tapes. As to the latter . . .

You hope to learn *that* off a printed page???

Indeed these principles are rigid. But not with the constricting rigidity of a corset—rather with the rigidity of a well-forged knife that will serve for a thousand tasks and never snap, or a bedrock foundation on which you can erect your towers, knowing it will never slip or slide.

NOTES

1. There are numerous exceptions; for instance, Samuel Delany had published five novels before "Aye. And Gomorrah" (his first short story to see print) won him a Nebula award. It is nonetheless true that sf magazines continue to serve as a nursery for writers long after most "category" periodicals, and many general ones, have been folded. Their role has moreover been supplemented by volume collections of original stories. Being blessed with a quarterly or even annual schedule as against a monthly one, the editors of the latter can afford to impose very selective standards.

2. Be warned. A lot of what look like vacant areas on the map have in fact already been explored. The reason this is not often mentioned is that the people who went there decided it wasn't worth the trouble. Or else their readers did.

3. Translated by N. K. Sandars and published in The Penguin Classics.

4. In Robert Heinlein's contribution to the symposium *Of Worlds Beyond*, edited by Lloyd Eshbach, which appeared originally in 1947.

5. It is notorious that when unexpectedly arrested and interrogated one is best advised to tell the truth even if only because later on it will be easier to remember what one said. Telling the truth is forbidden to writers of fiction, who are by both profession and definition systematic liars—and moreover liars who hope to be rewarded for the excellence of their falsehoods. It takes practice to achieve consistency in lying, though. This approach, the nearest available substitute for telling the truth, is accordingly recommended to all beginners.

6. One of the simplest yet most effective means of enhancing narrational

tension is to present separate groups of characters which the reader knows to be involved in a common overall pattern of events but which remain ignorant one of another until the story is well under way.

7. Although a photographer can.

8. Arthur Clarke's famous story "Rescue Party" succeeded in spite of being littered with topological transforms of it but cannot be recommended as a model since not everybody is lucky enough to hit on that strong a plot.

9. Phrases of the form "Had I but known . . ." should be avoided with the same diligence as their third-person counterpart.

10. After several false starts I hit on this trick and used it throughout *Quicksand,* the most subjective of my novels. It proved immensely valuable because so much of the action took place inside one person's head.

11. It is a matter for debate whether "quest" stories automatically qualify as picaresque. My view is that the majority fall under the sequential heading. Here again, however, I am relying on what is essentially a distinction between the states of mind they entrain in the author at work.

12. Contrary to popular belief, and especially to what most teachers will tell you, English is poor in synonyms, not rich. What we actually have is countless ways of saying *not quite the same* thing. The temptation to be imprecise is therefore tremendous. But what a waste it is if you give in!

13. To a greater extent than British English, American English is becoming an isolating language like Chinese, as witness phrases like "all stations go" and "I am into . . ." (writing/Zen/women's lib/what-have-you). Thus far, however, such tropes remain largely in the categories of slang or cant. And it should be borne in mind that vogue and faddish terms tend to be localized in time as well as space; those who rely on them often sacrifice a huge potential audience. People still read *The Diary of a Nobody* . . . but not *The Yellowplush Papers;* Mark Twain . . . but not Artemus Ward.

14. One takes it that Wyndham had in mind the "novel of sensibility," for the thriller and the spy story—to cite but two of many cases—are just as preoccupied as is sf with the external at the expense of the internal process.

15. Any attempt to sing the foregoing to the tune of *Widecombe Fair* will be undertaken entirely at your own risk.

John Brunner

John Brunner was born in Oxfordshire, England, on the 24th of September, 1934, and was educated at Cheltenham College, where he specialized in modern languages. He made his first sale of a science fiction novel while still in school, worked as an editor, served in the RAF, and in 1958—after making his first novel sale to the U.S.—decided to freelance full time. In that year he also married his wife, Marjorie. They have traveled extensively and now live in a small town in Somerset.

John Brunner has received the British Fantasy Award, the British SF Award (twice), the American Hugo for best sf novel of the year, and the major French sf award, the Prix Apollo. He has published more than sixty novels and short novels, nine or ten short-story collections, two volumes of poetry, and a translation (of Gérard Klein's *The Overlords of War*). His short stories have appeared in all the leading sf magazines in Britain and America and many of them have, of course, been anthologized. Translations of his work have appeared in nine languages. In addition, his stories "Some Lapse of Time" and "The Last Lonely Man" have been adapted for BBC-TV's "Out of the Unknown," and another, "Such Stuff," was sold to the American TV show "Night Gallery." He also wrote the film script for a Murray Leinster novel, *The Terrornauts.*

Of him, Frederik Pohl writes:

> As a writer he has been developing force in the field of science fiction since the early 1950s; his big novel of a couple of seasons ago, *Stand on Zanzibar,* was so big that the Modern Language Association devoted the whole of its annual science fiction symposium to that single novel. No other book has ever been so honored.
>
> Brunner writes with many voices. His early work is straight sf adventure, so good of its kind that only the most depraved addict of elegant prose would welcome the transition to more sophisticated work. But if he had not made that transition, he would not have novels like *Zanzibar,* or short stories like "The Totally Rich."

A few of the Brunner titles are:

The Brink, 1959
The Crutch of Memory, 1964
The Devil's Work, 1970

Double, Double, 1969
The Dreaming Earth, 1963
From This Day Forward, 1972
The Gaudy Shadows, 1970
The Jagged Orbit, 1969
Listen! The Stars!, 1963
The Long Result, 1965
No Future In It, 1962
Now Then, 1965
Out of My Mind, 1967
A Plague on Both Your Causes, 1969
The Productions of Time, 1967
Quicksand, 1967
The Sheep Look Up, 1972
The Squares of the City, 1965
Timescoop, 1969
The Whole Man (U.S.), 1964/*The Telepathist* (U.K.), 1965
The Wrong End of Time, 1971

HARLAN ELLISON

With the Eyes of a Demon: Seeing the Fantastic as a Video Image

One afternoon in (something like) 1965, I sat in a little treehouse in Beverly Glen, in Los Angeles, in Hollywood, writing a television script; and I typed these words:

> **The witch rushes down the spiral staircase and runs wildly through the lavish reception hall of the mansion. Her cape knocks aside a candelabrum that crashes to the floor and spins off a burning candle. The candle rolls across the floor and comes to rest in the heavy velvet folds of drapes covering one wall. The drapes catch fire and suddenly the entire reception hall is a mass of flames. The witch is trapped and burns to death.**

I wrote those seventy-eight words, only seventy-eight words, for a tv series called "Burke's Law," late one summer afternoon in something like 1965. It took me possibly one minute to type those lines. And three weeks later I stood wide-eyed in wonderment as they set fire to sound stage #11 at Four Star Studios. I stood stunned with amazement as one of the most beautiful actresses

I'd ever seen, Janet Blair, in the role of the witch, Purity Mather, ran down a spiral staircase and through the posh reception hall of a mansion with only three walls. I stood staring open-mouthed as she knocked aside a silver candelabrum, as a sausage-thick candle, specially made not to go out on impact, rolled across the parquet floor (drawn on an invisible thread), settled among swagged drapes, as the fabric actually exploded with flames, and half a dozen firefighters, a fire marshal, sixty-odd studio grips, gaffers, electricians, propmen, studio personnel, extras, stars, producers, associate/assistant/executive/and hemisemidemi producers, the director, and assorted others fell back before the awesome spectacle of that mansion dissolving in flames while Purity Mather writhed in pain and terminal anguish.

And when it was all done—because they could only do it once and they *had* to get it right the first time—the director yelled, "Okay, that's a take! Let's wrap for the night!" And everyone applauded like crazy, and I was hooked on writing for television.

Seventy-eight casually written words, one minute of the time I spent on that one-hour-long script, and they had called out half the population of the civilized world to put *my* dream on film.

Until you've been there, don't tell me about power.

I begin this discussion of writing fantasy and science fiction and other forms of magic realism for films and television with the previous comments and memories for a good reason. As we go forward in this essay, I'll be saying, again and again, that working in the visual media is very much like the old story about the moron who dug being beaten across the belly with a sawed-off ballbat because it felt so damned good when they stopped. I'll be saying that in *no other* creative medium is there such an attack on the writer's sensibilities (and often his or her life) than in the tv/film arena. It is an art-form by committee, a cobbled-up Frankenstein's Monster of arbitrary rules, imbecilic decisions, cowardly rationalizations and tasteless pandering to the lowest possible common denominators of public mass taste. I don't know what you have read about working in the Industry, I don't know what nonprofessional beliefs you hold about how things are done "on the inside," and I don't know what myths you believe or lies you've swallowed. But I would be a liar and a hypocrite if I didn't tell you *precisely* what it's like from the git-go. Bear in mind, of course, that everything I'll say here is drawn from almost fourteen years' working in the Industry, and the conclusions are based on where *I've* been and what *I've* seen. It's as responsible and accurate as I can make it; but it *is* an upfront subjective position.

So when I start with that story about "Burke's Law" and then instantly badrap the Industry, you're bound to ask, "If it's such a cesspool, why do you do it? Why should *any* sane, talented writer choose to indenture him/herself in a medium where the work itself is manhandled and corrupted and amputated, to be used, finally, as the come-on for selling trashwagons and paisley asswipe?"

The memory of that day at the Four Star Studios (now CBS Studio Center) is thus presented as partial explanation and rationale for a writer enduring attacks on his creativity one should *never,* under any other circumstances or in any other situation, tolerate. The explanation, of course, is that working in visuals is exciting and, when you can connect, when you can slip one past them, when you build up enough clout or somewhichway steal enough good karma to purchase some luck, it can be artistically rewarding in ways not even the print medium can approach. How heady it is to envision that witch and that fire, write those few words, and see them actually bring the vision to life. It is the closest contemporary paradigm for Aladdin's Magic Lamp. Merely rub the distended belly of a studio executive and whoosh! you get your wish.

That's part of it. The other parts are two.

One: if those with talent opt for sanity and peace, and refuse to fight the fight necessary to getting good writing on the tube, if they bolt and desert the arena, forfeiting the medium to the no-talents and the venal businessmen who conceive of themselves as creators *manqués,* then we abrogate our artistic responsibility and surrender without bloodshed the greatest medium for the dissemination of information and individual imagination the world has ever known. I work in television, *cum dissentiente.* With a dissenting voice.

Two: as I mentioned, when you *do* manage to get something produced that you've written with craft and skill and inventiveness and honesty, it is a thrilling experience; it reaches more people than those who usually read the printed word; and it vindicates the anguished times you've invested. But more, writing a script—as opposed to a short story, a novel, a quatrain, a play or an essay—is a complex technical undertaking. And learning to do it to perfection, so you develop a "voice" that marks your work and sets it apart (and hopefully above) all scenarios written by others, fills you with pleasure, pride and the knowledge that you have expanded yourself as a writer. Because writers should write in *all* forms, should not limit themselves, should constantly strive to enlarge the scope of their abilities.

Add to the foregoing, the financial rewards. If we're to be utterly honest here.

The going price for a one-hour teleplay, between one month and three months' work (depending how speedily and carefully one works), is about $6400. That is about double what a new writer can expect as an advance for a novel in the sf category. And if one is serious about one's writing, that kind of money can provide security and freedom to *spend* the year it takes to write a novel properly. (Well, let's say *two* scripts could provide that time.) So a writer invests three or four months' writing time to buy seven or eight to do what he/she wishes. And the time one invests is spent *writing,* not waiting table in a diner or working for the telephone company, so it is *invested,* not *spent.*

And that is the reason I've taken these pages to tell you *why* one works in a medium that can be terribly crushing for all but writers with stamina and a highly developed sense of their talent and direction. One labors in the House of the Dead to buy passage into Heaven for one's immortal soul.

I knew you would ask, so that's the answer.

And, of course, because it *is* a collaborative medium—where one's brainchildren are taken away and altered by producers, directors, cinematographers, editors and actors—the working conditions of the Industry, and the writer's mental attitudes, cannot be avoided as pivotal elements in the equation of creativity. I'll deal more with those conditions later in this essay. But at this point, let's get into the specifics of actually how to *write* a script for television, and by extension, for movies, using the special tool of sf/fantasy.

It is essential to understand, not just superficially, but all the way down in the creative core of your thinking, that writing for a *visual* medium is quite different from writing for the printed page. The form is different, of course, but more than that, the intellectual set is very different. If I were to write:

> Simonson sat across the memory-pool table from her, staring silently at the expression of hate in her lovely face. He knew what she was thinking: *this is the man who caused the death of my family.* He wanted to tell her that it had been her own father who had done it; her father who had destroyed

> himself and his wife and his son because of a sense of duty less courageous men and women could never comprehend. Less courageous men, like Simonson; less courageous women, like the grieving, hating daughter seated across the shimmering blue surface of the memory-pool.

I could get away with it perfectly in a story, because the printed page demands participation on the part of the reader. Unlike television, films, football games, the roller derby, wars in underdeveloped nations and Watergate hearings, which are spectator sports, a book requires the activation of its words by the eyes and intellect of a reader. As Isaac Asimov said recently in an article, postulating the perfect entertainment cassette:

> A cassette as ordinarily viewed makes sounds and casts light. That is its purpose, of course, but must sound and light obtrude on others who are not involved or interested? The ideal cassette would be visible and audible only to the person using it. . . . We could imagine a cassette that is always in perfect adjustment; that starts automatically when you look at it; that stops automatically when you cease to look at it; that can play forward or backward, quickly or slowly, by skips or with repetitions, entirely at your pleasure. . . . Surely, that's the ultimate dream device—a cassette that may deal with any of an infinite number of subjects, fictional or non-fictional, that is self-contained, portable, non-energy-consuming, perfectly private and largely under the control of the will. . . . Must this remain only a dream? Can we expect to have such a cassette some day? . . . We not only have it now, we have had it for many centuries. The ideal I have described is the printed word, the book, the object you now hold—light, private, and manipulable at will. . . . Does it seem to you that the book, unlike the cassette I have been describing, does not produce sound and images? It certainly does. . . . You cannot read without hearing the words in your mind and seeing the images to which they give rise. In fact, they are *your* sounds and images, not those invented for you by others, and are therefore better. . . . The printed word presents minimum information, however. Everything but that minimum must be provided by the reader—the intonation of words, the expressions on faces, the actions, the scenery, the background, must all be drawn out of that long line of black-on-white symbols.

I've quoted Isaac at length because he has summed up precisely the difference between writing a narrative and creating a screenplay. All of the things your imagination provides without effort as you read—intonations of words, expressions on faces, actions, scenery, background—all of that *plus* an exterior point of view, must be *invented* by the scenarist.

Watching television is a spectator sport. *Writing* for television is the most involving participation sport in the world of literature. Most people who sit plugged into the box like a patient with acute irreversible coma plugged into a respirator, don't realize that a scenarist not only has the initial dream—the subject matter, the story-line, the approach to the work—but he writes all them funny words them funny little actors—"Electronic Lilliputians," one commentator has called them—say to each other. The scenarist puts in what angles you'll see a scene from. He writes the moves and attitudes of the characters *within* a scene and the flow of the scenes as a totality, act by act, crisis to crisis. It is visual poetry, as carefully structured as the flow of words into lines and lines into paragraphs and paragraphs into chapters of a novel.

But unlike the written narrative, the script has to *show* all that. From the outside. Unless you use a *voice over* technique (V.O.), everything that goes on in a character's mind must be either spoken or shown in the actions of the character! For many writers, that is a handicap, a tether too short for them to endure. For others, it becomes a kind of challenge, to see how cleverly and *visually* one can interpret the interior monologue, the irrational impulse, the anguished moment, the inexplicable action.

So, from the very start, the writer of a screenplay must understand that *everything* will be shown. Or if not blatantly conveyed, at least clearly indicated through the use of camera angles, misdirection, point of view (POV) and electronic techniques.

(I'm wandering from my original point in this section, and in just a moment I'll get back to that paragraph of story I dropped in a little bit ago. But the suddenly discursive tack this piece has taken demands I illustrate the preceding paragraph with some examples. Please bear with me, it'll all come right in the end.)

What I just said, about indicating by misdirection and camera angles, and so forth, is the essence of using *film as film.* Film is not a stage production, it's not a printed page, it's not the "talking head" mode that one finds employed on television newscasts. It is a realization that the actual movement of the camera, the POV, can convey what would be pages of explanation in a story. For instance:

Let's say the character I introduced in that story paragraph, Simonson, has discovered that his enemies have developed a way to kill him by use of a remote control device keyed to the telephone . . .

No, hold it! Let's make it an even better example than *that.* Let's say *we,* the audience, have discovered that fact. That Simonson can be killed when his telephone is picked up. But *he* doesn't know it.

So there he is in his apartment, nervous, unsettled, knowing that the enemy will be making an attempt on his life, but he doesn't know when or how. In a story, in a book, we'd have to write all manner of interior monologue and observations from the viewpoint of the Omniscient Author. But in a teleplay, it can be done like this: (Don't worry about the form, or the numbers or abbreviations that you don't understand; I'll explain all that later.)

56 INT. SIMONSON'S APT.—NIGHT—
ESTABLISHING

LONG SHOT in UP-ANGLE PERSPECTIVE from telephone on modern writing desk LARGE IN F.G. across room to Simonson, pacing in the b.g. HOLD PHONE LARGE as he lights a cigarette, takes two hurried puffs, then comes to ashtray on writing desk in f.g., snubs the cigarette.

CUT TO:

57 REVERSE ANGLE—PAST SIMONSON—HIS POV

as he walks into f.g. and we SHOOT OVER HIS SHOULDER. The phone RINGS. Simonson turns FROM CAMERA to stare at phone. CAMERA ZOOMS IN on phone. HOLDS SEVERAL BEATS. CAMERA ZOOMS BACK to include Simonson in frame. As he moves toward phone the CAMERA GOES WITH. He reaches for the receiver as CAMERA COMES IN TIGHT on his hand poised above the phone. He hesitates. Phone RINGS AGAIN, seemingly louder, more tension in its ring. Will he pick it up or not?

Okay, now do you *see* what I mean? Not a word has been spoken; no one has had to announce in that cornball V.O. that Simonson is nervous—the action with the cigarette and the pacing says it all—that he is in danger from the phone—the angle with the phone dominating the foreground (f.g.) makes that clear—and all the suspense you need is built with camera movement—zoom in/zoom out, Simonson's hand poised above the receiver.[1]

Thus, we have our first lesson in using *film as film;* an absolute must if one is to be a good scenarist, an inventive script writer, something more noble than a hack or the hundreds of, well, call them "creative typists," who fill most of the endless hours of prime time with *dreck.*

Another, perfect example of the use of *film as film*—that is, film used to tell a story without the words or even the use of actors—is the ending to Francis Ford Coppola's extraordinarily brilliant motion picture, *The Conversation* (which is, for my money, the finest motion picture of the last twenty years, and utterly stunning in its sense of filmic movement).

The ending of the film, in case you haven't seen it—or even if you have seen it and didn't catch the subtlety of what Coppola was doing—is this: his protagonist, a professional wiretapper and bugger, has discovered something he was never intended to find out when he was hired. Now *he* knows a secret that is dangerous to a group of powerful people, and they have to bring him under their control. Rather than killing him, they make him paranoid by using his very own trade against him. They call him and tell him he's being watched. They call him on a private line he has gone to extreme lengths to keep secret. So he knows they're on to him. Now his innate paranoia takes hold. He has to de-bug his apartment. He begins tearing it apart. The phone, down to its parts, like an eviscerated animal. The furniture, stuffing yanked out. The frames of pictures, broken apart, scattered around the room. The walls, savaged to the stanchions, banged open like an empty rib cage. The baseboards ripped out. The ceiling fixtures yanked down. Everything a shambles. Nothing there. Nothing at all.

And the final shot is of the wiretapper, Gene Hackman, sitting amid the ruins, mournfully playing his saxophone. But. Where lesser directors—and Coppola is one of the heavyweights—would have either pulled up and back for one of those teddibly teddibly meaningful master shots, showing the hunter now crushed and broken, or given us the ho-hum standard freeze-frame, Coppola has done something absolutely original. He has made the point of the film subtly and artfully by doing this:

The camera is already moving right as the shot begins. It pans right slowly, a medium shot with a modified fisheye lens that shows the entire room as the camera sweeps past Hackman, going the full width of the room to the right-hand wall. The camera stops, holds a beat so we think that's all we're going to see, then begins panning back left at the same mechanically steady pace as before. The pan carries us back and we think it will stop when it holds Hackman centerframe. But it keeps going, past him, all the way to the left-hand wall, showing the debacle that we have now seen thoroughly from one side to the other. Camera holds a beat. Then starts panning back right again. All the way across. And if, by that time, the viewer does not realize what Coppola is doing, he or she should not have gone to a film that is intellectually beyond his or her capacities.

Had Coppola taken one pan right or left, and finally held on Hackman, it would only have been a grace note. But the steady back-and-forth movement of the camera, it abruptly dawns on us, is Coppola's way of saying, "We are watching this man through a spy camera, the kind they have in banks, that scans across the interior of the lobby, that feeds its image to the watchers who now have Hackman under their thumb. Coppola has not permitted Hackman to find even the slightest trace of bugging equipment in the apartment, though it's stripped to the outer walls of the building, so we cannot know whether this spy camera observation is actual, literally happening, or if it is a subtle clue that they have driven Hackman totally into paranoia, that he will *always* feel he is being watched, and is therefore no longer a threat. It is an artful fillip added to the final point, made by camera movement alone, permitting us to plot for ourselves. It is the use of *film as film.*

And it sends a final shiver up our spines.

Having illustrated what I mean about seeing film visually, not merely as the translation of, say, a stage production, with everything static and set out in long, medium and close shots, I'll return to that snippet of story I wrote many pages ago. It's almost entirely an uneventful segment, from the outside. (Go back and re-read it if the digression has flensed all memory of it from your mind. Go read; I'll wait, come back and we can go from here.)

All right, you're back. Now. The story as written from techniques that would be acceptable in a novel, would be unacceptable in a script. How the hell do you lay in the backstory about the woman's father and her family? How do you show what he's thinking, or what she's thinking? How do you illustrate her hatred of Simonson, or his innocence? How do you show that he *knows* what she's thinking; and how does he convey to her the true story?

Well, there are many ways for a scenarist, but they *all* involve thinking visually. Here is the way I would do it, in script form, using videotape, not film.

25 INT. MNEMOSYNE—EXT. CLOSEUP ON MEMORY POOL

CAMERA CLOSE on the shivering aquamarine radiance of one of the memory-pools set into the center of every dining table at the famous Mnemosyne. Strange colors flicker and dance through the liquid, and in the b.g. we HEAR strangely compelling music, like the songs of the Sirens.

CAMERA PULLS BACK to show Simonson and Klara sitting across from each other. They stare into the pool. CAMERA BACK as we see the rest of the dining spa, a futuristic restaurant all angles and planes of metal and plastic, with colors flickering inside the walls. From time to time we CHROMAKEY the walls of the Mnemosyne so they change subtly from red through violet to blue and on through the spectrum. CAMERA PULLS BACK to ESTABLISH the scene, then moves again, TRUCKING IN SLOWLY on Simonson and Klara.

26 MED. CLOSE—SIMONSON

as he stares across at her.

27 MED. CLOSE—KLARA

as she looks up, registers acknowledgment of his presence and his attention. Her expression is as cold as the surface of the memory-pool.

28 MEDIUM SHOT—ARRIFLEX—ON SIMONSON & KLARA

as they talk, the CAMERA MOVES AROUND THEM, first holding Klara past Simonson's shoulder, then circling to give us the REVERSE ANGLE.

KLARA
(coldly)
I don't like this place. I've never liked it. Why did you insist?

SIMONSON
The Mnemosyne specializes in more than good food.

KLARA
I don't have any memories I'd care to let you see.
(beat)
It ought to be enough that I agreed to meet with you in the first place.

SIMONSON
(earnestly)
What if I could prove to you that you don't need to hate me?

She reacts to the suggestion with a tenseness that fills her face with even

(CONTINUED)

28 CONTINUED:

greater animosity. She draws herself up and looks around as if expecting someone.

KLARA
I'd like something to drink.

Simonson presses his hand against a transparent plate set into the arm of his chair. Light shines up.

SIMONSON
Klara, what if you've read all the signs wrong? What if . . . just what if . . . I had nothing to do with the death of your family?

KLARA
(levelly)
You'd remove the only reason I have left for living: hating you.

CUT TO:

29 SHOT WITH WAITER—MOVING TOWARD TABLE

CAMERA CLOSE ON WAITER'S BACK as we SHOOT PAST HIM to Simonson and Klara at the memory-pool table. He comes to their table and they stop talking. She looks up, speaks very quickly, in a manner we might take to be imperious.

KLARA
Sting martini, over bubbles.

The waiter looks at Simonson. We have not seen any part of the waiter but the back of him.

(CONTINUED)

29 CONTINUED:

SIMONSON

Absinthe and coffee.

WAITER

Very good. Thank you.

Waiter turns DIRECTLY INTO CAMERA and we see it is a robot, immobile metal face oddly melding with the ornate waiter's costume. He moves TOWARD CAMERA and out of FRAME to left, leaving us with a MEDIUM CLOSE SHOT of Simonson and Klara.

SIMONSON

If you're fair, you'll let me see the memory.

KLARA

I'm not fair.

SIMONSON

Then, if you're curious.

They look at each other without speaking for long moments, then Klara nods slowly.

KLARA

Perhaps this _is_ the best way to show you the depth of my hatred.

She looks down into the memory-pool.

CUT TO:

30 VERTICAL SHOT—STRAIGHT DOWN—MOVING IN

on the MEMORY-POOL. We can see their hands on either side of the liquid, and

(CONTINUED)

30 CONTINUED:

the tops of their heads, bent toward the circular pool in the center of their table. As CAMERA COMES DOWN, the liquid begins to ripple, like a placid lake suddenly producing wavelets as a breeze comes up. We HEAR the SOUND of water hissing through a channel and then what might be wind-chimes. CAMERA DOWN and HOLD the pool.

31 SEGUÉ SHOT—INSERT—MATTE

Preceding shot of pool alters as MEMORY INSERT shimmers and takes form in the rippling blue liquid. We HOLD it MEDIUM CLOSE:

31A INSERT—WHAT WE SEE—SEQUENCE OF MEMORIES

31B ESTABLISHING SHOT of a sleek spacecraft in outer space. CAMERA MOVES IN on the ship, passes through hull to BLACK FRAME.

31C OUT OF BLACK FRAME to interior of spacecraft. We are in a ship's saloon, with four people. An older, gray-haired man, Klara's father; an attractive, imperious woman of middle years, Klara's mother; a frightened young boy of twelve; and Simonson. All three of Klara's family are ravaged by angry red sores on faces and hands. Simonson seems untouched. Still seeing this in the pool, we HEAR tiny voices SPEAKING.

(CONTINUED)

31C CONTINUED:

FATHER
You've got to go back. Before it passes to you, too.

SIMONSON
There has to be another way.

MOTHER
Please, John, do what he says. You can't help us.

SIMONSON
At least let me take Kenni with me.

FATHER
Why? To spread it? Take the lifeboat and go, John.

Klara's mother moves to the side, out of Simonson's sight.

SIMONSON
I can't just leave you here to drift, with this thing killing you. There's a quarantine station on Ganymede. They can—

Klara's mother has come up behind Simonson, with a small disc in her hand. Now she lunges at him, presses it against the back of his neck. His eyes roll up and he collapses. Klara's father looks at his wife, and their eyes meet with understanding.

31D Preceding SHOT FADES and DISSOLVES THRU TO shot of the father and mother

(CONTINUED)

31D CONTINUED:

loading Simonson into a tiny rescue craft. His eyes are open, and he's trying to speak, but he cannot move and cannot articulate.

FATHER
Goodbye, John. Do us this one last favor. Klara will need someone . . .

They close the transparent hatch and we see through SIMONSON'S POV the boy, Kenni, crying, being held by his mother.

CUT TO:

31E EXT. SHOT OF SHIP as the rescue craft is blown free. DISTANCE SHOT TOWARD SHIP as it comes TOWARD CAMERA. Suddenly, in b.g., the ship silently explodes and at the same moment of the explosion the liquid in the pool roils and bubbles and then . . . subsides to its former placidity.

CUT TO:

32 CLOSEUP—KLARA

with a horrified expression. Her eyes are filled with tears. We are back in the Mnemosyne.

KLARA
You bastard! That wasn't <u>my</u> memory! It was a fake, some awful lie you dreamed up!

33 TWO-SHOT—FAVORING SIMONSON

He leans across, tries to take her hands. She pulls them back; she is still crying.

SIMONSON
(softly)
You're right, it wasn't just your memory. It was mine, too. I had to trick you a little. I knew how you felt, I knew you thought I'd killed them, that I let them die; but I didn't, Klara. So help me God it was just the way you saw it.

KLARA
No!

SIMONSON
He had more courage than either of us. I can't tell you I'd have stayed . . . to catch that . . .
(beat)
I can't say that.
(beat)
But they never made me have to face the question. They sent me away and he dumped the pile himself.

KLARA
(with pain)
I can't stand any more of this.

SIMONSON
He wanted me to take care of you. That's what they wanted, all three of them. If you don't believe me, if you don't believe the memory, then you've killed all of us. Not just three . . . five.

(CONTINUED)

33 CONTINUED:

KLARA
(softly)
What do you want from me?

Simonson looks at her, and shadows from the changing colors of the room's walls cast planes of darkness across his features. All but his eyes are suddenly hidden. They shine with reflected light from the memory-pool, and his voice comes across a wasteland:

SIMONSON
Peace. Just peace. I'll always feel guilty, even if I believe I didn't do anything wrong. But you can give me peace.

She stares back at him and we HOLD the SHOT as we:

FADE TO BLACK
and
FADE OUT.

Hmmm. Some day I'm going to have to write that story and that teleplay. I like that scene. A bit wordy, perhaps, but essentially solid. Now, do you see what I mean—and what Isaac meant—when we say that you have to give the viewer *every*thing? What took only a few lines in a story, took many pages of script. Of course, I grant you that I got so involved in my own story that I went on past the point of the narrative segment, but even so it would have been a good deal more complex and a lot longer than what was needed to convey the scene in short story form.

Not only was there plot progression in that scene, but there was characterization, dialogue, camera angles, setting, incidental background, interior tension, conflict, backstory and action. And I wasn't doing anything particularly special just for your benefit here; I'd have written as much for *any* script assignment.

If there is a sure-fire test you can give yourself, to ascertain whether or not you are equipped with the bare essentials for writing screenplays, it might be this one:

Hopefully, I've established by this point that you must *think visually before you write.* There can be no scenes of "talking heads" sitting in a bar, telling each other what happened. You must *show,* not *tell;* it's a basic rule for any kind of muscular writing, but it's absolutely mandatory when working in films and television. So test yourself by using this secret method I use for writing a script. Pick a bit of a story you want to translate into script, as I did here. Close your eyes. Now run that scene through your mind as if you were watching a movie. Do you see the scene from various angles? Does the camera in your mind's eye move? Do the characters have positions in relation to each other and to the scene as a whole? Can you see what they look like, what they're wearing, the way they gesticulate? Can you hear the inflection in their voices? How are transitions effected: wipes, cuts, dissolves, lap-dissolves, swish-pans, fades? Is it all flat or does it have three-dimensional corporeality for you?

If you can *see* that movie in your mind, and can set it down on paper so the vision is translated into the kind of directions I gave in that sample script, then you have a chance to become a scenarist. If you can't translate it, if it's all flat and merely vague shadowy movement without definition . . . forget it. You may be a writer of narratives, but you very likely don't have the visual capabilities to write for films and television.

Don't feel badly. The sensory equipment of human beings varies greatly. Some people hear their memories, some see them in color and wide-screen, some people only have recall of odors or tactile impressions. There are people who are tone-deaf and people who are color-blind. It's nothing to be sorrowful about; but it's something you must realistically assess before committing yourself to the grueling life of a tv/film writer.

Warning: don't ignore these caveats. I've seen very talented writers, in several cases the biggest names in science fiction, who set themselves to become scripters, who simply couldn't write visually, who beat their wings against the Industry like moths against a windowpane, and whose hearts were finally broken after wasting months and years bombing out with one project after another.

It is a remorseless and unsympathetic Industry, and the only thing that counts is ability. You can be the biggest shit in the world and, if you can write the words, they'll hire you again and again; you can be a sweetheart, a charming guy or gal, a pleasure to dine with and share conversation with, but if you cannot produce, they will reluctantly, sadly, helplessly cast you aside and you'll starve before they let you write a beach party flick, or even anything as undemanding as a segment of, say, "The Six Million Dollar Man."

You have been given this warning in all honesty. If you ignore it, don't come crying to me.

For those of you left after the preceding weeding-out, let's examine the mechanics and terminology of a script.

You saw a gang of words and numbers and abbreviations in that section I wrote. Most of it will seem like gibberish unless you've read a good book on screenplay writing or had the blissful fortune of obtaining a script somewhere.

Let's take form first.

A motion picture screenplay is not divided into acts. It is all of a piece. It starts with FADE IN and just goes to FADE OUT.

A teleplay is quite different. I'll deal with the one-hour form here, because half-hour sitcoms and 90-minute or two-hour movies are merely expansions or contractions of the one-hour layout.

The teleplay is usually divided into six parts. (On some series either the *teaser* or the *epilogue* is dropped, but most use both. In no case is the four-act form departed from.) The six parts are:

TEASER
ACT ONE
ACT TWO
ACT THREE
ACT FOUR
EPILOGUE

These divisions are not like the ones you'll find in a stage production, a Broadway show, for instance. They are wholly artificial dismemberings devised to permit the advertisers as much opportunity as possible to sell you their goods. But they exist, they're real, and when you plot, you have to take them into consideration.

Hold it. Another digression. (I'll grant you this isn't the best-organized essay ever perpetrated, but as I keep getting into cul-de-sacs and side-tunnels of the craft of screenwriting, I keep remembering all manner of little tips that I've picked up that you won't find in rational studies by learned savants . . . but these are the stray bits of data that only experience and being beaten with that ballbat can teach, and I think you should have them at your command; so bear with me.) I'm not going to lay on you all that esoteric jiggery-pokery about how long an act should be in terms of minutes of actual play-time (as opposed to the "stolen" minutes for commercials). It isn't necessary for you to have the timing down, if you follow a general rule of thumb that I've never seen fail, and it is this:

Each act of a one-hour dramatic show should be about fifteen pages in length. The pages are, of course, full pages of copy such as the ones I cobbled-up with that imaginary scene just a little bit ago. Sometimes, if you run extensive set description or a great deal of action that takes pages to set up (such as an involved, choreographed fight scene), you'll run over that fifteen. But a fifteen-page act will play in about twelve minutes, give or take some seconds. So we're talking about a 60-page script, divided into the parts already named. Okay? Digression over.

The arbitrary divisions of a series segment into the six deadly parts was devised by the clever lads upstairs at the advertising agencies and the networks. The use of the teaser and the epilogue provide two additional breaks that permit sales-time for two more commercials, a piggyback, a billboard or two, and the credits the Writers Guild and Directors Guild insist come at the outset of the show.

When plotting, the business-wise professional will write his or her script in such a way that the *strongest* point of the story, the most teeth-clenching crisis, the most terrifying moment, comes at the end of act two. Now, normally, that moment usually comes at the *end* of a story, leaving you limp with awe at the writer's cleverness, because he's held the big punch for the final moment. But not in television. In tv it comes at the end of act two. Why? I'll tell you why.

Because the break for commercials between act two and act three is double the length of the breaks between the other acts.

There are fifteen hundred one-minute commercials, public service announcements the network hates to have to put in valuable money-time (but is required to dole out by the FCC), billboards, local station spots, network identification spots, and a host of etceteras that might cause you to turn to another channel to see if anything better is happening over there with that private eye. So the writer gets the responsibility dumped in his or her lap. "Write it so goddam exciting they'll come back even if they're having a cardiac arrest." That's the unspoken ultimatum. And so, whether story-logic demands it or not, you have your hero in the most dreadful straits possible at the end of act two.

The second strongest high point of viewer interest is at the end of act one, then act three, and finally, at the end of act four. And if you recall from those old Cisco Kid shows, they don't give a damn if *anything* happens at the end, because by that time they've sold everything but their ancient grandmothers. So, as a consequence, all sitcoms and most dramatic shows end with Cisco and Pancho giggling at each other like a pair of schoolkids.

Remember all that, nasty as it is, artistically corrupt as it is, when you start writing the plot of your script.

Interior tension should be sustained from act to act, hopefully; but producers don't know what the hell interior tension is, in most cases, so all they insist upon is that the tension is maintained *within* an act. If you don't know what I mean by interior tension, it's the progression of events that dramatically lead you from scene to scene within the story. The dramatics. The suspense. Got it? Good.

I've found that each act should have four scenes of major importance. There can be more, such as short linkages between scenes to move the action from place to place, but there should *never be less* than four scenes per act, or you're going to wind up with a very static, stagey act. Let me demonstrate what I mean by four scenes to an act, using our old friend Simonson from that earlier snippet of script. Here's a synopsis of, say, the first act of the script.[2]

FADE IN deep space. CAMERA MOVES IN on a shape reflecting back light faintly from the stars. We approach it slowly, and discover it to be a kind of clear tubelike coffin with a naked man in it. Our POV turns out to be an Earth-bound freighter plying through space toward the home planet. They pick up the coffin and bring it aboard.

On shipboard, the coffin is opened after great difficulty with laser-torches (it is made of some alien substance never seen on Earth) and the man is taken out, unconscious. He is taken to sick bay and slowly, as weeks pass, he's nursed back to health. He confides in the female captain of the ship, HERTA LORAY, that he was the captain of a small space yacht named *The Nightwind* that has been destroyed somewhere beyond the Asteroid Belt. He tells her he is the only survivor, but says no more. He feigns amnesia, but can remember his name, DEN SIMONSON.

The freighter makes Earth, Simonson is the only one kept by Port Authority officials, and he is questioned closely by representatives of some top-secret Earth government agency. They want to know where he was piloting the yacht when it met its fate, and what has happened to the three members of the BOWKER family who perished in the accident. They put him in protective custody, against his wishes, and take him to a hospital where he is little more than a prisoner.

There is something about him that they find out under examination. That he has almost perfect and total regenerative powers. He discovers this himself, before they do, when he tries to escape one night and tears the skin off his chest against a rough metal wall. As he watches, the skin grows back in a matter of seconds.

He discovers, purely by accident, that he is not the first person to return from space with this linkage to immortality, and that the government wants to keep him in custody forever. He realizes he has some strange destiny involved with this power, and plots to escape from the prison hospital.

Before he can effect his escape, however, he is permitted a visit from KLARA BOWKER, surviving child of the family that died in the yacht accident in space. She calls him a killer and swears she will see him as dead as her mother, father and young brother.

Simonson knows she has the story wrong, but at that moment decides not to defend himself. First, he must get away from the ones holding him prisoner.

That night, he uses a clever ruse to escape, and flees into the city. As the act ends, the agents of the government discover he's gone and start after him, calling him, "the greatest threat to humanity the world has ever known." FADE TO BLACK AND FADE OUT. End Act One.

Okay. Now let's examine that portion of the treatment for the scenes. 1. Deep space. Simonson found and brought aboard freighter. 1a. A linkage sequence showing him taken to sick bay; time-lapse of him recovering. 2. Simonson in conversation with captain of the ship. 3.

Landing on Earth and immediate arrest. 4. Interrogation by government agents. 4a. Linkage sequence; Simonson taken to prison hospital and locked away. 5. Discovery by Simonson of his abilities. 6. Discovery of immortality by doctors. 7. Overhearing of background information Simonson needs to move his future actions and his escape. 8. Visit from Klara. 9. The escape sequence. 10. Grace note; the agents' saying he's a menace.

Now, since it was the first act, and a great deal of background information had to be laid in before-the-fact, the act comes out longer and with more scenes. I'd say it would come out around twenty pages, with heavy set descriptions. You'll notice there are several conversation scenes, which occur in between scenes in which there's movement, some action. That's called pacing. You take the viewer up and down the hills; bring the audience to a peak, give them some respite, then start yanking them up again. In that way you build interior tension. Pacing.

But let me digress for just another moment.

Until Simonson discovers he's immortal, this is not science fiction. Oh, I hear you mumbling, it has spaceships and alla that junk in it, so it's *gotta* be sf! Nonsense.

Just transpose the setting to the South Seas and make it a pleasure yacht cruising through a chain of obscure, uncharted islands. They pick up a plague, they cosh the stalwart Captain over the head, put him in a lifeboat and set him adrift and then blow themselves up. He's picked up by a freighter blown off the well-traversed seaways, he's brought back home, and then quarantine officials put him in protective custody. See? It ain't sf. Which brings us to one of the absolute necessities if you're going to specialize in writing the fantastic for film and tv.

The fantastic.

It has to be there.

But it has to have internal logic. That is, the plot *must* fall apart and be untellable *without* that sf element. This is hardly a fresh concept. It's been said by every sf critic since the genre became a viable commercial medium. It is what identifies the form. Without the science fictional linch pin that holds it all together, it might just as well be a story that can be told as a western, a gothic, an adventure saga or a mystery. Or, to quote the classic comparison, consider the following, taken from the back cover advertisement that was featured on the first issue of *Galaxy* science fiction magazine, September 1950:

Jets blasting, Bat Durston came screeching down through the atmosphere of BBIlzznaj, a tiny planet seven billion light years from Sol. He cut out his super-hyper-drive for the landing... and at that point, a tall, lean spaceman stepped out of the tail assembly, proton gun-blaster in a space-tanned hand.

"Get back from those controls, Bat Durston," the tall stranger lipped thinly. "You don't know it, but this is your last space trip through this particular section of the Universe."

Hoofs drumming, Bat Durston came galloping down through the narrow pass at Eagle Gulch, a tiny gold colony 400 miles north of Tombstone. He spurred hard for a low overhang of rimrock . . . and at that point, a tall, lean wrangler stepped out from behind a high boulder, six-shooter in a sun-tanned hand.

"Rear back and dismount, Bat Durston," the tall stranger lipped thinly. "You don't know it, but this is your last saddle-jaunt through these here parts."

Sound alike? They should—one is merely a western transplanted to some alien and impossible planet. If this is your idea of science fiction, you're welcome to it.

And so, until Simonson discovers he's got the power of regenerating his body, until that moment in the teleplay or film script, all we have is a transplanted South Seas adventure story. But from that moment *on,* it's science fiction. (Oh, and by the way, while I was plotting act one of that treatment I figured out the entire story. That happens sometimes. Terrific idea for a story or a teleplay. I may just sit down and write it soon. Good thing this piece is copyrighted. Which brings me to the subject of protecting your work against theft. But it's too soon for that. I'll get to it later. I'll be damned if I'll digress off a digression.)

Back to where we were. I've shown you the form for writing a treatment—and *always* write the treatment, not the screenplay first; only fools and amateurs try to write and/or sell a screenplay without a treatment—and I've detailed how you pace the work in scenes. Now let's tackle those strange terms I used in the script pages.

The words in caps are the camera terminologies that form the directorial guide-lines for setting up shots. There are writers who have been in the business for decades who'll tell you only to write "master scenes" and to forget all the fancy camerawork, that it's the province of the director or the cinematographer. Any writer who says that is a hack and ought to be out honeydipping Andy Gump chemical toilets. "Master scenes" are sloppy donkeywork cop-outs used by lazy and usually untalented writers so they can do ten scripts in the time it should take them to do one. A "master scene" is set up like this:

```
15  THE SMITH HOUSE—LIVING ROOM—DAY—
    ESTABLISHING SHOT

    John enters the room. He sees Martha.

                        JOHN
      So! At last! You're home!

                        MARTHA
      Where was I supposed to be?

                        JOHN
      That's what I want to know!

                        MARTHA
      What are you suggesting?

                        JOHN
      I'm suggesting you were out with
      Rick.

                        MARTHA
      I won't dignify that remark with
      an answer.

                        JOHN
      Easy enough for you to say.

    Martha slaps him.

                   JOHN (CONT'D.)
      That's what I'd expect of you.

                        MARTHA
      Put 'em up! C'mon you turkey, up!

                                     (CONTINUED)
```

15 CONTINUED:

JOHN
Violence is the last bastion of the coward.

MARTHA
How about I bust you one in the pudding trough?

JOHN
You don't love me any more.

MARTHA
I don't love you any less.

They rush into each other's arms. John smears his mascara, Martha's tattoo runs; their tears spoil the artwork.

FADE OUT.

Etcetera, etcetera, etcetera, *ad nauseam.* Sorry I had to do that to you, but I wanted to get across my revulsion at the "master scene" philosophy. It's part of the whole corrupt *auteur* theory that directors have been using to hype gullible film students and cinema critics for years. For those who *really* believe the director is the author of the film, I offer these two direct quotes. The first from George C. Scott, very likely the finest actor this country and its film industry have produced in the last thirty years.

> "Directors come in different levels of competency like all of us," Scott said with a look of innocence. "They may be fascinated with technique at the expense of the acting and even of the writing. You can mess with the acting a little but start tearing up a good piece of writing and you're in trouble. Screen writing is an extremely difficult craft; the writer should be applauded and be given the respect of constancy, of having his work done the way he intended it to be done."[3]

And the second quote is even more on the button. It comes from one of the five directors in the world today whom I consider wholly and totally *sui generis,* with voices so distinctive and powerful that they dominate the directorial landscape like the Colossus of Rhodes: utterly without competition. The other four are Luis Buñuel, Stanley Kubrick, Federico Fellini and Robert Altman. But the quote is from Francis Ford Coppola, who said:

> "I like to think of myself as a writer who directs. When people go to see a movie, 80 percent of the effect it has on them was preconceived and precalculated by the writer. He's the one who imagines opening with a shot of a man walking up the stairs and cutting to another man walking down the stairs. A good script has pre-imagined exactly what the movie is going to do on a story level, on an emotional level, on all these various levels. To me, that's the primary act of creation."[4]

The *auteur* theory denies the (to me) inarguable truth that FIRST CAME THE WORD. Without script, the director has nothing.

Without a solid script, the director and his/her players can have all the charisma and verve in the universe, and they'll wind up standing around the sound stage with fingers up their noses.

The most obvious current example of that condition can be seen in the films of John Cassavetes, an enormously talented director who, inexplicably, has yet to learn that he cannot write very well, no matter how muscularly he directs. His schema for making a film, from his first (*Shadows,* 1961) to his latest (*The Killing of a Chinese Bookie,* 1976) is to sketch out a plot with the barest essentials, and then to permit his players to ad lib their way through the shooting. It is a testament to Cassavetes' talent that there is *anything* of merit in such films as *Faces, Husbands, Minnie & Moskowitz* or *A Woman Under the Influence.* (It should be noted that these represent his "personal" films, as opposed to projects such as *Too Late Blues* and *A Child is Waiting,* the former a disaster artistically and commercially, the latter a success in both respects, which were undertaken for major studios and for which full scripts were written. In the case of *A Child is Waiting,* the script was written by Academy Award winner Abby Mann [*Judgment at Nuremberg, Ship of Fools, Report to the Commissioner*] and has always seemed to me the high point of Cassavetes' directorial career.) In his most representative films—*Husbands, A Woman Under the Influence* and *The Killing of a Chinese Bookie*—Cassavetes runs on like a senile old relative telling an anecdote the punchline of which he's forgotten. The actors posture and mumble, ramble endlessly, bore interminably, and the films come out at twice the length the material will support. I urge you to go see *Chinese Bookie* (a failure in many other ways, as well, but interesting for our purposes here as a startling proof of the contention that without script a director is nowhere), a film that clocks out at two hours and sixteen minutes . . . and could have been done as a sixty-minute film-for-television.

Actors who, puffed with self-importance, tell a director or a scenarist on a sound stage, "I can't say these lines," mean *precisely* that. Not *these are badly written lines*, but *they* cannot say them. In short, they are incapable or inadequately talented to say them. Yes, it is a scenarist's job to write speeches that are flowing, rational, artful and concise without being tongue-tying, but it is the actor's job to bring skill and soul to the reading. In this way it is a collaboration between Art and Life. And when actors or directors fool themselves with tragic little delusions that *they* are the authors of the film, they condemn themselves to the making of a bad film.

If you retain any vestige of doubt that what I say here is core truth, and if neither Scott nor Coppola convinces you, check the credits of those directors you consider the most innovative, the most daring, the ones with the longest string of successful credits (and I mean not only artistically, but commercially, as well). Josef Von Sternberg, Billy Wilder, John Huston, Robert Rossen, Sam Fuller, Lina Wertmüller, Charles Chaplin, Bryan Forbes, Mel Brooks, Ingmar Bergman, Preston Sturges, Claude Chabrol, Joseph L. Mankiewicz, Sergio Leone, François Truffaut, all of the giants I listed above—each director also writes. And brilliantly. Most of them were writers before they expanded their activities into directing. Even Orson Welles, credited with all the glory for *Citizen Kane*—though the script has been almost universally acknowledged, finally, as being the creative vision of Herman J. Mankiewicz—began as a writer and continued writing throughout his early and mid-career.

These comments are made at this point to invest you with the feeling that writing is a holy chore; that writing for film can be equally as holy, and that even in the face of the massive promotion for directors that permits jingoistic journals such as *Newsweek* to list actors, cinematographers and directors in their reviews, while omitting the name of the scenarist . . . if you decide to pursue a career as a writer of films/tv, you will be the foundation of *any* production, the cornerstone of the Industry. Take my word for it: you can have Redford and Newman and Streisand and Steven Spielberg all signed on the dotted line, but the banks who put up the money to finance films won't give you a dime without a strong script.

Which brings me back, at long last, to script terminology, hoping that by these digressions I've purged the thought of writing bullshit "master scenes" from your world-view.

Script terminology. Hmmm.

When I started writing this essay, I thought I would lightly skim over the basic facts and refer you to other, more detailed studies. But apart from an excellent reference work by Coles Trapnell[5] there isn't a book on the subject I think worth your time. Oh, I've added some supplementary readings to this piece, but mostly they are for insights into the way the Industry works. And as I've progressed through this discussion of translating the fantastic to the visual media, I've found it's very much a case of trying to explain in simplistic terms something that's incredibly complex. I guess it's even more complex to explain than I'd ever considered; even having worked in the media as long as I have.

There were two choices. One was to brush across the surface and touch only the high points; the second was to give you everything I've got. But that means a rather extensive glossary of film/tv terminology. And clearly, you won't need it all immediately, nor is there space here to insert forty pages of terms. So I've weeded down the lingo to ninety-five of the most used terms, hoping they'll cover any questions you might find yourself asking. There is a wealth of terminology that applies to camerawork, lighting, set decoration and special film/tape technology that I have excluded; you won't need it unless you become a full-time practicing scenarist.

What you have in this glossary is a basic vocabulary.

Trapnell's book can give you more.

But a general rule of thumb that works extremely well is that the simpler and more direct your language in writing a script, the easier it is to visualize and to shoot. That is, and should always be, a paramount consideration. Also a 20th Century–Fox, Warner Bros. and Universal consideration.

A SHORT GLOSSARY OF FILM TERMS

NOTE: Laboratory and highly technical and specialized terms have been omitted.

ANIMATION	The bringing to apparent movement of inanimate objects set before the camera by employing the joint capacity of film and eye to fuse disparate images into an apparently continuous flow. Among the objects set before the animation camera are cells, cutouts and puppets.
ANIMATION (CONT.)	Table-top animation. A type of animation in which small objects are photographed in close-up and moved along a frame at a time to produce magical results.
ARRIFLEX SHOT	Specific name of a type of hand-held camera used for filming action and extreme close sequences where space limitations or a desire for "jerky" sense-of-movement exclude the use of large, standard-size cameras. Other trade names for the equipment include Eclair, the Beaulieu R16B(PZ), the Mitchell Mark III and the Panaflex. But generically, shots using these hand-held cameras are called Arri Shots.
BLOW-UP	The optical printing process by which a picture image on a large gauge of film is produced from a picture image on a small gauge of film. A common application is the production of 35mm separation negatives from 16mm monopack color originals. Sometimes also refers to the enlargement of the film image in an optical camera.
BOOM, CAMERA	A mobile camera mount, usually of large size, on which the camera may be projected out over the set and/or raised above it. Provision is made for counterbalancing, raising and lowering, rotating, and bodily moving the boom, these motions being effected either by electrical motors or by hand.
BOOM, MICROPHONE	A simple version of the camera boom, designed to project the microphone over the set and twist it in any direction required by the mixer.

CAMERA ANGLE	The field of view of a camera when it is set up to shoot. The qualifying terms "high," "low," and "wide" are based on an imaginary norm which more or less corresponds to a 35mm camera with a 2-inch lens pointed at a scene from shoulder height.
CAMERA MOVEMENT	(1) Movement of the camera as a whole (i.e., not pivotal movement on its horizontal or vertical axes) while shooting a scene. (2) Same as intermittent movement.
COMPOSITE	The presence of one piece of film of corresponding sound and picture images, either in editorial, camera or projection synchronism.
CONTINUITY CUTTING	A style of cutting marked by its emphasis on maintaining the continuous and seemingly uninterrupted flow of action in a story, as if this action were being observed by the audience as spectator. Contrasted with DYNAMIC CUTTING.
CONTRAST	In a scene, this term popularly denotes the difference between the brightness of the most illuminated and the least illuminated areas; and, in a negative or print, the difference between the densities of the most exposed and least exposed areas. Generally measured in gamma.
COOKIE	A variegated flag, perforated with a pattern of leaves, branches or flowers, etc., which is set so as to cast a shadow on an otherwise uniform and monotonous surface. Sometimes opaque, sometimes translucent like a scrim.
CRANE	A large camera boom.
CUT	An instantaneous transition from any shot to the immediately succeeding shot which results from splicing the two shots together. The cut, a simple and timeless occurrence, is at the root of many of the creative powers of the film, and is primarily responsible for its ability to construct a new framework of time and space.

DEPOLARIZER	In optics, a device for eliminating the polarization of a polarized ray of light, that is, for restoring the vibrations of the ray in all directions at right angles to the ray itself. Commonly used to photograph through glass (which is reflecting sun or other light) so that contents behind glass can be seen and also for eliminating glare from highly polished surfaces.
DEPTH OF FIELD	The range of object distances within which objects are in satisfactorily sharp focus.
DISSOLVE	An optical effect between two superimposed shots on the screen in which the second shot gradually begins to appear, the first shot at the same time gradually disappearing. Also called lap dissolves and in England, mixes.
DOLLY	A light and compact wheeled mount for a camera, often used by small units for making dollying shots and for moving a camera from place to place on a set. See also BOOM, CAMERA.
DOLLYING	Movement of the whole camera when making a shot. Sometimes referred to as trucking or tracking.
DOPE SHEET	An analysis of film material prepared for purposes of library classification.
DOUBLE EXPOSURE	Successive exposure of a light-sensitive emulsion to two scenes, so that two superimposed images are visible after development.
DYNAMIC CUTTING	A term used in film aesthetics to mean a type of cutting which, by the juxtaposition of contrasting shots or sequences, generates ideas in the mind of the spectator which were not latent in any of the synthesizing elements of the film.
EFFECTS FILTER	An optical filter which distorts the rendering of natural objects to such an extent that a special effect, light at night or fog effect, is produced.
EXTERIORS	Any outdoor scene.
FADE	An optical effect occupying a single shot, in which the shot gradually disappears into blackness (FADE OUT) or appears out of blackness (FADE

IN). The most usual convention for this is to note the passage of time as opposed to the dissolve, which usually notes related or continuous action of longer intervals than a cut.

FAST MOTION — Motion of the film through the camera slower than the standard speed, which therefore results in action appearing faster than normal when the film is projected at the standard rate. See also SLOW MOTION.

FLIPOVER WIPE — A kind of wipe in which the image appears to turn over, revealing another image on the "back," the axis of rotation being either vertical or horizontal.

FOCUS — The point at which parallel rays meet after passing through a convergent lens. More generally, that position at which an object must be situated in order that the image produced by a lens may be sharp and well defined; hence an object is spoken of as in focus or out of focus.

FOLLOW FOCUS — A continuous change in camera focusing necessitated by relative movement between the camera and its subject, greater than can be accommodated by depth of field. Following focus is usually a function of the first assistant camerman.

FOLLOW SHOTS — Another name for DOLLYING or TRUCKING SHOTS. A shot in which the camera moves around, following the action of a scene.

FRAME — The individual picture on a strip of film.

FRAMING — Most commonly used to denote the setting up of a camera in such a way that the image framed by its lens and aperture plate is precisely that required by the director and cameraman.

GAFFER — In studio parlance, the chief electrician who is responsible, under the first cameraman, for the lighting of sets.

GRIP — The person who, on the studio set, has charge of minor adjustments and repairs to props, camera tracks and the like.

HOT SPOT — A small area in a scene which has been lighted excessively brightly.

INKY-DINK — A popular term for a miniature incandescent lamp, usually 250w. Its main use is an eyelight, being a spotlight, not a fill.

JUMP CUT — If a section is taken out of the middle of a shot, and the film respliced across the gap, a jump cut is said to result, since there is a jump in the shot's continuity. When the shot is motionless, this is a useful device for eliminating dead footage. Shots, however, are usually moving, and if there is movement, an unpleasantly visible jump will usually occur.

LAP DISSOLVE — See DISSOLVE.

KEY LIGHT — The main light used for the illumination of a particular subject.

HIGH-KEY LIGHTING — When the key light forms a very large proportion of the total illumination of the set, resulting in a low lighting contrast and an effect of general brilliance in the scene. Still the recommended method for color shooting.

LOW-KEY LIGHTING — When the key light forms, in comparison with high-key lighting, a lower proportion of a smaller total illumination. The result is that many objects are allowed to fall into semi-darkness or even total blackness, thus throwing others into correspondingly stronger relief. This more dramatic style of lighting, which has now won general acceptance for certain types of commercial films and is advancing even in color photography, makes greater demands on emulsion characteristics and on processing techniques than does high-key lighting.

LONG-FOCUS LENS — A relative term describing lenses of longer focal length than normal, and consequently giving greater than normal magnification. Incorrectly called TELEPHOTO LENS, which see.

NORMAL-FOCUS LENS — 16mm—1 inch; 35mm—2 inch

SHORT-FOCUS LENS — A relative term describing lenses of shorter focal length than normal, consequently giving lower than normal magnification and a wider field of view. Also called WIDE-ANGLE LENS.

LIGHTING — Photographic lighting is designated, like wind, by the direction from which it comes.

BACK-LIGHTING — Lighting from behind the set or toward the camera, the actual light sources being shielded so as not to shine into the lens. Back-lighting increases lighting contrast up to the extreme condition of silhouette (no front light).

CROSS-LIGHTING — Lighting intermediate in its direction and effect between front-lighting and back-lighting.

FRONT-LIGHTING — The main lighting of a set is directed on it from behind and beside the camera, i.e. from in front of the set. The greater the proportion of front light to other kinds of light, the flatter in general will the lighting be, i.e. the lower will be the lighting contrast.

HIGH-LIGHTING — Additional illumination applied to a small area.

TOP-LIGHTING — Light resulting from sources mounted above the subject and shining down onto it.

LOCATION — Any place, other than the studio lot, where its units may be shooting a picture.

MATTE — A light modulator which consists of an obstruction to the passage of light on its way to form a photographic image. Thus MATTES are not essentially different from masks, but the former term is applied more often to the camera, the latter to the color and optical printer.

MONTAGE — As used in commercial studios, the term montage means a type of cutting using numerous dissolves and superimpositions rapidly following one another to produce a generalized visual effect.

NEGATIVE IMAGE — A photographic image in which the values of light and shade of the original photographed subject are represented in inverse order.

OVERLAP — In dialogue cutting, the extension of a dialogue sound track over a shot to which it does not belong, usually a reaction shot of the person being addressed on the overlapping sound track.

PAN, PANNING — Movement of the camera in a horizontal plane. Sometimes the term is used generally to describe movements of the camera in any plane.

PARALLAX — The difference between the image seen by the eye through the view-finder and that seen by the camera lens. In framing a picture, this has to be taken into consideration, since areas may be cut off due to this error. Parallax is eliminated in cameras with reflex viewing systems, since the eye sees through this lens itself.

PUSH-OVER WIPE — A type of wipe in which the first image moves horizontally across the screen, as if propelled by the second image which immediately follows it, much as in a lantern slide projector when slides are being changed.

SCRIPT — The written prescription for the making of any film. In its early stages, it is often designated a TREATMENT. In its final stages, a SHOOTING SCRIPT.

SEQUENCE — A section of a film which is more or less complete in itself, and which sometimes begins and ends with a fade. However, sequences frequently end with dissolves or even cuts, which give a better flow to the action than fades. In a comparison with writing, a shot may be taken as equal to a sentence, a scene, a paragraph, a sequence, a chapter.

SET — An artificial construction which forms the scene of a motion picture shot or series of shots.

SHOOTING SCRIPT — The final working script of a film which details the shots one by one in relation to their accompanying dialogue or other sound.

SHOT — An elemental division of a film into sections, within which spatial and temporal continuity is preserved. In commercial practice, a shot is more often called a scene, especially in referring to the script. The common descriptions of shots are necessarily relative to the kind of picture of which they form part:

CLOSE SHOT (CLOSE-UP) (CU) — A shot taken with the camera close, or apparently close, to the subject, which is often a human face filling the field. Abbreviated CS or CU.

DOLLY SHOT — A shot in which the camera moves bodily from one place to another on a special camera support such as a dolly or boom. Also called a TRUCKING or TRACKING shot.

ESTABLISHING SHOT — Long shots, usually in exteriors, which establish the whereabouts of the scene.

HIGH SHOT — A shot which looks down on the subject from a height.

INSERT SHOT — A shot of some object, usually a piece of printed matter, which is cut into a sequence to help explain the action.

LONG SHOT — A shot in which the object of principal interest is, or appears to be, far removed from the camera. Abbreviated LS.

LOW SHOT — A shot which looks up at the subject, often from ground level.

MEDIUM CLOSE SHOT — A shot intermediate in distance between a close shot and a medium shot. Abbreviated MCS.

MEDIUM LONG SHOT — A shot intermediate in distance between a medium shot and a long shot. Abbreviated MLS.

MEDIUM SHOT (MID SHOT) — A shot which shows a person at full height, or views a scene at normal viewing distance. Abbreviated MS.

MOVING SHOT	A shot from some normally moving object such as an airplane or an automobile.
PAN SHOT	A shot in which the camera pans across the scene.
REACTION SHOT	A shot inserted in a dialogue sequence to show the effect of an actor's words on other participants in the scene, usually in close-up. More generally, any shot displaying the reaction of anything.
TWO SHOT	A shot containing two characters, as a rule close to the camera. The term THREE SHOT has a corresponding meaning.
ZOOM SHOT	A shot taken with a zoom lens.
SLOW MOTION	Motion of the film in the camera faster than the standard rate, which therefore results in action appearing slower than normal when the film is projected at the standard rate.
SOFT-EDGE WIPE	A kind of wipe in which the boundary line between the two shots is softened or blurred, often by shooting the wipe masks out of focus. The degree of softness can be brought perfectly under control.
SOUND EFFECTS	All sounds, other than synchronized voices, narrative and music, which may be recorded on the sound track of a film. Prior to re-recording, these effects usually occupy a separate sound track or tracks called sound effects track(s).
STOCK FOOTAGE (MEASURE)	The material in a film library which consists of shots, such as establishing shots, historical material, and footage of other general application, which is likely to be used on many productions over a period of time.
STOCK SHOTS	Shots which are kept in stock for general studio use. They record historical events, famous places, and in general whatever it would be impracticable to shoot for each production.
STORY BOARD	Sometimes used in film preparation when it is often convenient to make sketches of key incidents in the

action, which are then arranged in order on a board called a story board and captioned.

SWISH PAN — A type of panning shot in which the camera is swung very rapidly on its vertical axis, the resulting film producing a blurred sensation when viewed, which is quite unlike that produced by a corresponding movement of the eyes.

SYNOPSIS — (1) A short or preliminary version of the script of a film.
(2) A summary of a completed film, often intended to catalogue its contents for a film library.

TELEPHOTO LENS — A lens, usually of greater than normal focal length, so constructed that the back focus is different from the effective focal length of the lens; usually less, in order to increase compactness, sometimes more, in order to allow for the use of a wide-angle lens in a camera where a prism must be interposed between lens and film. More generally, this term is mistakenly used to designate a long-focus lens.

TILTING — Pivotal movement of the camera in a vertical plane, contrasted with PANNING.

TITLE — Any written material which appears on a film and is not a part of an original scene is called a title.

CREDIT TITLES — The titles which enumerate the actors in a film and the technicians who made it.

CREEPER TITLE — A title, often carrying the names of the cast of a film, which creeps slowly round on a large unseen drum in front of the camera. Sometimes called a ROLL-UP TITLE.

TRACKING — See DOLLYING.

TRAVELING SHOT — A shot in which the camera moves bodily in relation to its object. Same as DOLLYING SHOT.

TREATMENT — A more or less detailed preparation of a story and idea in film form, which has not yet been clothed in the technical terms which convert it into a script.

TRUCKING	See DOLLYING.
WIPE	An optical effect between two succeeding shots on the screen in which the second shot appears and wipes the first off the screen along a visible line, which may run from top to bottom, side to side, or in any one of a large number of patterns.
ZOOM, ZOOMING	Real or apparent rapid motion of the camera toward its object is known as zooming.
ZOOM LENS	A lens of variable magnification which enables zooming effects to be simply achieved without moving the camera toward its object. Parallactic effects, which usually accompany real movement, are of course, absent from zoom lens shots, which are therefore most useful when the object is at a great distance, e.g. a sports field. This lens has achieved great use in television where cameras often cannot move, e.g. a convention, a football game, etc.

And that's only the tip of the iceberg. There is, of course, a fairly large supplementary language for opticals and special effects that would be used in sf/fantasy films or tv shows. Most of them are in the area of videotape and the uses of *Chromakey* (a term I used in that script portion earlier). *Chromakeying* is quite literally altering the picture that is being put on the videotape through electronic means, regulated from a control booth console. It can be used to produce special effects such as flames, ghost shapes, multiple images and other opticals usually associated with expensive special effects productions. Videotape thus becomes a key to beating the heavyweight production costs of sf shows. I'll say a few more words about that before I close. No need to remind me, I'll remember.

Chromakey is what I did to the background in the restaurant in the script portion, so the walls changed color while our principal actors were talking. It's all done in the machine.

But beyond electronic alterations, the sf vocabulary makes use of such new terms as SMASH-CUT. Now, to be flat-out truthful about it, there's only one kind of cut, and that's a CUT. From one scene to another. But a SMASH-CUT *seems* more violent, *seems* faster, because of what you cut from and to. For instance:

If you cut from a shot of a knife descending toward a person's back, in let's say, MED CU, to a shot of a meat cleaver smashing down on a steak in EXT CU, you get the *sense* of a much more dramatic cut than if you'd cut from a man approaching his victim with a knife in LONG or MED SHOT to a DOLLYING IN SHOT on a woman lying on a slab in the morgue. It's all a matter of technique, and the use of visual dramatics.

There is no need my going into further terminology here. You've got virtually everything you'll need unless you're a *very* advanced and visually oriented scenarist, in which case you can make up your own language (such as DIMINISHING MOTE STROBE EFFECT). And if you're that far along in your craft, you're probably already working in films or tv, so why should I insult you by telling you what you already know?

One final thing about form, about what a script should actually *look* like.

If the typesetters and designers of this book have set the pages of that script portion as I wrote them, exactly, using typewriter type-face, all you have to do is follow the form and you'll be doing it in a professional manner. But here is a tip that was given to me by Alex Gottlieb, a producer who was working in the office next to mine at 20th when I was doing the first treatment (never used, but paid for very handsomely) of *Valley of the Dolls* about ten years ago.

Alex and I got to know each other, and he was a fount of those obscure little tips that, if followed, save you endless hours of wrong directions. One afternoon, having written a half dozen pages of script in which two people have a long exchange of dialogue, I carried the pages in to Alex, to have him read them, to see if he thought they'd "play" (that is, if they'd be fast and perky and easy for the actors to work with). He took the pages from my hand, flipped through them without apparently reading a word, and dropped them on the desk.

"They won't play," he said.

I was stunned. "But you didn't even read them!"

"Doesn't matter," he said, with unassailable *sang-froid.* "They won't play."

"How the hell can you say that?"

"I can tell by looking at them. They don't *look* right."

I picked them up and leafed through them. "They look fine to me."

Alex pulled a note pad over and began making marks. "Look," he said, "here's what your pages look like."

They all looked about like this:

Excuse my slovenly drawing. The short line in the upper left is the shot sequence information, the short line in the upper right is the page number. The short lines centered on the page are the indications of which character is speaking, and the long lines (which are, in reality, as you can see from the script portion earlier, much shorter) are the speeches.

"And here," said Alex, drawing on another piece of scratch paper, "is what that page *should* look like to flow and move for film." And here, approximately, is what he drew:

At first, I just stared at them without understanding what I was seeing. But after a moment I began to perceive what Alex was telling me. Do *you* see the difference?

Of course. You've got it. *My* script had speeches that were six, seven, eight, ten lines long; very long; too long. Prolonged speeches. Lectures. Alex's version had the speeches broken up, short "leader" lines that prompted the other character to elaborate . . . but not too much. There were three and four word interrogatives that pulled the conversation forward; sharp dialogue that compressed the wordy messages of my version; the establishment of *interior tension* in the dialogue because the conversation was now a tennis match, not a series of pontifications. Alex hadn't rewritten my script, he simply showed me that you can tell whether or not a page of dialogue will work from the physical appearance!

I've repeated that tip to professional tv writers—several of whom have even won Emmys—and they were amazed and delighted. Yes, they said, that's *right;* you *can* tell just by looking at the page. So check over that script portion and see if it'll work. Except for one thing: there are *always* exceptions to the rule. Check out Linda's speeches at the close of *Death of a Salesman.* They're long, but they play like a baby doll. This is a general rule that is a good one to follow, but when you have someone speaking intensely, full of emotion, it is often permissible to let the character run on.

Oh hell. *Any* rule can be broken!

I was going to do a section here on Magicam, matte techniques and miniaturization, which are the coming thing in sf on tv, but I've come into possession of a dynamite article that has everything you could possibly want to know about this new videotape technique—the one so badly misused on a series I created called "The Starlost"[6]—and so, rather than trying to paraphrase it, and getting it wrong (not to mention having to explain in a belabored prose what is clearly demonstrated in color photos and diagrams and schematics in the article), let me suggest you try and obtain the January 1975 issue of *American Cinematographer* magazine, wherein reposes an exhaustive article on this new camera control system that makes possible complete freedom of camera movement during a matte.[7]

Let it suffice as my opinion here that while these new technological developments *can* permit a network or studio to put the equivalent of *2001: A Space Odyssey* on the screen *every* week for less money than it took to produce a segment of, say, "Star Trek," these visual techniques are still only ways of telling a story more excitingly. Without a parallel development of sensibility that sf is about *people* and the effects on people of technology, the future and the fantastic . . . what we'll see on the tube or the big screen will merely be more Technicolor tomfoolery. It is the *story* that counts!

(Incidentally, additional data on Magicam can be obtained by writing to Mr. Robert C. King, Jr., Vice-President, MAGICAM, Inc.; 3100 Airport Avenue; Santa Monica, California 90405.)

(And for the very best assessment of the state of the motion picture industry today, I urge you to locate the August 5th, 1974 issue of *The New Yorker* containing Pauline Kael's long, absolutely brilliant article, "On the Future of Movies." It provides a view into the Industry that I can only touch on briefly here; Ms. Kael's perceptions will stun and enlighten you.)

(And for a television market list, featuring every show of the current season; to whom scripts should be sent and the shows that are either staff-written or that will only read agent-submitted manuscripts; *précis* of the plot-lines of the new shows and what material they're seeking, $1.00 should be sent with such a request to The Writers Guild of America, West; 8955 Beverly Boulevard; Los Angeles, California 90048.)

And now let me tie up all the loose ends I promised to tie up, so we can both sit back and think about all this.

The Industry is in Los Angeles. Some tv and film work is done in New York; and there's a smattering of independent filmmaking throughout the rest of the United States; but if you are planning to write for films or television, your chances of breaking in are incalculably enhanced by living in Los Angeles. Unless you happen to have a talent roughly equivalent to that of S=Shakespeare
H=Heinlein
A=Aesop
Z=Zelazny
A=Anhalt
M=Melville you'll be batting your head against a putty-soft wall from any other base of operations than Los Angeles. There are exceptions, of course. Jerry McNeely, who created "Lucas Tanner," "Owen Marshall" and other television series, lives and teaches in Madison, Wisconsin, at the U. of Wisconsin. Theodore Fox, who has written a screenplay for Warner Bros. based on Heinlein's *Stranger in a Strange Land*, lives in Douglaston, New York. John Mes-

ton, who wrote the most outstanding segments of "Gunsmoke," the segments that made it a quality show head-and-shoulders above all other tv westerns, has for years lived on the Riviera.

But these are the exceptions to the rule, and each of these writers spends a portion of his business year in either New York or Los Angeles, assessing the markets, firming up contacts, getting assignments if possible. And don't forget, all three of them are well along in their careers: they have credits.

For anyone who has mastered the form of writing a screenplay or teleplay (and you'll need a helluva lot more instruction than what I've been able to adumbrate here, as exhaustive as it may seem), there is still the stately pavane of *working* in Los Angeles, within a spiderweb of concretized social and economic and "through channels" systems second only to those epitomized by life at the Versailles court of Louis XIV, the "Sun King." Most of these rigors need not concern you unless you try cracking the market, but once you commit to such a course of career activity, you'd damned well better know what you're up against.

For instance, television scripts are sold in stages: story-conference, treatment, first draft, final (or shooting) script. That first step, the story-conference, involves an art-form many people find themselves incapable of understanding. It is, quite literally, the job of selling a story by talking, not writing. Because of space limitations here, I cannot go into *all* the socially oriented aspects of getting work in Hollywood, but at least I can explain how a story-conference works. And from this one facet of the scenarist's work-pattern, you can extrapolate to the whole.

It is necessary, first, to understand that the tv arena and the magazine/book publishing field are structured differently, when it comes to selling something. If you write a short story for a magazine, you write it and submit it, and if they dig it, they buy it. Period. If you want to sell a book, you write ten thousand and an outline, submit them, and if they swing for your action, they give you a contract, on the strength of what you've already done. In Hollywood, they make the commitment *before* you do the writing. You go into a story-conference and pitch your idea to the producer, or the story editor, or some *schlepp* used as a figurehead, to keep all the kooks out of the way of the people really getting the job done. The Writers Guild contract with the studios forbids a writer to set anything down on paper without being paid for it. In theory. It's a nice theory, too; and even granting that before the Writers Guild jammed their Minimum Basic Agreement down the collective throat of the studios and networks it was hell and thievery for all but the biggest name writers, still the situation is a shifty one when it comes to that first tentative move toward getting an assignment. It all rests with the story-conference.

The story-conference usually runs like this:

Your agent tells you that the new hour western "The Upchuckers" is open and buying, and he has set up an appointment for Wednesday at 11:00 with Morrie Wheedler, the story editor. (It's always eleven o'clock, or three o'clock, for appointments, for obvious reasons.)

You get past Morrie Wheedler's secretary, and you enter the inner sanctum. Morrie is on the phone. He motions you to a chair. You siddown (as opposed to the act of "sit down," which is performed in every other city in the world) and you begin to wait. Morrie is dickering with an agent about the cost of a guest star needed for an upcoming segment. When you hear the figures being bandied about, you wonder why you're bothering writing, when you could make so much more mouthing other people's words.

Morrie grins his capped-teeth smile at you, around his Nat Sherman in its Aqua-Filter. He'll be with you in a minute. Half an hour later, three phone calls later, five secretarial interruptions later, he settles back in his swivel chair, ready for you to do your quaint native dance.

The story-conference is half idea session, half burlesque show. If you are introverted, shy, slow on the tongue, or if you cannot think on your feet, like Reynard the Fox, you are probably two strikes toward the showers for openers.

Because no matter how good an idea is, and how good it will look on a screen, when you have to capsulize it, synopsize it, boil it down to one-liners, it sounds like dogmeat. *The Philadelphia Story, War and Peace, Moby Dick* and *Catcher in the Rye* all sound like pablum or insanity when broken down to the sort of primary-level plotting needed for a story-conference. Here's a frinstance. Say you've gone in to write an NBC Movie of the Week, with an idea to develop for a two-hour film. The name of your idea is *Huckleberry Finn.*

"It's about the growing up of a wild kid on the Mississippi River," you say. "He has a black friend named Jim, and they get into all sorts of adventures. It's a morality play, sort of." The story editor looks at you and his eyes get hard. "We got enough race problem stories. Thanks, anyhow."

Back to Morrie Wheedler. He lights a fresh Sherman and says, "Well, have you seen the poop sheet on the show? We call it *The Canons of the Upchuckers.* It tells pretty much what we have in mind, and what we're looking for. We want hard-hitting one-hour ideas that you can hand in by next Monday." (N.B. The philosophy out here is generally: it doesn't have to be good, just fast.) Morrie beams at you. The guy is sincere, he's honest, he really means it when he says, "We want ideas that will really sizzle. No taboos! Just let fly and hit whatever you aim at, that's all we ask. Now, what's your idea?"

Now, unless you are able to dazzle him with your verbal pyrotechnics, unless you have as many trick voices and phony accents as a Mel Blanc or a Paul Frees, unless you can capture him with a spiderweb of storytelling (your image is closer to that of a medieval minstrel than to Joseph Conrad), he will sit there and get The Look.

The Look is compounded part of pity, part of annoyance that you've wasted his time, part of disappointment, part of boredom. It is a mask-like thing that slides down as smoothly as the shield in an atomic pile. It means you're locked out, talking to yourself. You hem and haw, you *fumfuh* and grasp at straws. "Well, if that one doesn't seem right," you whine, "I thought it might be interesting to try one about a renegade who has been with Quantrill's Raiders and has been regenerated by his childhood sweetheart after the Raiders burned out this town. But he is being hounded by three members of the band who think he has buried some money stolen from the bank, and . . ."

"Too close to a segment we're shooting next week," Morrie tells you. No further word is expected on that topic. So you quick like a bunny think of another one, off the top of your head (if you're that good), and you throw it at him. If you're lucky, somewhere in the dozen or so one-liners, he'll find a germ that either pleases, interests or stops him, and he'll ask you to expound on it. Now you've no more thought of that story than you have of cutting your toenails with an oxyacetylene torch, but you start jackpotting, praying that the dredge of cliché ideas and old movie plots salted away in your cortex will hurl up some tidbits that fit in. If you're lucky, he'll like what you tell him. If, as more often happens, you haven't really got anything (that first idea was the one you were hot about, the one you wanted to do, these others are just second-thoughts, backstops), he'll politely but firmly get you out of his hair with, "Why don't you call me when you have something closer to what we want?"

But let's pretend miracles still happen, and you have someway managed to stickum-and-pray an idea together that is not (a) exactly like a segment already bought, (b) too controversial, (c) too difficult for this show's actor-excuses to do, or (d) too expensive to shoot. Let's say he likes it. Then comes the Wheedler gambit.

Writers Guild says he can't ask you to put it on paper. Breach of Agreement. And all reputable producers, studios, networks, agencies, outfits, etc. are signatories to this Agreement. And you can't work unless you belong to the Guild. So there he sits, with your idea intriguing him, and he wants something to show you can write, something he can give to the higher-ups in case you foul out along the line. But he can't ask for it. So he sits and stares at you, with Another Look.

This one says, very simply, *Well, keed, it's your move. Give me something for nothing.*

"I can't ask you to write any of this," Morrie wheedles, "Guild regs and all, but I think it needs a little more form before I can give you an assignment." So your greedy, hungry little mouth opens and you *volunteer* to write it all down "in two or three pages." (It is, of course, truly impossible to do a competent story treatment that reads as if it's worth shooting, in less than half a dozen to eight pages.)

So you've sold him by talking, not writing.

Then, let's say, you write up the idea, and he digs it, and it gets accepted. Then you have a contract for story and teleplay with cut-offs. (See previous footnote 2.)

The mention of cut-offs brings us to the terms of the much-lauded Writers Guild MBA (Minimum Basic Agreement). Every year or two the MBA goes through contract revisions with the MPAA (which is the motion picture and television producers' guild), and so it would be foolish for me to try outlining its terms here, in a book that would be outdated almost by the time it was published. Earlier in this essay I gave you an address for the Writers Guild (referred to as the WGAw). Use it to obtain a copy of the MBA. It will fill you in on what you can and should do, what you can expect, and how to go about getting a square deal.

If you're worried about being plagiarized, should you come up with a series format or a screenplay idea, you can use the WGAw registration service (I think it's $4.00 per item) even if you're not a member of the Guild. The Guild has many such services. It is, in short, the only writers' organization with which I'm familiar that spends its time and effort and money to protect and better the working conditions for writers. Once you've sold something, you can join for a very nominal fee, and you'll find the Guild a guardian angel of not inconsiderable power.

Okay. That brings me to a couple of life-style comments about Los Angeles.

If you decide you want to write for film/tv, you've got to come to live in Los Angeles. First, ignore the dopey stories about smog and earthquakes and cuckoo people who are supposed to run amuck out here. Charlie Manson and his crowd are no loonier than Birchers in Montana or KKK'ers in Missouri or snipers in Minnesota. We live in perilous times, and the whackos are everywhere; but the tv/film arena is only in Hollywood and New York. Calculate your risks as opposed to the benefits and make your decision accordingly.

But if you opt for Los Angeles and the pain of trying to break into the film/tv life, bear two things in mind:

The first is that you must have some money laid-back to support you while you write treatments and story-ideas and scripts on speculation, while you try to get an agent, while you go to those story-conferences and try battering down the producers' doors . . . and you *must* have a car. L.A. has a very weak public transportation setup, and you'll need wheels to get you around. Without a car, you're sunk to your knees in nowhere. So: money and a car.

The second is that you'd damned well better know if you have an acceptable talent. Not just an ability to mimic the script writing format, but a *talent;* something to say. Don't delude yourself, as thousands do every year, that you can be a writer if someone just gives you a chance. Do a lot of writing. Find yourself a good college-level course on writing for films and tv *TAUGHT BY SOMEONE WHO HAS DONE IT,* like Jerry McNeely at the University of Wisconsin, not some dip who read a book once and got the assignment to teach the course because he once had a couple of drinks with Martin Milner when "Route 66" was shooting location footage in his town. Check out the credentials of the instructor carefully: a course taught by an inept is worse than no course at all. Do some reading in the field. There are dozens of books on the subject. But, again, check out the credentials of the author before you take it as gospel.

But . . .

And this is important . . .

DO *NOT* SEND ME YOUR SCRIPTS, OR LETTERS ASKING ME TO READ YOUR SCRIPT, OR REQUESTS TO FIND YOU AN AGENT, GIVE YOU SPECIFIC MARKET INFORMATION,

A PLACE TO STAY, OR ENCOURAGEMENT. I HAVE DONE MY SHARE BY WRITING THIS ESSAY. IF YOU SEND ME SOMETHING, NO MATTER HOW CLEVERLY YOU WRITE THE COVER LETTER, I'LL ONLY BURN THE DAMNED THING!

There. That ought to be direct enough.

A final word. Writing science fiction and/or fantasy for the visual media is a tougher row to hoe than writing a western or a caper film or even a searching, penetrating study of life in America today. It takes great skill, a fertile imagination, and the stamina of an Outback Abo.

Watch what comes across the tube, go to see the sf movies, and study them for technique, not just how good or bad the storyline might be.

And, in an effort to weed out those of you who will be deluding yourselves about your abilities or the toughness of this gig, even after all I've said here, let me close with the words of a great critic, the late Cyril Connolly, who said in his book *The Unquiet Grave:*

> The more books we read, the sooner we perceive that the true function of a writer is to produce a masterpiece and that no other task is of any consequence. . . . All excursions into journalism, broadcasting, propaganda and writing for the films, however grandiose, are doomed to disappointment. To put of our best into these forms is another folly, since thereby we condemn good ideas as well as bad to oblivion. It is in the nature of such works not to last, so it should never be undertaken. Writers engaged in any literary activity which is not their attempt at a masterpiece are their own dupes and, unless these self-flatterers are content to write off such activities as their contribution to the war effort, they might as well be peeling potatoes.

I'm not sure I agree with all of that, but he's right on the most important count. If you aren't prepared to produce work of a masterpiece brilliance, don't come out here, don't try to become a scenarist, don't muck up the water with more inferior work. Be prepared to embark on a writing career whose sole purpose is to refute Connolly's admonitions.

It *can* be done. I've seen enough superlative screen writing to know it *can* be done. But if you are arrogant enough to think *you* can do it, just remember: you have to be a very fast gun, indeed; and there are those of us here already who will challenge you to draw against us.

And when the smoke clears, there won't be any Cisco and Pancho giggling their way into the sunset.

You've been warned.

A VERY INCOMPLETE LIST OF SUPPLEMENTARY READINGS ON THE SUBJECT

Ellison, Harlan: *The Glass Teat* (Pyramid Books, 1975); *The Other Glass Teat* (Pyramid Books, 1975).

Elwood, Roger, Editor: *Six Science Fiction Plays* (Washington Square Press, 1975).

Dann, Jack, and George Zebrowski, Editors: *Faster Than Light* (containing the entire screenplay of *Phoenix Without Ashes*) (Harper & Row, 1976).

Friendly, Fred W.: *Due to Circumstances Beyond Our Control* . . . (Random House, 1967).

Hoopes, Ned E., and Patricia Neale Gordon, Editors: *Great Television Plays,* Vol. 2 (Dell Laurel Original, 1975).

Johnson, Nicholas: *How to Talk Back to Your Television Set* (Little, Brown, 1970).

Kaufman, William I.: *Great Television Plays* (Dell Laurel Original, 1969).

Lang, Kurt, and Gladys Engel: *Politics & Television* (Quadrangle, 1968).

Laughton, Roy: *TV Graphics* (Reinhold Publishing Co., 1966).

Miller, Merle, and Evan Rhodes: *Only You, Dick Daring!* (William Sloane, 1964).

Sopkin, Charles: *Seven Glorious Days, Seven Fun-Filled Nights* (Simon and Schuster, 1968).

NB.: The book by Nicholas Johnson (an ex-FCC commissioner) has an extensive bibliography included; though I haven't read all of the titles or government-issued reports listed therein, I recommend the book and the bibliography for those who wish to pursue the subject further, particularly Michael Arlen's *The Living Room War,* which I neglected to include in my list above.

NOTES

1. You've got to be chary in your use of "indicators" such as the phone large in f.g. It draws attention where you need it drawn, but you'd damned well better pay it off and ring that phone before very long. It ties in with what Chekhov once said: "If, in Act One of a play, you show a dueling pistol hanging on the

wall, you *must* fire that pistol before the end of Act Two." Otherwise, you're a cheat.

2. This is written in the form of a "treatment." The term *treatment* is interchangeable with the term *story* in the parlance of film/tv deal-making. It is the first step in writing a script. It is a present-tense, straight-line description of the entire plot scene-by-scene, with the barest minimum of dialogue and characterization and camerawork. It serves several purposes, most of which benefit the producer: it tells him what your story will be and how it will move, so he can "cut off" the scenarist before the first draft stage of the assignment if he doesn't like where the story's going or he doesn't trust the writer; it gives him an opportunity to force the scenarist back onto the track he thinks the show should have if you've wandered; and it minimizes the chances of a script going wrong from the start. For the writer it provides a chance to plot succinctly and without holes. I'll talk more about this later. Remind me.

3. George C. Scott, as quoted by Charles Champlin in the Los Angeles *Times* "Calendar" section.

4. Francis Ford Coppola, as quoted by Hollis Alpert in *Saturday Review/ World.*

5. *Teleplay: An Introduction to Television Writing* (Revised Edition) by Coles Trapnell; Hawthorn Books, New York; 245 pp., $4.95.

6. For those interested in how badly a good tv series idea can go wrong, I refer you to a paperback novel, *Phoenix Without Ashes,* by myself and Edward Bryant. The introduction to this novelization of a script I wrote for *The Starlost,* included in the volume, is titled, "Somehow, I Don't Think We're in Kansas, Toto," and provides another view of working in the Industry. (Fawcett Gold Medal Books; M3188; 1975; 95¢)

7. "Magicam," pp. 34–37, 72–73, 112–13; by Joe Matza; in *American Cinematographer* (Vol. 56, No. 1, January 1975).

Harlan Ellison

Harlan Ellison has won more Nebula and Hugo Awards than any other sf writer —ten at the last counting, including two Special Citations for editing the "giganthologies" *Dangerous Visions* and *Again, Dangerous Visions.* (The final volume in the trilogy, the half-million-word-plus *The Last Dangerous Visions,* is scheduled by Harper & Row for Fall 1977.) His published and scheduled book titles now number more than thirty. He has also won the Edgar Allan Poe award of the Mystery Writers of America for best short story, and is the only writer to ever win the Writers Guild of America award for Most Outstanding Teleplay *three* times.

His wide experience with sf in the visual media qualifies him uniquely to discuss this aspect of the craft of science fiction. His TV scriptwriting credits include "Star Trek," "Voyage to the Bottom of the Sea," "The Chrysler Theatre," "Cimarron Strip," "The Man from U.N.C.L.E.," "Outer Limits," "Batman," "The Alfred Hitchcock Hour," "The Rat Patrol," "Route 66," "The Young Lawyers," and "Circle of Fear." For the past three years, his work in the visual media has been concentrated almost exclusively on the creation of pilots for series of his own devising and films for television.

Among these projects have been *Stranglehold* for 20th Century–Fox, *Esper* for Universal, *Flintlock* for a proposed "Our Man Flint" series at 20th, *Astral Man* for Warner Brothers, and currently *The Tigers Are Loose,* a two-hour prime-time dramatic special for NBC based on the work of a prison psychiatrist, and *Dark Destroyer,* an original fantasy for ABC-TV and Dan Curtis Productions.

In late 1971 and early 1972, he moved briefly to the other side of the desk to work for the highest weekly fee paid to any story editor on the Universal lot, for the ABC-TV series "The Sixth Sense," a job he deserted happily—despite the money—after seven weeks. (He describes the experience as akin to "reading Voltaire to a cage of baboons.")

Continuing his list of pilot projects: he created (in collaboration with Larry Brody) and sold to Screen Gems and NBC an original fantasy/occult TV series, "The Dark Forces," featuring a modern-day sorcerer. (A series of "Dark Forces" novels has been commissioned by Pyramid Books as part of their Harlan Ellison program; the first, *The Salamander Enchantment,* in 1976.) An sf series (with Ben Bova, editor of *Analog*), entitled "Brillo," about the first experimental robot cop sent to work a beat in upper Manhattan, sold to ABC; and an earlier sf series,

"Man Without Time," sold previously but withdrawn by Ellison, is currently under consideration again.

Harlan Ellison was born on May 27, 1934, in Cleveland, Ohio, and attended grade and high schools in Painesville, a small town thirty miles away. His childhood and early youth were tempestuous and included such episodes as running away from home at thirteen and, before his eighteenth birthday, working as a treetopper in Ontario, a tuna fisherman off Galveston, an itinerant crop-picker down to New Orleans, a hired gun for a wealthy neurotic, a dynamite truck driver, and much else which later contributed notably to his fiction. He attended Ohio State University for a year and a half, was thrown out after being told that he had no talent for creative writing, and went to New York to pursue his career, working at all sorts of jobs until he got started. He made his first sale to *Infinity Science Fiction* for forty dollars—a story called "Glowworm," which the late and much-missed author-critic James Blish termed "the single worst story ever written in the field."

He seems to have come a long way.

FREDERIK POHL

The Science Fiction Professional

Time was when a professional science fiction writer knew what he had to do with his working time.

He wrote stories.

When he had finished writing them, he mailed them off to *Astounding* or *Thrilling Wonder* or *Weird Tales,* and sometimes he got a check back and sometimes not. Either way, that was about all there was to it. If he spent forty hours a week writing, all the rest of his professional activities combined might add another thirty minutes. He could spend the remaining 127 hours thirty minutes of each week eating, sleeping, having fun, studying Help Wanted ads and cursing his fate.

It is no longer that easy.

Being a science fiction writer is also, by the way, changed in other significant ways—money, fame and prestige, to name three—and for the better. But all these things come at a high cost. Sf writers don't spend as much time writing as they used to. They don't have time. I don't believe I know a single writer who puts in a forty-hour *writing* week any more, year round. I know many who work longer hours than that, but they are lucky if half the time is actually spent putting real words on paper for publication. The other jobs of the sf professional keep them jumping.

What are those other jobs?

There are at least a dozen of them. In order to be a real sf professional, you have to be able to function as:

1. A literary agent.

2. A contract lawyer.

3. A publicity man.

4. A performer—TV, radio, lectures.

5. An apparatnik, helping to keep professional and fan organizations functioning.

6. A teacher.

7. A critic.

And it helps if you are also skilled as:

8. A secretary.

9. An editor.

10. A proofreader.

11. A futurologist.

12. A scientist—at least to the extent of being able to understand and communicate what is happening in the marches of science.

13. An artist.

And, oh, yes—

14. A writer.

I suppose it is possible to shed all these cares, retreat to some remote Bolivian fishing village with a typewriter and a native wench and do nothing but *write.* I keep intending to try it. So do a lot of other writers I know. But it doesn't happen; the world doesn't let you.

You may think you can hire people to do these things for you. Indeed you can, most of them. But any boss knows that he can't hire intelligently unless he knows enough about the job to know who can do it. In order to hire an agent, you have to know what it takes to *be* an agent. In order to supervise a secretary, you have to have enough skill to recognize when she's doing a satisfactory job.

Literary Agents

The first thing you need to know about literary agents is when you need to get one.

That time is not when you feel the need most strongly—i.e., when you first begin to write.

You will not want to believe this. Very few new writers do. Obviously, when you are brand-fresh-new and have had no experience in submitting to markets or dealing with editors you will feel very alone in the world and wish very hard for expert professional help.

So you will go looking for one. You will ask your professional writer friends to give you an introduction to their own agents. Or you will pick an agent's name from your local library's copy of the *Literary Market Place*[1] or respond to an ad in one of the writers' magazines.

None of these is likely to do you much good. *Good* agents cannot waste much time with beginners. They can't afford to. Sometimes one will take a freshman on, as a sort of a lottery ticket for the future or out of some benign impulse to help the kids along. But for every new writer they take there are fifty they won't even talk to, and you are much more likely to be one of the fifty.

Besides that, you may be better off without an agent. Partly because you can learn a great deal from the personal dealing with publishers and editors (even if those dealings are only printed rejection slips). Also because there may be real disadvantages in having an agent too early. If he is a really big agent, he may well price you out of the market. If he is a really bad agent, you may find yourself inextricably tied to him before you find out how bad he is.

The second thing you need to know about agents is what they do.

For one thing, they sell your work for you.

That is, they read it, think of an editor who might buy it and offer it to that editor. Usually all that amounts to is putting a note on it, putting it in an envelope and dropping it in the mail. If it doesn't sell, he tries again with somebody else.

This is perhaps what you think an agent does all day long. Wrong. It is a very small part of what they do with their time. Much more of their time is spent on negotiating contracts, selling subsidiary rights and *un*selling your work—i.e., getting you out of deals that have outlived their usefulness, or never had any.

An interesting thing about what your agent does is that he does a lot of it, as much as he possibly can, over a lunch table. Usually somebody's expense account picks up the tab, which confers certain obvious benefits of its own, but the other benefits are real enough: there aren't any phone interruptions, and an informal chat can reach a happy agreement more readily than twenty telephone calls.

An agent basically has one source of income. Every time one of his clients makes ninety cents, he makes a dime. His 10 percent commission is where it's all at, and out of it he has to pay for his office rent, his secretary, his stationery, his house in the country, his car, his wife's alimony, his kids' tuition, his phone bill and those double Gibsons, very dry with a twist, on the occasions when the editor's expense account is feeling poorly at lunch. (A few agents charge "reading fees," but we'll come to that later.) So it is to his advantage to *handle money.* This is not the same thing as making sales. Obviously, the more sales he makes, everything else being equal, the more money will flow through his account and the more dimes will accrue to him. But everything else isn't equal. A short-story sale to *Amazing Stories* may mean a lot to the writer, but it means maybe five bucks to the agent, and there just isn't any profit in five-dollar commissions. A novel that goes through fifteen printings and keeps generating royalties for twenty-five years is something else again. The actual time involved may be as much to sell the short story as to sell the novel, so if you were an agent, which would you concentrate on? That's right, you would. He does. So if you are at the short-story now-and-then stage of your career, do not expect an agent to do it for you.

The time you really need an agent is when there is fairly big money involved, and he can do something for you that you can't do for yourself. For instance, if the phone rings and it is Hollywood offering to make a movie out of one of your stories, *then* you need an agent. Or if a publisher expresses interest in a book, then you need an agent. What you say to the potential customer is, "Thank you very much, I'm delighted, and I'll have my agent call you." Then you go out and get an agent. You select one from LMP or wherever, pick up the telephone, tell him the circumstances and ask him to represent you.

Which brings us to the third thing you need to know about agents—namely, which agent should you get?

Unfortunately there is no answer for that. An agent is like a wife.[2] An ideal match for one person is sheer misery for another. If you move in the company of other writers keep your ears open for gossip about agents—you'll hear a lot of it, don't worry—and don't hesitate to ask for recommendations.

When you do pick one, try to avoid signing a contract that ties you to him for a period of time. Divorces are expensive.

I mentioned reading fees a moment ago, and that relates to another major function of agents—namely to act as literary critics and coaches.

This is a useful function, and some agents are very, very good at it. A young sf writer once came to see me in some despair; he thought he could write but was selling very little. I turned him over to the late Rogers Terrill, who spent a lot of time coaching and advising the man. Now he's a major figure who gets six-figure advances and last year won a National Book Award. Very few agents are as good at this as Rog. But many are good enough to help you a lot.

Sometimes you can get this part of an agent's services without having him handle your sales, by paying a "reading fee." Generally speaking, this is a bad idea. It costs you maybe $25 to get a three-page appraisal of your latest story. The price isn't bad, but what do you do if the advice is? It may be. Most "reading fee" agents don't actually read the stories themselves; they hire hungry would-be writers at so much a manuscript, so the advice you are getting is often from somebody with no more writing skills than your own. Even so, it can be worthwhile—it's easier to see flaws in someone else's work than in your own. But if you want to be involved in reading fees, consider doing it the other way around: ask for a job writing them rather than paying them.

Marketing

Supposing you don't have an agent to sell your stories for you, how do you do it for yourself?

The first thing you do in order to sell a story is this: you take it out of your desk drawer, put it in an envelope and mail it to somebody who might buy it.

If I seem to be putting this in very elementary terms, it is because this question keeps coming up whenever I talk to aspiring authors. "How do I get published?" is always the second question I hear.[3] There appear to be certain superstitions prevalent among unpublished writers: that they can't get their stories read by editors, that editors won't buy from anyone who is not vouched for by some substantial figure, etc. None of these is true, at least not in most sf markets. (There are a few book publishers who return unsolicited manuscripts unread, but even they in most cases make an exception for their science fiction editors.) Nearly every science fiction editor I have ever known, which is most of them, is highly anxious to discover new talent, and the only good place to discover it is in the slush pile.

Let me run down some of the other questions that come up over and over again:

Q. How do I submit a story?

A. You put it in an envelope (manila clasp envelopes from the five-and-ten are fine; if possible, you should always mail your manuscripts flat). You enclose with the story an SASE ("self-addressed stamped envelope"—again, one big enough to hold it). You address it to an editor. You put a stamp on it, and you drop it in the mail.

Q. Should I enclose a covering letter?

A. If you have something to say that the story doesn't say for itself, maybe. Generally not. If you must send a letter, make it brief.

Q. What editor should I submit to?

A. Well, what do you read? If it's a science fiction magazine, the editor's name and the address of the editorial office are on the contents page or somewhere nearby. Send it to your favorite magazine first, if you have one.

If he bounces it, try elsewhere. Keep trying as long as there are markets. If the manuscript gets dog-eared, retype the first page from time to time.[4] Any manuscript can be bounced a few times. Editors make mistakes. Maybe they're wrong, and it's really good. Or maybe the ones who bounced it are right and it's awful; the next editor might make a mistake in your favor and buy it.

Q. Should I ask an editor for criticism of my story?

A. No. Just no. Don't do it. You probably won't get it unless he has something specific he wants to say for *his* reasons. Then you'll get it whether you ask for it or not.

Bear in mind that an editor may get maybe 100 manuscripts a week. If he spends ten minutes on each one, reading it, putting a rejection slip on it and putting it back in the mail, that's about seventeen hours' working time. If he has to write a carefully thought-out letter on each one, that ups the time to maybe thirty minutes each, or a total of fifty hours. There just aren't fifty hours in a forty-hour week. So he can't do it for everybody, and he probably will not do it for you.

Q. How do I sell to a book publisher?

A. About the same way you sell to a magazine. You don't need to write the whole book first. Write maybe three chapters. Put them in finished form. Write an outline of the rest and mail the whole shooting-match off to the science fiction editor at the book publishing house of your choice. You get the name of the publisher by seeing what the name is on some science fiction books you've read. You get his address from *LMP*.

You may, in spite of the above, want to work from market lists rather than going after the publishers you like best. There's no real harm in it. You can get such lists in science fiction by subscribing to *Locus* or the *SFWA Bulletin.* Writers' magazines also publish them from time to time, but they are not as reliable.

Q. How long should it take to get a decision?

A. God knows.

Some editors respond almost overnight. Some—well, I've heard of *eight years.* The average is maybe three or four weeks. But to that you must add travel time, which, with the present slovenly state of the mails, can easily double that.

Q. What terms should I accept?

A. Ah, that is a question, isn't it? It depends on how much the editor can offer, how valuable your story is to him and how good you are at bargaining. This is where an agent can be extremely helpful.

Without an agent, you should *try* for the following:

In magazine sales, try to sell First Serial Rights Only. Do not sell "All Rights" unless you are absolutely desperate, and try to get out of it even then. "All Rights" means you no longer own any part of your story, and they can make a movie out of it or sell the Swedish comic-book rights or anything at all, and you have nothing to say and no part of the profit.

In selling to a book publisher, try to get advice from someone who has negotiated book contracts before. Don't bother going to your family lawyer; he won't help. Go to a writer or an agent.

If you can't do that, at least try to avoid signing a contract that doesn't let you recapture your book if things go bad. There should be a clause which says that if the book goes out of print for ninety days or so you can demand it back (and get it, or a new printing). And there should be a clause that says that if the publisher goes bankrupt you get the book back.

For the rest, try to get as much money in advance (a couple of thousand dollars, anyway), as high a royalty (at least 10 percent on a hardbound and at least 6 percent in paperback) and as large a proportion of the subsidiary rights as you can.

Let's talk about the fine art of contract negotiating in further detail.

Contracts

There are three basic things to know about contracts:

1. Everything in a contract, including the date at the top of it and the publisher's address, is negotiable.

2. The way to write a contract is to make believe that you and the nice person who bought your book will both drop dead tomorrow, and your heirs will hate each other's guts.

3. A contract is basically two sets of promises (one what the publisher promises you and the other what you promise the publisher) and an agreement for dividing up the loot. The rest is hardware.

In negotiating a contract, it is to your interest to promise as little as you can get away with. If you can, you strike out the option clause; you try to avoid agreeing to pay part of the costs if there is a lawsuit; etc. It is to the publisher's interest to promise you as little as he can— in the way of money and also in a commitment actually to publish the book, or to be bound by a particular timetable, etc. And it is to the interest of both of you to grab for as big a share of all the money involved as possible.

Think of your book as a great goose in the sky, excreting golden eggs in the form of dollar bills. You and the publisher are standing underneath as the dollar bills float by, and each of your wants to grab as much as he can. Some of the dollar bills come from retail sales. Some come from foreign editions. Some come from book clubs. Some come from serialization. How many of each kind each of you grabs depends on what the contract you have signed says about it. If a packet of dollar bills from a Swiss edition comes by, and you have given him 25 percent of translation rights, he is entitled to grab and keep one out of four of them. If a batch from a book club comes by and he has 50 percent of that, he gets to grab one out of two.

Do not assume that there aren't going to be any subsidiary rights. Don't even assume that there won't be a lot of money involved. Of course, when it's your first book and you're looking at the subsidiary-rights percentages in the handsomely printed contract, it all looks like fantasy. "Commercial rights." That means, like, maybe somebody will put out a line of T-shirts with your picture silkscreened on them. Would anybody in his right mind do that? Maybe not—but you never know.

So ask for what you want—but, please, *ask.* Don't demand, and above all don't get into a fit of moral anger. There is nothing moral about a contract. It is a business deal.

If your contract calls for your publisher to get 25 percent of all translation rights, you may view this as a way of putting his hand in your pocket. You may be right. On the other hand, if he acts as agent for you and does a good job of selling the translation rights he is entitled to something for his trouble. Twenty-five percent is more than an agent would charge you. But it is not necessarily more than the publisher's services are worth to you.

How much revenue do you think he will produce? (That's a rhetorical question. You don't know the answer; you have to guess.) How hard will he work to earn it? A publisher may maintain a subsidiary-rights department of twenty people; he may keep up relationships with other publishers in thirty countries and send someone every year to the Frankfurt Book Fair to make contact with new ones. He may send out scores of copies of your book and aggressively seek out new markets for you.

Or his whole subsidiary-rights operation may be a part-time assignment for a bookkeeper, and the only activity is to say "yes" to whatever offers chance to float in. In one case he's worth 25 percent. In the other, probably not (although just the fact that he has a known address that foreign publishers may come to visit once in a while means he may be able to make some sales you can't make for yourself).

So in order to make an intelligent decision about what share of foreign rights your publisher should get, you need to know his track record. Unfortunately, you may not be able to find that out. So you guess.

And in practice, what you do is say, "All right, let's horse-trade. You can have 25 percent of foreign sales, but let's strike out the option clause on my next book."

But don't press too hard!

Try to limit your requests for contract changes to what is really important to you, especially when you are new and not in the best of bargaining positions. It is very easy to price yourself out of some markets —either in dollars, or in trouble. If you price yourself too high in dollars the publisher will probably bargain, and you lose little by trying. If you price yourself too high in trouble you may lose a publisher.

To you your book is a unique thing, your baby that you have at great pain of parturition brought into this world.

Your editor has some of these feelings too, or else he would be making more money writing advertising copy or running a publicity operation for some big corporation. But he also has dollar bills in his head. He wants to make money for the publisher. He doesn't have much choice about this; if he doesn't do that, he gets fired.

So in his eyes your book is a line of merchandise. He can calculate a certain amount of profit from it. If there is enough profit, he wants to publish it. If there isn't, he doesn't. He can publish only so many books a year—maybe one a month in a science fiction line. Next November he can publish your book, or he can publish somebody else's. If the books are equal in merit and equal in cost, but he can get a bigger share of the subsidiary rights from the other fellow, then your book goes back.[5]

Your editor also has limited time. So when it comes time to fill his November slot, suppose he has a choice between dealing with you and dealing with someone else. If you take up a lot of time and effort in contract haggling and the other fellow is a pussycat, then (everything else being equal) you are in trouble.

You are not the only person he has to deal with, you know. You want to keep your foreign rights; but every Thursday afternoon the subsidiary-rights lady drops by his desk complaining she doesn't have enough product to sell. You want a big advance, but he has a steady stream of memos from Accounting pointing out how much capital he has tied up in advances already. So you should ask for what you want and even bargain as hard as you have to when it is really important to you. But when push comes to shove he can't fire the subsidiary-rights lady or the Accounting Department, but he *can* fire you.

Of course, if what you have to sell is so valuable that you are *worth* a great deal, both in dollars and in trouble, then you can do what you like.

Publicity

You turn on your television set at 11:30, and there's Johnny Carson talking to a guest about his latest book tearing the veils off Hollywood, or Washington, or the feminine-hygiene industry. And you say to yourself, Ah, that's what I need, *publicity.*

Maybe you do. Sometimes it happens, I've seen it myself; exposure on the Carson show, or the *Today* show, or any of half a dozen other major TV talk programs can make books melt right off the shelves. It doesn't even have to be that big a show. If the audience is right, and the book is right, even a local radio program can send a lot of listeners down to the bookstore. The audiences are *huge*—twenty million or so for a network TV show, hundreds of thousands for even local radio. If you can persuade even one percent of them that your book is a good buy, you move a lot of books.

But the book has to be right.

Over the years I've had a lot of publicity. I've been on the Carson show; in fact I've been on four or five hundred talk shows, on most of the English-speaking radio and TV networks in the world, plus a few foreign-language ones where my voice was dubbed by a local, and uncounted single-station appearances. I've been interviewed by maybe a thousand newspaper and magazine reporters, sometimes in press conferences with twenty-five there at a time, representing everything from high-school quarterlies to the *Times* (both New York and London). I've lectured all over the place. You can buy some of my lectures on film or cassettes. I quit trying to keep press clippings years ago, for sheer lack of room.

Well, enough. What I want to say is that, with all this publicity, the only thing I am pretty sure of is that it has not actually *hurt* the sale of my books. I am far from sure that it has helped much.

The reason for this is that science fiction, which is what I mostly write, is a very special taste.

In relative terms, the audience is small. Not by any means insignificant; I would guess that there are two million people in the United States who read sf. But that means that 99 out of 100 Americans don't. So if you appear before an electronic audience of a million people, only 10,000 of them are realistically ever going to be customers for your book. And if you persuade one percent of them to rush out and buy it, you'll never notice the sale.

What you *may* do, if you turn out to be an attractive broadcast personality, is persuade a few of the 99 percent of Americans who are *not* sf readers to try a science fiction book or magazine. Not necessarily yours.

So why bother?

Well, two reasons. One reason is that publicity may be wasted effort, but it also may not be. You never know. There's an old adage in advertising that goes, "We know that 75 percent of what we do is wasted. The trouble is, we don't know *which* 75 percent, so we have to do it all."

The other is that selling books is not the only thing that may be gained from publicity. You may get lecture invitations, writing assignments, invitations to prestigious events—if nothing else, perhaps at least the respect and affection of your local banker, grocer, friends, children and wife.

So you should not scorn even the lowliest of publicity outlets, not the campus closed-circuit TV station or the shopping newspaper that clutters your mailbox every Wednesday. Accept. Even go looking for it.

How do you go about looking for it?

The easy and obvious thing for you to do is to call up the editor of the local paper and say, "Hey, I have a novel coming out next week. Why don't you interview me?" Often as not he will.

Of course, that sounds like a dreadfully pushy thing to do. Most of us don't want to do that sort of thing. It is the way things are that we all want to be famous, but we don't want to let other people see the nakedness of our desire.

So perhaps you will want to try it through a third party. For instance, the publicity department of your publisher. Go see the publicity girl (for some reason there is hardly every a publicity *man*, or even a publicity woman) and confess to her in all candor that you want fame. You will catch her unawares, because in all probability she has never heard a writer say that before, even though that is what her job is all about. But you can ask her to send out a news release to your local news media, both press and broadcast. She may let you write your own release. You might even offer to pay for it. You might ask only for a blank sheet of the publicity department's letterhead and some envelopes; write your own release, Xerox a bunch of copies and mail them off yourself.

Why (you may ask) do you have to do this? Isn't that what a publicity department is for?

Well, yes, sort of. But in practice you will find that the publicity department is all choked up with two other kinds of chores. Most of their time is spent writing obligatory in-house things like newsletters to salesmen, bookstores and local distributors. What's left goes into selling the hell out of whatever their Number One Best-Seller happens to be that month. The theory is that publicity sells most when it concentrates on selling *more* of something that is already selling *very well.* The theory is right. Nevertheless they should spare a few crumbs of time for you, and that's all you really need.

If your publisher can't do that for you (or if you don't have a publisher), almost any institution will do—a college where you teach (or attend!), a company you work for, your church, any charitable or social organization you help out. They all want publicity, and if you can show them that they can get some by tying in with your own desires in that area, they can help.

The important thing is to let the media know you exist.

In order to do this, you should send them a story—a "press release." They may or may not ever use it, probably not. But if it interests them, they will interview you.

The story can be quite short and simple:

> John Smith, 35, has just published his first novel, *Darker Than a Darkling Plain.* He is a graduate of Bowdoin, a 32nd Degree Mason and a twenty-year resident of Upper Scotch Plains.
>
> For further information:
> Bantam Books
> Tel. (212) 765–6500

You also include an 8 × 10 glossy photograph of yourself in a suitably literary pose, probably with pipe and dog.[6] Be sure to include a contact phone number for further information, either your publisher's or your own, if not both.

That's all. The rest they will do. And you send it to *everyone.* Your local papers, area magazines, radio and TV stations. Shopping newspapers. Church newsletter. College alumnus magazines. Nearby big-city papers—they may have local editions that will be interested in you, even if you don't make the core-city section.

And you keep on doing it. Not just once. But every time you have a new book out, or receive an award, or attend a conference. Any kind of a news peg is enough to hang a story on. ("John Smith, 35, of Upper Scotch Plains, has just returned from Wichita, where he completed research on a novel in progress. He is best known for his novel *Darker Than a Darkling Plain,* which placed seventh in the Prix New Jersey awards last year.")

The term "press release" sounds as if it is meant just for printed publications, but the same thing goes to radio and TV stations. They won't use it. You don't expect them to. What you expect them to do is invite you to be a guest on one of their talk shows.

Start with your local stations. Listen to them from time to time. When you hear a talk show that has a guest, or might have a guest if the host could think of anyone to invite, make a note of his name. See that he gets a copy of the release as well as the one that goes to the station itself. If you like, you can include a note saying "John Smith is available as a guest for you," although they will probably deduce that such is the case without it.

Having conquered all of Scotch Plains, move on to the rest of the world. Do the same thing with nearby big-city shows. If you travel, try to do the same with shows in cities you visit. Here your publisher can help you a great deal, unless you are exceptionally lucky in your contacts and knowledge; the publisher can tell you what the talk shows are in, say, Los Angeles or Chicago, so you can send them the release before you get there, with the phone number of your hotel and dates you will be available. If you're really with it, you may even get your publisher to set up the dates and fly you around the country to fill them.

In most big cities there are services that sell lists of talk shows, with phone numbers and the names of contact people and some idea of the range of their interests. Each talk show should be contacted individually. Happy Halloran's Pre-Game Chat may be back to back with Betsy Bliss's Women's World, but they will probably do their booking in fiercely guarded independence of each other. Address each show by name, in care of the station or network.

Once you're on a talk show, what do you talk about?

Well, now you're in an area where you're on your own. You try to be interesting. To the extent possible, you try to get people to want to know you better, or to know more about what you're discussing, and of course the hope is that the way they will try to do that is to buy your book.

If you think you are afraid of microphones and TV cameras, be reassured. You forget they exist in short order. It is good if you can keep some marginal awareness of them, so that you don't rock back and forth out of microphone range or look into the wrong camera,[7] but that's really the control room's worry, not yours. Just talk.

Most talk shows are on a set that is designed to look as much as possible like an idealized living room or study. Your host says something; you respond to it. Don't worry about running out of things to say. If it does happen, that's the host's worry. He is more likely to interrupt you than to let you hang twisting in the wind. In any case you'll be interrupted every couple of minutes for commercials.

There are a few other things to think about, but we'll take them up under the next heading.

Lectures

Traveling the lecture and talk-show trail inflicts a lot of psychic trauma. It's no good at all unless you like to travel. If you hate it, find some other way to push your books. Even if you do love wandering around the world there are drawbacks, because you will find that, although you go to a lot of interesting places, you seldom are in any one of them long enough to take much joy from it.

It's helpful to have some continuing interest you can indulge in your travels. Alvin Toffler insists on making time to rent a light plane and fly around by himself. Arthur Clarke takes every chance to skin-dive. What I usually do is rent a car and drive away to whatever local point of interest I can find, either by myself or with as few other people as possible. I also travel with a portable typewriter and a cassette tape-recorder. Some of my most productive writing time has been holed up in a hotel room, waiting to make a speech.

The psychic shock is mostly interpersonal. There is something traumatic about walking into a room of anywhere from six to six thousand people, every one of whom is a total stranger to you, especially when you do it over and over again. You fly into, say, St. Paul. You are met at the airport by someone who whisks you to a hotel and sits tapping his feet in the lobby while you check in, hang up your other suit and go to the toilet. Then you join a few other people for cocktails and are joined by still others for dinner, and all of a sudden you are on your way to the lecture hall wondering if you will be able to read the notes you jammed in your pocket six hours and two thousand miles ago.

It is not all bad. Sometimes it is very good. Some very dear and enduring friendships have come to me this way. But it is a strain, and unless you make some space for yourself somehow it becomes more strain than joy. Not only does that take the fun out of it, but your performance suffers.

Still, lecturing is well worth doing; not only does it spread the word about you, but they give you money to do it.

How do you get lecture invitations?

The best way to be invited to lecture is to lecture. I used to do a great deal of talking for the American Management Association. They didn't pay a lot, but almost every audience I spoke to contained a couple of people who themselves were program chairmen for some future event and would come up to me after my talk to inquire if I were available to address a state Kiwanis convention in Alabama or a testimonial dinner for Mayor Daley in Chicago. The other recommended way is publicity. The more prestigious and personal the publicity, of course, the better. The *New York Times Magazine* once ran an article about me; *Business Week* gave me space in a feature; after each of those my phone was jumping for a while. I've given up most of that out of fatigue. I can hear myself talk just so many times a year and then I don't want to hear myself talk any more.

You have to start somewhere, of course. It's easy enough to start small and local. There is always a local Rotary or church discussion group. The publicity release you send the local papers can also go to all the local groups you can get an address for, with a letter saying you are available as a speaker. You will be good news for some of them. Especially if you work cheap.

Should you get a lecture agent?

It is exactly the same as with a literary agent. You can't get a good one when you feel you need one most. You have to get started on your own.

Lecture agents take enormous fees. Thirty percent is common; if they pay your travel expenses, the commission is even higher. Whether or not one is worth that to you depends on how good you are at doing your own booking and how much of that sort of thing you want. You usually have to pay starting-up costs in addition to the commission. The agent will want a brochure about you to send his clients, and he will probably want you to pay for it. That can cost $1,000, and there's no guarantee it will get you any dates.

The Summing-Up

The foregoing by no means exhausts the skills one needs to be a science fiction professional. I haven't touched on teaching—and yet, with hundreds of courses in sf being given in the colleges and uncounted additional ones in the high schools, there is a very great need for a few teachers who know something about sf; perhaps you should be one of them. Nor have I discussed criticism, but that's important too.[8]

And there is a disclaimer that is somewhat overdue but which I would like to make.

Having written all this, I must now confess that I am not entirely sure what it means to be a "professional" science fiction writer.

I suppose I am one. I don't always feel that way. I am capable of grave self-doubts and of periods of wondering what the hell ever made me think I had a chance of making it as a writer.

When we speak of "professionals" we generally mean doctors, lawyers, engineers—people, that is, who have been trained in a skill and who practice what they have learned.

Being a writer is not quite the same thing. What you learn is only a part of what you do. What you cannot learn—because you create it yourself, so that others can learn from you—is far more important. The writer who only does the things he does well is dead. I would hate to think that any of us was so professional that we no longer had to try new and difficult things, testing the limits of our ability—and thus never be quite sure that we were succeeding.

Arthur Clarke once told me that he had established three criteria for himself and that he never undertook any new writing job unless they were met.

First, the money had to be good. Second, the task had to be something he thought was worth doing. Third, it had to be something that nobody else could do as well as he could.

I like those rules, although I have one reservation about them. The first one, the one about the money, doesn't seem to be applicable in my own experience. It appears to me to have turned out so that anything I really wanted to do for its own sake has, sooner or later, produced pretty good material rewards. The only real failures I've ever had have been ill-advised attempts to go for the money.

In order to be a professional, I think you have to be enough of an amateur (which means "one who loves") to *care.* To take chances. To push yourself a little farther than you've ever gone before.

And when you do that, sometimes you push yourself too far. You fall flat on your face.

That's discouraging, even if you bury the creature stillborn, so that no one sees your failure but yourself.

It seems to me that that is an occupational hazard that you must face, or find some less demanding occupation.

There's a story someone told me once that seems worth repeating. It has to do with failure, and professionalism, and the sickening realization that you are not doing a job as well as you thought you would be able to. It may be apocryphal, but I like it.

It is supposed to be about the director Mike Nichols and about a playwright and an actor whose names I don't know. Nichols is directing a scene in a new play. The actor is rehearsing it, and the playwright is standing by, biting his nails.

Nothing goes right. The actor keeps changing his interpretation. Nichols keeps inventing new bits of business. The playwright keeps changing the lines; and the harder they work, the worse it gets.

So they adjourn for a drink, brooding over their failure.

Says the actor after a time, "Look, fellows. It's my fault. I'm just not a good enough actor for this part."

Says the playwright, "Christ, that's not true. It's the play. It's not actable. I've blown it. It just never comes to life."

Says Nichols, "Bullshit, both of you. You're fine. It's me. I am not up to directing an actor like you in a play like this, and that's the whole trouble."

So they have another drink, and then Nichols says: "Look, I've been thinking. What we just said, it's all true. You don't know how to act. You don't know how to write. I don't know how to direct. But," he says, "when we open our eyes and look around us at everybody else, none of *them* is even as good at this as *we* are. So let's go back and try it again."

It seems to me that in that realization of limitations, and dogged determination to transcend them, is where the core of professionalism lies. It is no disgrace to try something hard and fail. But to surrender in advance, without making a fight—*that* is sin.

NOTES

1. *The Literary Market Place*, or *LMP*, published by R. R. Bowker Co., New York. Make a note of that name. *LMP* contains more information on current publishers, agents and everything else than any other source in the world. It covers only the U.S., but there is a companion volume called *International LMP* or *ILMP* which is almost as good for the rest of the world. Your library should be made to carry its annual editions if you don't want to buy them yourself.

2. Or husband. I do not *mean* to inject sexist bias into these remarks.

3. The first question is always, "How do I get to be a writer?" The answer is, "You write." That is, you put words down on paper. There isn't any other way to do it.

4. Or better still, make a *good* Xerox copy of your original and submit the copy. When it wears out, Xerox another.

5. In practice the decision-making is never that simple, of course. No two books are exactly equal. But the principle is sound.

6. My friend and collaborator Cyril Kornbluth produced such a photograph on demand, but he had the dog smoking the pipe.

7. The right one is the one with the red light on it.

8. Reviewing someone else's book is a good way of keeping your name in front of the book-buying public until your own next book comes out.

Frederik Pohl

Frederik Pohl, four-time Hugo winner (thrice as author and once as editor), has edited some thirty science fiction anthologies and is the author, co-author, or editor of more than seventy books, mostly fiction.

From 1960 through 1969, he was an editor at Galaxy Publishing Corporation, publishers of *Galaxy* and *If* science fiction magazines and is now science fiction editor at Bantam Books.

He was the author, with C. M. Kornbluth, of *The Space Merchants* (1953), which has been translated into more than thirty languages. His most recent sf novel is *The Age of the Pussyfoot* (1970), and his next novel is to be *Man Plus,* scheduled by Random House. His latest nonfiction book is *Practical Politics,* a handbook of the political process in America, and he is the Encyclopedia Britannica's authority on the Roman Emperor Tiberius, whose biography he has written.

He is also the author of *The Case Against Tomorrow* (1957) and *Drunkard's Walk* (1960) and the editor of *Star Science Fiction Stories, The Expert Dreamers, Galaxy Reader,* and *Nightmare Age.* His current titles include *Farthest Star* (a novel in collaboration with Jack Williamson, Ballantine, 1975) and *The Best of Frederik Pohl,* a short-story collection (Nelson Doubleday, 1975).

His work has appeared in more than 300 publications worldwide, including all the sf magazines and such periodicals as *Playboy, Family Circle,* and others in England, Romania, Japan, the U.S.S.R., etc.

A native of New York City, he lives in Red Bank, New Jersey, with his wife and family.

Index